SO GLAD THEY TOLD ME

SO GLAD THEY TOLD ME

WOMEN GET REAL ABOUT MOTHERHOOD

JESSICA SMOCK & STEPHANIE SPRENGER

The HerStories Project Press

SO GLAD THEY TOLD ME: WOMEN GET REAL ABOUT MOTHERHOOD

Copyright © 2016 by HerStories Project, LLC

ISBN: 978-0-692-79655-3

Printed in the United States of America

For Shawn, the most devoted, courageous, and tireless parenting partner anyone could hope for, and the roots of my tree. And to Sophie and Izzy, constant sources of inspiration. — SCS

For my mom, whose support and love through every stage of my life has meant the world to me. — JAS

Contents

Foreword

My work centers on one important word: LISTEN. Like an apple for the school teacher, after seven seasons of running LISTEN TO YOUR MOTHER shows, videos, social media—and editing a book by the same name—the word "listen" appears all over my clothing, jewelry, and hangs on my walls. Were I truer to my generation, I'd already have it tattooed between my shoulder blades. While *listen* serves as a mantra for me when it comes to supporting parents, another word feels almost as all-caps important to me: TELL. Tell the truth, tell *your* truth, tell how you really feel; tell how your baby fell on his head when you turned to grab a diaper off the table (mine did), tell how you let her sleep in the crook of your arm for eight months—not out of conscious choice, but rather out of desperation (I did). Tell how your relationship went from smooth-sailing on sunny waters pre-kids, to code brown and stuck in the baby pool postpartum (ours did). Tell it like it really is, and in doing so find yourself feeling less alone. That's exactly what these gripping, soulful, funny, wise SO GLAD THEY TOLD ME stories offer you, reader. If you find yourself stuck in the code brown baby pool, you might as well join all the other parents trapped alongside you, sharing stories like you'll find in this book.

Ahhhh, other parents. I remember all too well my own attraction/repulsion to parents as a new mom. Bjorn-ing along Chicago's north side with my firstborn, I experienced an intense attraction toward any other baby-schlepper in my purview, often directly followed by an intense repulsion. Suddenly they appeared *everywhere*, like the day my fiancée and I registered for our wedding; the department store was teeming with couples I'd never noticed before, scanners drawn like weapons, and fighting over $200 rabbit-eared wine openers. Seemingly overnight, my neighborhood became overrun with new parents draped in burp rags—unremarkable to everyone, save other parents draped in burp rags. Instead of wish-lists, our lists itemized fears, needs, questions, and opinions—especially opinions.

A stroll around the neighborhood often resulted in my beelining across the street toward a parent, introducing myself, and in short order getting right to one of the most fraught personal questions you can ask a parent of a baby or young child: *So how's he sleeping? Does your kid take a bottle? What are you doing about vaccinations?* In a dating scenario, the apt comparison might be asking someone five minutes into a date, *So, how do you feel about me as a marriage prospect?* No sooner would the words leave my mouth than my index fingers itched to plug my ears. If she had all the answers, I felt inadequate. If she offered me yet another book title, I'd shut down. If his opinion differed from my own, I changed my mind for the 297th time. But, on the off chance she seemed as clueless, impressionable, and overwhelmed as I did, and told it to me straight, à la *it takes me two hours to put her down and I'm afraid no one will ever be able to get her to sleep but me, and if I open my mouth all the rage I feel will come flying out and eviscerate my beloved partner whom I suddenly hate because she can sleep and I can't.* In those rare moments, a spark of connection sometimes flew out—along with the fear and helplessness—and breathed hope into our overwhelmed parent hearts right there on the street corner. Sometimes a friendship even took root then and there, and all because they told me.

Dear reader, instead of interrogating innocent baby-wearing civilians willy-nilly as I did, you can read these pages from the comfort of your home. Honestly, if you have wee ones it's easier not to leave your house anyway. In The HerStories Project, collaborators Jessica Smock and Stephanie Sprenger not only create an award-winning anthology series amplifying women writers, but also curate a motherhood literary community built with bold true stories, scaffolded with supportive classes and services, and shared online with outstretched arms. The personal essays in SO GLAD THEY TOLD ME offer hope, humor, and truth about parenting at all phases—from pregnancy, infancy, toddlerhood, all the way up through empty nest parenting, including topics such as special needs diagnoses, pregnancy loss, surviving colic, parenting a transgender child, and balancing work and family. I'm so glad they told me, and you will be too.

Ann Imig
Founder, LISTEN TO YOUR MOTHER
annimig.com

Introduction

It's no secret that motherhood has become a competitive sport in our culture. Parenting advice is often given from a vantage point of smugness, superiority, and perhaps even a touch of schadenfreude, that condition in which we derive satisfaction from another's misfortune. In this climate of motherhood perfection, it's tempting for moms to want to pretend they have it all together: their kids are always perfectly groomed when it's time to meet the bus, their babies slept through the night from Day One, nursed until exactly twelve months, and were potty trained just weeks later. Their precocious offspring are all in the gifted and talented program, practice martial arts, play the violin, speak several languages, and volunteer for a sustainable living committee. These moms have never questioned their discipline strategies, raised their voices, or felt like they had no idea what in the hell they were doing as parents.

But we all know the truth, don't we?

In January 2015, I read a blog post that really pushed my buttons. The author wrote about how much happier she was now that she was a mother, how smoothly her transition had gone, and how wrong all those people who "warned" her about motherhood were, the ones with the horror stories and scare tactics.

I am all for women speaking their personal truths—especially about motherhood—and I applauded this writer for embracing a positive attitude about her new role and expanded family. But her glowing account didn't leave much room for any other aspects of motherhood. Particularly the parts that aren't so fantastic.

Like sleep deprivation or nursing problems. Like marital tension or a lack of interest in sex. Or postpartum depression, maternal ambivalence, body issues, or identity crises. Sharing only the rosy parts of motherhood does a great disservice to mothers—and families in general—everywhere. While it's wonderful to celebrate the joy of motherhood, it is irresponsible to gloss over the hardships, whether they are fleeting, clichéd struggles like grocery store tantrums, diaper

1

blowouts, or pregnancy mood swings, or more serious issues like grief and loss, special needs diagnoses, divorce, or single parenting.

Sharing our truths—*all* of them—makes mothers stronger. In my response to the blog post that fired me up, I wrote:

> "I believe that all mothers, regardless of how smoothly or horrifically their transition to motherhood unrolled, should be part of changing the cultural dialogue about new motherhood. . . . I also think our society is at major risk of internalizing this kind of glorified commentary of motherhood as fact. Yes, yes, I'm well aware that many people are tired of the negativity and complaining. But it's about more than that. It's about our culture's absolute lack of support and understanding when it comes to the postpartum period. We embrace an archaic view of motherhood and more disturbingly, of the smooth and natural transition to motherhood. This mindset does not serve the 38-year-old former career woman who is sobbing over her bleeding nipples and wondering what the actual fuck just happened to her life. It does not serve the 29-year-old woman who has been dying to become a stay-at-home mom for her entire life and is now in the throes of undiagnosed postpartum depression."

I believe this with all my heart. After I wrote the article, I was blown away by the response from mothers all around the world. They wrote to me, sharing their stories about the women who helped them when they needed it, or confessing how alone and inadequate they felt as a new mom. They thanked me for giving voice to their own motherhood struggles.

We at The HerStories Project realized how many mothers wanted to talk about this, and the #sogladtheytoldme movement was born. Hundreds of women shared their own messages of honest, supportive advice they received, or *didn't* receive, about motherhood. It became clear just how many women were ready to start getting real about motherhood. Here's how we described our movement:

"**#SoGladTheyToldMe is a social media movement aimed at uniting mothers through support, compassion, and honesty.** It is a chance for parents everywhere to share the honest, helpful, real advice they received when they became parents, or, contrarily, the advice they *wish* they had received. The objective is not to share horrifying "warnings" or unkind "Just you wait . . . " scare tactics, but rather to exchange reality-based, compassionate truths with the purpose of providing support and solidarity to moms.

The campaign is a way for women to share their motherhood truths, even the hard, darker ones we may not want to hear. So Glad They Told Me has a larger goal of changing the cultural dialogue about motherhood, to dispel myths of idealized, unrealistic images of what it means to be a mother and instead provide a broader, more balanced, and more realistic depiction of motherhood. It is not about negativity, competitiveness, or complaining. It is about openness, honesty, and eliminating the adversarial one-upmanship that often characterizes modern motherhood."

We need to find a way to both celebrate motherhood and to encourage new mothers with positivity and hope, while still honestly disclosing the challenges that come with raising children to prevent parents from feeling isolated or defective. This is no easy task, and it requires finding a balance between bombarding mothers-to-be and new moms with negative, shocking "warnings" and blowing smoke up their maternity skirts.

But I believe it can be done, and the key to doing it is embracing a spirit of camaraderie and support rather than competition and alienation. In fact, I *know* it can be done, because the contributing authors to this book have done it. They share their stories of motherhood in a way that will teach, inspire, and unite the mothers who read them. The essays you will read in this book span pregnancy, adoption, toddlerhood, parenting school-age kids and teens, all the way through empty nest-hood.

You will read about pregnancy and birthing realities, breastfeeding mishaps and challenges, special needs diagnoses, grief, single parenting, and the bittersweet pain of letting go of your children. You will laugh until you cry, your heart will ache, and you will feel a kinship with these authors that comes from recognizing a fellow parent warrior in the trenches.

Some of these women share stories about the friends, parents, grandparents, sisters, and doctors who threw them a lifeline when they desperately needed it, and others write about the things they *wish* they had known but were never told.

You may learn something from many of these stories, and you will recognize yourself in others. Most importantly, reading these honest, real accounts of motherhood will make you realize that you are absolutely not alone, that you are not defective, and that you are enough. For all who are reading this book, we hope you will embrace your own real story of motherhood: it is beautiful, it is valid, and it deserves to be told.

—Stephanie Sprenger

Stories To Tell

Emily Gallo

*I could feel the weight of responsibility to pass the torch of
information and break motherhood's code of secrecy that left its
members reeling from being sucker punched by the truth.*

"And then it fell off."

"Wait. What did? What fell off?" This was the first time my
gaping mouth closed enough to form words. Until then it mirrored the
ten centimeters she demonstrated with her two hands. Ten centimeters
isn't much until it's a vagina you're talking about.

"My nipple. Part of my nipple fell off onto the vanity."

I wouldn't have thought it anatomically possible, but just like that
my nipples recoiled. I couldn't blame them really. I would have folded
inside myself if I could have. I wondered if I closed my eyes if I could
disappear.

She kept talking, her words firing like BBs: episiotomy, forceps,
witch hazel pads, mesh underwear, ice pack crotch pads. I could endure
BB shots indefinitely if they weren't hurtling toward my privates, well,
the parts formerly known as private. I cringed.

I was just a girl, after all, a newlywed. In my mind, babies were
still adorable accessories, sweet little handbags that cooed and smiled
and completed the motherhood ensemble. When my new husband
and I decided to visit my brother and sister-in-law with their new
baby, I fully expected to see the cosmopolitan couple I always believed
my husband and I would become—the well-traveled, put together,
adventuring duo who gave fabulous Christmas gifts—only with a new
perfect gift of their own.

Years ago, when I first met my sister-in-law, we were both
meeting my in-laws for the first time. I was a shy high school girl,
and she was an effervescent career woman. She sparkled. She was like
champagne, and we all giggled with each little carbonated bubble of
personality that tickled our lips as we sipped her in. I was intoxicated

5

by her unapologetic affection for my boyfriend's brother. Their syrupy adoration coated us. I watched with my arms folded and my legs crossed, a stiff and silent observer from my perch on the arm chair. I had worn mascara and flavored lip gloss for this meeting, but I know no one noticed.

Another girl may have resented her gregarious nature. Another girl may have hated the bright lipstick that framed her open-mouthed smile, both a stark contrast to the neutral décor. Another girl may have tried to compete. Not me. I faded into the background like a figurine that's forgotten until it's time to dust. All eyes were on her. She saved me.

I was unprepared for this conversation that was more a monologue or a somber soliloquy in a Shakespearean tragedy. My sister-in-law nannied in Paris; she ran a marathon; she was an executive in cutthroat companies; she stalked rhinos in Africa. None of this prepared her for motherhood.

Clearly she looked at me, a naïve girl who had done none of those things, and felt compelled to save me again.

"No one told me it was going to be like this," she confided. "No one prepared me for this," she whispered. Her eyes were wild from months of irregular sleep. Her once-straightened hair was pulled back in an unruly ponytail.

I was speechless.

When we left that evening, she hugged me a little longer and a little harder, and I think if she could have, she would have slipped notes from our conversation in my pocket to keep in case she didn't make it out alive. As we drove home in the dark, I stared out the window and replayed her words in my head, committing them to memory until they became the soundtrack that played like the poems I memorized in elementary school: "I have a little shadow that goes in and out with me, and what can be the use of him is more than I can see," ". . . part of my nipple fell off onto the vanity." It didn't have the same rhythm or rhyme, but it was sacred information.

"And then her nipple fell off," I said to rooms full of my wide-eyed girlfriends preparing for childbirth or muscling through motherhood. I felt it was my duty to prepare them . . . for my sister-in-law. I could feel the weight of responsibility to pass the torch of information and break motherhood's code of secrecy that left its members reeling from being sucker punched by the truth.

Years later, my baby boy arrived. A sledgehammer through drywall, a sprinter through the finish-line tape, a loosed cannon. My son was born.

My lady bits lay in pieces on the birthing table, and three doctors' heads bobbed between my legs like buoys trying to restore my land down under to its former glory despite the fleshy shrapnel. My husband described my delicate flower as the open end of a cleaned out turkey. But I was prepared for the raw unbridled gore of childbirth. I'd been warned.

Five days later, I stared at the purple bathroom tile of our little apartment and prayed to become the first woman to never have to use the toilet again because, "Please! Hasn't there been enough destruction!" But I remembered my sister-in-law: "And then you'll have to go to the bathroom!" There was fear in her eyes. I understood.

It was two hours before my son's first well-baby check that nature called. I tried not to answer, but it was relentless. The witch hazel discs, the plastic squirt bottle, a mountain of gigantic pads lined the back of the commode, prepped and ready.

I knew what I needed to do. My sister-in-law had survived. Surely I would, too. I had to be brave. I used the Lamaze breathing I had forgotten during childbirth. And it was done. When the toilet overflowed into my closet and all over the heels I wore in what felt like a previous life, I thought of her, choked back the tears, and cleaned up the mess until my bundle of joy cried the rattling cry that only I could soothe. When seedy yellow poop erupted all over the clothes I had so thoughtfully prepared, I swallowed my pride, checked the clock, and quickly resurrected a sleeper from the drawer.

We were ten minutes late for his appointment.

The days, the weeks, the months marched on. Sometimes I didn't recognize my reflection. Breastfeeding and play dates and doctor visits kept time. I thought of her.

My sister-in-law met my boy when he was nearly one. We flew

across the country for the meeting. She greeted us wearing bright lipstick that framed her familiar open-mouthed smile.

It was good to see her. She had saved me, more than once. But the girl who greeted her back with a baby on her hip and a fully stocked diaper bag slung over her shoulder had been forged by the fire of motherhood. This girl? She had her own stories to tell.

Then I Saw Her Face

Elizabeth Bobst

How do you love as someone's mother when you have a choice?
Is love a choice you can just turn on or off?

Night after night, as soon as my boys were tucked in and asleep, I flipped on the computer and searched. Website after website, photo after photo, I scrutinized the faces of the children, skipping over the faces of the boys. I knew that no matter what, my next child wasn't going to be a boy. I loved my two boys with a ferocity that often astounded me, but I wasn't going to go halfway around the world to adopt another one. It was China in 1999. The baby would be a girl. So each night, I stared into the eyes of the girls in the photos, searching for a connection, a spark. Could this one be my daughter? I saw nothing I recognized. I was searching for love in the photographs and I couldn't see it.

My plan to adopt came together quickly and decisively. I did not waver when my husband voiced his concerns and then finally gave his consent. I floated the idea to my friends and family. Wonderful! Terrific! Their responses were positive, but always given with a hint of bemused concern. Once we signed on with the agency, I became a paperwork demon. If "paperwork" had been a college course, I would have been sitting in the front row, answering all the questions, turning in assignments before they were due and asking for extra credit. I handled the home study and the social worker with practiced ease. I was already raising two biological boys who were gorgeous, smart, polite, and well adjusted, so I was not worried about being judged as a mother.

With the paperwork complete, the waiting began. This waiting period was when the Internet prowling began. Website after website, face after face, I scrutinized intently. That one is too small, I thought. This one? Her hair is too thin. That one looks very needy and not very well adjusted. I thought horrible thoughts about some of these girls and

9

not very positive thoughts about most of them. A few of them, I was able to consider seriously. "If this child were to be my daughter, I *might* be able to love her," I thought to myself.

I would turn the computer off and crawl into bed, my head reeling from all the ridiculous thoughts that had been flowing. I became sure, after all my previous certainty, that I should *not* be adopting. What kind of a mother would I be if I couldn't even bring myself to like a child in a photo? I had found fault with every single one of them. What kind of mother does that?

I cautioned my friends to back off talking about the adoption, but I wouldn't talk about why. "Nothing to do but wait," I would say cheerfully. "Nothing to report." Then I would change the subject. Yet I couldn't stop myself from moving forward with the adoption process. I felt like I was involved in the slowest train wreck ever conceived. I knew the crash was coming and I couldn't stop myself. Instead of saying stop, I packed like an experienced professional. One large and one small suitcase, packed with just the recommended number of outfits, able to mix and match for variety. Gorgeous baby girl outfits. Diapers. Wipes. Formula. Medicine. Paperwork. Checked and rechecked.

But I did not want to go. I had stopped looking at the photos. I despaired. I was stuck. This was quite possibly the worst decision I had ever made and I couldn't reverse it. I had rallied my family, my friends, my kids. Everyone was behind this. Everyone was lending his support.

Fraudulent. That's how I felt. Cheap and dirty. What sort of a person sets up an adoption and then backs out? Someone weak and spineless. Someone with no convictions whatsoever. The talk in my head convinced me of my worthlessness as a mother. But time kept rolling forward. People would ask me how I could stand the waiting and I would say breezily, "Oh, it's not so bad. I'm so busy with work and the boys that I just try not to think about it!" But I thought about it all the time and I wanted the waiting to go on forever. It would keep me from facing up to what I had done.

And then, one day, I got "the call." I was in the car, driving with the boys, and the agency called. Our referral was in. "A beautiful six-month-old girl," she said. "She looks healthy, everything looks great.

I'll FedEx the paperwork to you tomorrow. You will need to accept the referral in the next few days and then we can start working on the travel plans."

I thanked her, although I was having trouble breathing, and drove home. I cooked dinner mechanically. I called my husband at work. I tried to tuck away the giant destructive thoughts that were attempting to overtake my brain by playing with the boys and keeping as busy as possible. I had a glass of wine. I put the boys to bed. I had another glass of wine. And then one last one for good measure. I did not want to find myself surfing the Internet for photos again. I wanted to sleep and try to figure out how to get out of this.

Maybe there is something wrong with her, I cautioned myself. Maybe it'll be as simple as that. We can't handle a special needs child or a child with an illness. If there is something wrong with her, we can say no. Maybe it's not a health issue but a developmental issue. Maybe there was a clerical error. Maybe a mistake in the documents. These thoughts and more swirled around with the wine in my head until I fell asleep straight through them.

Five o'clock FedEx delivery. I had to wait all day. I went to work in the morning and taught my classes. I didn't mention to anyone that the referral had come through, making it easier to back out without having to explain myself to too many people. I studied the students in my classes and thought about what they had been like as babies. Could I have loved any of them? Could I have been their mother? How do you love as someone's mother when you have a choice? Is love a choice you can just turn on or off? How was I supposed to love someone I had never even met?

By 4:30, I was ready to start drinking again. Good that I was a rule follower and couldn't break the five o'clock start time for cocktails. The boys rode their bikes in the drive way and cul-de-sac. I sat on the stoop, miserable. Never in my life had I created such a mess. I called my husband. The package will be here soon. Are you coming home? Should I wait to open it? He told me to go ahead and he would see it when he got there.

I watched the FedEx truck round the corner and pull around into my driveway. I couldn't make myself stand up but then I was standing anyway, walking to the truck to greet the driver. Package in hand, I walked back to the stoop, pulling away the thin strip on the top to open the package.

Cover letter from the agency. Chinese paperwork. I flipped until I found what I was looking for. A small photo—maybe 2×3 inches. Staring at the photo, my body was flooded by a wave of relief. It started in my hands and flooded through my arms, up and down my torso into my head and my feet.

Oh, I said simply. I took in a breath that made up for months of shallow breathing. I exhaled and my shoulders dropped. Oh, of course, I said to myself, incredulous at my own ignorance. I studied the photo, taking note of her pale skin, her short, dark hair, her rosy cheeks. She wore a brightly patterned snowsuit, too big for her, which made her look stuffed. She was a tiny, tiny girl being made to look like a sumo wrestler.

I giggled. Then I laughed. I shook my head and could hardly believe how stupid I had been. All those nights and all those photos had convinced me that I couldn't love a child I didn't know, that I wasn't capable of loving someone else's child like my own. All that time and it had never occurred to me that I was wrong. I could love a child like my own. I could love *my* child like my own. Here she was, in this photo, looking at me with her determined, fixed expression, begging me to bring it on. In my hand, in this photo, was my child. And the relief I had felt was replaced with gratitude and love.

"Oh," I spoke softly to my daughter in the photograph. "There you are."

At Least Your Hair Looks Gorgeous

Ellen Nordberg

*When I'd had anxiety attacks about becoming a mom, about
whether I could handle it, and about whether I would suck, all
mothers said I'd fall in love with my babies. "You can't help it,"
they told me.*

When I was eight, my sister told me to sit still at the kitchen table,
she'd be right back with a special surprise. This turned out to be a
whiffle bat strike to the head. Similar to this whiffle bat encounter, my
experience with motherhood has not turned out the way I expected.
No one warned me about the "special surprises" that were to come.

While I was nervous about becoming a mother, I looked forward
to being pregnant. I recalled the image of the near-naked seven months
along Demi Moore on the cover of Vanity Fair, and thought "Sign me
up! How hard could this be?" I'll have fabulous hair, giant boobs, skin
to match my upcoming newborn, and the sex drive of a twenty-year-
old! With no PMS for nine months, who wouldn't be on board?

Except that I ended up pregnant with twins. And nobody warned
me that the seventy-five pounds I'd gain would make my ass wider
than my stomach and my upper arms comparable to my pre-pregnancy
thighs. Nor was I given a clue that fluid retention would mean my
football-sized feet could wear only men's slippers, and my eyeballs
would swell so badly I could no longer read or watch TV. My husband
nobly read out loud to me—his favorite book, "A Prayer for Owen
Meany." But the errant baseball to the head that kills the mother and
the Mary Magdalene statue decapitation did little to calm my pre-
delivery jitters.

As far as the dewy skin prediction went, I ended up with melasma,
or the "Mask of Pregnancy." The brown and pink splotches covering
my cheeks and forehead made me look as if I had fallen face first into a
giant patch of poison ivy, and then endured a discount chemical facial
peel.

The only bright spot in my appearance was highlighted by a model-gorgeous Texan friend who looked from my puffy ankles to the hot-air balloon sized skirt to my blotchy face with the expression of one who has observed an impressively grotesque Halloween costume. She recovered, and then drawled, "Well, at least your hair looks gorgeous!"

While no one warned me about the surprises in the looks department, plenty of people offered other "helpful" cautionary advice.

Friends told me strangers would touch my belly and talk to the babies. But I wasn't prepared for the ladies in the health club locker room who checked out my stomach sighing, "Motherhood is the hardest thing I've ever done," with a look in their eyes that said, "You won't make it." Or blurted, "You'll never get your figure back," while staring at me as I tried to paste two XL bath sheets around my middle and Sumo Wrestler waddle toward the showers.

Experienced mothers assured me that the lifelong soul-mate family friendships made in their birthing classes were the best part of being pregnant. My husband and I eagerly drove forty-five minutes to a highly recommended birthing coach's group. The coach shared crucial insights into the birthing process, then shook her head at me, saying, "Not for you. Twin births are risky." Then at the end of class, a tiny, barely pregnant-looking woman eyed me up and down and suggested "eight almonds" as a good portion for a healthy snack. I wanted to tell her "eight almonds" wouldn't be enough to get me off the couch and into the kitchen for my double sausage, egg, and cheese breakfast sandwich, but my husband hustled me to the car. So much for the potential soul mates.

Then I went through the delivery that resembled none of the birthing coach's descriptions, and eventually ventured out with the babies. In Costco, women would approach me, asking, "Are they twin boys?" This question I had expected. "Are they identical?" Also predictable. Then, the conversational twist I hadn't seen coming: "Because I was married to a twin. He could NEVER let go of his brother!" They'd glare at me as if I were personally responsible for all the bad choices of every identical twin husband in the history of womankind. "I lost TWELVE YEARS of my life!" they'd roar after me as I fled for the bakery.

After all these useless warnings and unhelpful advice, I actively sought input from mothers I trusted.

I queried other twin moms about breastfeeding. Most said they either A) nursed both babies no problem, or B) gave it up as a bad job and stuck with formula. No one told me I'd end up with one infant who could latch on, and one who couldn't. Nor did they mention that milk would spew from my breasts like an out-of-control kitchen spray hose as I attempted to have the skilled latcher start boob one, then switch to boob two, and then attach the struggler to the first boob. (Although I suspect prior knowledge of this scenario would not have made it any more successful.)

Then my mother assured me all her children were potty trained by eighteen months, so I assumed it was easy. Yet by age three-and-a-half, my boys were still shaking their heads at M&M bribes, sitting naked on the potty for an entire Muppets movie, then standing up and peeing all over the floor.

There were unexpected surprises on the positive side too. Twin A would wake up serenading us with songs from the Disney Cars movie, and Twin B would hide in any closet or cupboard, and burst out literally shouting "Surprise!" dozens of times a day. It was funny every time.

Eventually I stopped listening to all the advice-givers, and somehow made it to the kindergarten phase on my own. Slowly, I got back on my bike, laced up my hiking boots, and was able to wear at least some of my pre-pregnancy jeans.

When I'd had anxiety attacks about becoming a mom, about whether I could handle it, and about whether I would suck, all mothers said I'd fall in love with my babies. "You can't help it," they told me. After countless nights where the only comfort for a child with an ear infection was sleeping on my chest, and many images of muddy faces at the back door holding long stemmed sunflowers, I realize it's the only thing anyone told me about motherhood that turned out to be true. And I'm so glad they did.

Colicky Residue

Christi Clancy

*We tell all our pregnant friends, look, the odds are long that
you'll have a kid with colic, but if you do, call me. I am your red
phone. I am your in-case-of-emergency-break-glass. Any time
of day or in the middle of the night, I'm here for you.*

I never thought I'd be the mother on the front porch calling my
screaming child bad names, thinking about shaken baby syndrome
as something I could understand. I didn't shake my daughter, but
eighteen years later, I'm still haunted by my darkest moment when I
really wanted to, when I took her outside in our crowded Chicago
neighborhood so I'd be *seen*, knowing that I couldn't harm her if other
people were watching. I didn't want to hurt her. All I wanted was for
her to stop screaming for a god-loving minute.

Colic is three months of root canals, jackhammers, metal music,
nails on a chalkboard, forks scraping against teeth, tea kettle whistles,
horns honking, alarms blaring, raging seas. Colic is extreme parenting
when you're least ready for it—you're sleep deprived, sagging, leaking,
bleeding, engorged, insecure. It was an experience that penetrated
every border of patience and sanity that I thought I could maintain.

I loved Olivia, of course I did, and for a few hours of the day
she was perfect. She'd make those baby faces I swore were smiles, and
I counted her ten perfect little fingers and ten perfect little toes. She
wouldn't let me take her for walks, but sometimes she'd nap. That's
when I did my homework. I consulted *What to Expect the First Year*
and read that the typical baby sleeps sixteen hours a day. *Sixteen hours
a day?* I became so frustrated and incredulous that I threw the book
down, and the sound of the book hitting the floor woke her up the way
any small noise could wake her. I knew the creaky spot on every stair,
every loose floorboard. I feared the slightest cough or sneeze. When
she slept, I silenced the phone, prayed the mailman wouldn't come and
a car alarm wouldn't go off.

It started with a wind-up, somewhere between a wheeze and a squeal, and I'd think *no*. Please, please *no!* But in zero-to-sixty she was mad as a hornet, unleashing the full-throttle ear-splitting cry I never thought could come from someone so small and beautiful. I'd try to feed her but she'd pound me with with her little fists and roll her head away, hungry but too worked up to eat. My husband would call from work to check in as one might check on an inmate in an asylum, never sure which version of me he'd get. I'd say I am in hell, and he'd say sorry, I'll be home early, around seven. *Seven isn't early!* I'd shout, slam the phone down, and think dark thoughts about our marriage.

When the football hold and over-the-shoulder and knee bouncing didn't work, I'd put Olivia in her car seat, set her on top of the washing machine and turn it on, and then the dryer, because the only cure for noise was more noise. She'd keep crying so I'd turn on the vacuum and roll it back and forth with one hand while holding the car seat steady with the other. Nothing worked. Olivia shrieked until her hair was soaking wet and her face was cherry red. Her discontent . . . no, discontent is too polite a word. *Rage* is what she felt; why, I didn't know, because she wasn't ready to be born yet? Was it a mistake to have been induced? I had all kinds of useless theories that couldn't explain what fueled her seemingly bottomless source of pure, unbridled rage.

I assumed her colic was my fault, and so, it seemed, did everyone else. I heard every theory: I was eating too many vegetables, or too little dairy, or too much dairy. My Polish friend said I should eat only white food. The red spaghetti sauce and green beans upset her stomach. I switched to every formula on the market, but she was apparently allergic to life itself. Well-meaning people told me I didn't let her sleep enough. She didn't get enough air. I took her outside too much. She was feeding off my distress. If only I could relax. I should let her be; I should attend to her more.

My sister offered to watch her. I think she thought she'd have the magic touch I lacked. We went to a play at the Steppenwolf and slept during the first act. I called during intermission. "Come home!" she wailed, and I could hear Olivia echoing her cries in the background. "I literally can't do this for another minute."

The pediatrician looked like Lily Tomlin. She took one look at me, gave Olivia to the nurse, shut the office door, and said, "Let me guess: you aren't sleeping. Your husband is at work. Your mom went back home. You just moved here and don't have many friends. You aren't sleeping, and your baby has colic. Honey, it's your turn to cry." In an act of compassion that I swear to this day saved my life, and maybe even Olivia's, she let me sob into her chest. I have all the time in the world, she said, just let it go, and I did. I wasn't embarrassed or ashamed, just supremely grateful.

She told me that Olivia didn't have gas. She wasn't allergic to anything and my diet was fine. Her problem had more to do with her electrical wiring. Here's what you do to get out of the tunnel, she said. Go home and get a calendar and put an X on weeks five and six. That's when she'll be worst. That's when every baby is worst, because it's when the nervous system goes through rapid development. Then put another X on your calendar at eight weeks. That's when things will start to get better, and you won't trust it, but it will. Finally, put an X on the calendar at three months, and live for that day like it's the rapture.

There's a bright side to colic, she said, and I listened to what she'd say next as if my life depended on it. I didn't care if what she said was rooted in science. She told me colicky babies are special. They tend to be left-handed, and they usually have artistic inclinations. She told me Olivia would be sensitive to stimulation her whole life, and that's not a bad thing, because it's easier to raise teenagers who don't need too much stimulation. She said I was getting the hard part out of the way early, and her teenage years would be a breeze.

We somehow crawled out of that dark, clamorous tunnel. Eventually Olivia started to sleep like a normal baby. She smiled more, cried less. She was left-handed. When she was seven, we took her to a baseball game and had to leave after the second inning because she couldn't handle the lights or the noise in the stadium. In second grade she quit Brownies because the girls made too much noise in the cafeteria where we met. She's always liked small, quiet spaces, and could only handle one or two friends at a time. There's something about her that I see in other kids who had colic—a reticence that's mistaken for aloofness, a wary watchfulness, a desire for solitude and a tuning-fork sensitivity that I find hard to describe but easy to identify.

I also see something in other parents who have gone through that particular form of hell. We're more accepting about needing breaks from our kids. We understand that a good night's sleep will always be a priority. We tell all our pregnant friends, look, the odds are long that you'll have a kid with colic, but if you do, call me. I am your red phone. I am your in-case-of-emergency-break-glass. Any time of day or in the middle of the night, I'm here for you. I'm serious. I won't say anything is your fault. You will leave the house, even if just for five minutes, and I'll listen to your baby cry so you won't feel like you need to shake him. Put an X on your calendar at five weeks, and at eight, and at twelve. Your baby will be extra special. Maybe she'll be left-handed. Maybe he'll be an easier teenager. Colic will end, but it'll always be part of both of you.

Best Laid Plans

Brooke Takhar

"Don't have a birth plan. You will inevitably be disappointed."

I was hovering over a table laden with party snacks, hoovering one of each into my mouth as my nine-month-full belly dunked itself into dip; this wasn't what I wanted to hear.

My friend was a nurse, currently stationed in Labour & Delivery, so I considered her wise. She was college educated. She took proper vacations. She was a real adult.

So I cornered her and accidentally ruined the dip only to hear advice that rudely slammed up against my own ideas, like the tiny feet currently internally rearranging my lower ribs.

Artisanal gluten-free cracker crumbs sprayed everywhere as I moaned, "Don't have a birth plan? BUT I LOVE MY BIRTH PLAN."

This was my Birth Plan.

On my due date my water would break and we would slip and slide with glee into the back of a cab with my pre-packed (casual, cool, and colourful) overnight bag and get whisked to the hospital.

Once I was admitted, we would unpack the portable sound system and hit "play" on the playlist we had carefully curated so that our child would be serenaded by our favourite songs upon arrival, and thus one day be destined to take home a Grammy.

I would labour until I couldn't remember my name and then I would ask a kindly nurse named Gloria for an epidural to end the madness. After six (or maybe seven) well-timed pushes, shouts would ring out, "It's a boy!"

We would all cry and hold him aloft and pretend we were naming him Tyrannosaurus to make our moms have to lie about loving the name and then we would laugh and laugh and laugh.

That was my Birth Plan.

As you might have guessed, my wise friend was correct.

21

The plan *was* executed, but more along the lines of the "killed on sight" dictionary definition.

Nine days past my due date my water broke for three hours. I soaked through the back of two cabs as we were sent home again and again. The small sedan-sized bag I'd packed and the accompanying king-sized pillows turned my husband into a sweaty Sherpa and I was lucky he didn't dropkick everything down the elevator shaft of the hospital elevator that took nineteen minutes to arrive as I lock-jaw moaned like a moose in heat.

We played forty-five seconds of one song on our special speakers before we realized the beat interfered with the all-important soundtrack of the baby's heart rate being monitored. We listened to that noise like it held the secrets of life, because it did. It was beautiful and terrifying.

I laboured for hours. I don't remember how many. Time didn't matter. But it did. And then it didn't. I crawled along hallways, clinging to door frames when it got particularly unbearable. I tried laughing gas. I sucked so hard the canister turned inside out but didn't experience any relief.

I begged for an epidural. The needle was the size of my arm and I was gently warned that if I didn't stay perfectly still they might slip, and that needle would slice through my heart and out through my chest, and then everyone would laugh, shake their heads and elbow my husband, "OH WELL. Better luck next wife!"

The drugs entered my body and everything was the best. I read a magazine. I dozed. I had a conversation with an assortment of visiting friends that didn't involve me having to pause and grip someone's hands until their fingers turned black and fell off.

Feeling nothing after feeling everything was the greatest gift I had ever received.

Until I was handed a magical button. When I started to feel even the whispered tingles of a contraction, I was allowed to hit that button and release more sweet nothing juice into my pulsating lower half.

But then it was time to push. And I couldn't feel anything. So I pretended and did an Oscar-worthy job of portraying a woman who can feel her butt pushing something out of her butt. But not really her butt. But they kept saying to reference that sensation, so I listened really well and grimaced and pushed and *absolutely nothing happened.* Baby was stuck. Baby was wedged and we needed forceps. My crotch was stretched into a Joker grin and there was blood everywhere and my mom wept in the corner and my husband looked and acquired an "I can top that" gross story for the ages.

At 6:45 a.m. while the pillows we brought lay piled in a corner, our music sat silent, and my body was maneuvered open with metal, out was yanked an angry, fuzzy-eared girl.

My best laid plans, just like my vagina, had been blown apart. But this end result, this girl who made me a mom and made us a family, was never, and could never be, a disappointment.

Be Where You Are

Alison Lee

Wherever I happen to be, I only had to be 100 percent there. No distractions, no worrying, no wishing I could be somewhere else.

The incessant loud beeping caught me by surprise, but it was the bright lights that pierced my brain, sending a strange chill into my heart. It was my first "welcome" into the Neonatal Intensive Care Unit (NICU), where the noise of machines would become strangely comforting over the next two weeks, once I began to understand what each did, and what each beep meant.

Do you remember the final weeks of your pregnancy, when you would talk to your belly and whisper the words, "I can't wait to meet you" to your baby? Then when you are truly in the throes of labor, you think (or yell), "Just. Get. Out. Now!" And the joy and all the big feelings when your baby is finally placed on your chest, where they fit just right, as if they were made for that space between your heart and your breath? Do you remember?

I do. I remember with my first two children.

I did not have that experience at my third and final labor.

My twins were born too soon at thirty-four weeks. I did not see my daughter and son immediately. I do not remember hearing them cry. I only remember asking if they were all right, if they were alive. I remember worrying about where my husband was, as the medical team had instructed him to stay outside, because they didn't know what to expect. I remember my doctor telling me that it was the first time in many years that the hospital had a natural twin delivery.

I remember lying in recovery, shooting questions at the doctor: "Are they okay? How much do they weigh? Are they in NICU? Does my husband know? Do they need ventilators? *Are they okay?*"

Five hours later, I was wheeled into that brightly lit, noisy room, and saw my twins for the first time. She was tiny, just shy of four pounds, the little diaper swarming her skinny limbs. She had a plastic box over her head, tubes in her nose, and the entire back of her left hand was covered by a black bruise. There were other wires attached to her right hand and feet. She was in an incubator, and she was teeny.

He was slightly bigger, four pounds, six ounces, which was a good weight for a preemie. His brow was furrowed, his mouth seemed crooked because of the tube. When he cried, there was no sound because of the intubation. He was covered in wires and tubes, hooked up to at least three machines, one of which was helping him breathe. I didn't know where to look.

These were my children, and this was our first meeting. The lump in my throat nearly choked me.

I only touched patches of too-thin skin where it wasn't attached to a wire or a tube. When my children should have been skin-to-skin with me, there I was, looking at them in a too-bright, too-loud room, separated by things that kept them breathing and warm.

Those machines were their mother for the first few hours of their life.

Leaving them was hard. Coming back again and again was harder. I couldn't live in the hospital indefinitely with two older children still needing me at home. I had to figure out how to be the mother that I could be to my boys, while being a mother to two babies in the NICU who didn't know they needed me.

I turned to my online community (one of the perks of being a freelance writer is the people I "meet"), asking mothers who have had children in the NICU, "What do I do? How do I go home and leave my children here? How do I juggle all the needs of everyone? How can I split my heart and mind two ways?"

The advice came pouring in. All good, all wise, all loving and caring. One stood out—Be where you are.

Simply put, she said, when you are with the twins, be there fully. Hold them. Talk to them. Touch their hands. Get involved. Know how they're doing. Ask questions. When you're at home, do all the daily things as you would. Get the boys dressed, fix them food, get them to school and back, put them to bed at night. Be their mother.

Wherever I happen to be, I only had to be 100 percent there. No distractions, no worrying, no wishing I could be somewhere else.

Those four words saved my mental and emotional health. I could not have the typical postpartum experience of new-again motherhood, so I had to find a way to make it work somehow.

The once-scary beeping machines welcomed me back every day for two weeks. Every morning for a few hours, they were my reality, and I learned to live with them. Every minute at the NICU, I allowed myself to be a new mother of infants, albeit in the minefield of NICU life—navigating the many wires, mastering the thorough sanitation process, learning to understand the babies' progress in numbers and medical terms. I celebrated every ounce gained and each milestone, big and small.

I also did what new mothers do—I held my children, fed and changed them, sang softly to them, and said quiet prayers for their good health. I sniffed their little heads, held their small hands, and marveled at the fact that they were alive and here. I felt all the big feelings that new mothers feel when their babes are finally on their chest, after months of being under it.

Be where you are.

I was. I continue to be. With four children seven and under, it's easy to be buried in daily minutiae (and diapers). I can only do so much, but with everything I do, I am where I'm supposed to be, fully.

Thank you, friend, for those four special words.

The Visitors

Kelly Hirt

If any of the other mothers had taken more than one attempt for their visit, they didn't tell. If any of them were tired or overwhelmed, they didn't share. If any of them were experiencing doubt or fear or loneliness, they never said.

For years, I watched the same show with different lead actresses.

A teacher would leave her students to have a baby. She would be absent from our school campus for a few months and then, one day, she would casually and unexpectedly drop by so that everyone could meet the newest bundle of joy.

Each time, these mothers were showered and sported clean hair. The baby weight had almost disappeared and they were dressed in pre-bump jeans. The lip gloss that highlighted their smiles and their freshly manicured nails painted a picture of what I thought every new mom looked like.

During these visits, which usually took place in the main office or teacher's lounge, each baby seemed cuter than the last. They were held up and pronounced the newest member of our tribe while the onlookers ate up their baby freshness. The babies were happy and clean and excited to be out and about in a world that happily welcomed them.

With bright eyes the mothers each said, "Oh yes, he's a great baby. He already sleeps through the night." Others shared, "I love being a mother. It's so much better than I expected." Those of us who had witnessed these presentations would talk about the beautiful baby and how great the newest mother looked during her visit. "Motherhood most certainly agrees with her" was often repeated as the new mom happily carried her baby back out to the car.

They all seemed to say the same thing. These mothers all seemed to be handling their new roles, the most important of their lives, with ease and unbridled joy. I grew to expect that this was always true, but it was certainly not my experience.

When we finally received "the call" to pick up our five day old son from the hospital, it was the happiest and scariest day of my life. I walked through the aisles of Target with my mind spinning as I wondered if all of the items on the Internet's "Must Have for Newborns" list were truly necessary. I had to consciously remind myself to breathe so I wouldn't pass out from all the choices of diapers, formula, and tiny clothes.

My baby came to me just after the Fourth of July. The timing was wonderful since I could take a family leave for a few months before returning to the classroom to educate other parents' children. I dreaded the prospect of going back almost immediately, but knew I needed to enjoy this short time.

In the beginning, showering wasn't a priority. Certainly lip gloss or mascara was completely out of the question. I was too busy keeping track of how much food he consumed. I dutifully recorded what soiled his miniature diapers and when. In the dark, I watched him sleep and hovered my finger just under his nose to feel his breath when I couldn't see his chest lift under the swaddled cloth.

My needs were not simply second to my son's, they were even lower than that on my list. Both the dog and the tidiness of the house received more care than I allowed myself. I was exhausted and overwhelmed in a way that no other job had left me.

I knew that I had been given the greatest gift possible, but I was confused by my feelings of loneliness. I didn't have the desire or the energy to get dressed and all made up for others and at the time, I didn't know when or if that urge would return.

Finally, when the long summer days began to get shorter and the school year had begun, I decided I would make my own surprise visit to school.

I had showered the night before, which seemed sufficient compared to most of my previous days. I put on a pair of *real* jeans instead of my usual sweats or stretched yoga pants and I found a clean black t-shirt. I stood before the mirror and gave my looks the "it's-as-good-as-it-gets" approval before searching for matching shoes.

I spent only a few minutes on my hair and face before I switched my attention to what my son should wear. After all, he would be the star of the visit.

My bouncing boy cooperated as I pushed and pulled him into a fresh outfit. I loaded up my diaper bag and placed my baby in the carrier before we headed out for our adventure. To some, an outing like this might seem easy. To me, the courage that raced through my body made me feel like I was about to tackle a mountain. It was far easier to stay home, but those walls had been closing in on me.

I let out a sigh once my baby was buckled in. Looking in the mirror, I found that my hair was already out of place and I hadn't even left the garage yet. I was about to depart when I heard the familiar rumble of a diaper explosion from my backseat.

I stopped the car and looked behind me, however, I couldn't see anything but the back of my son's car seat. I sighed again, this time deeper than the first as I got out of the car to check on my all-important passenger. His face was scrunched up and red and his hands were balled up into little fists. I knew that he was either going to scream or he was in the middle of delivering another explosion.

I returned to the driver's seat and pulled my car back into the garage. I had seen the sunshine, which was more than I could say for some days, and I wasn't sure that I wanted to attempt this outing again. But I did. All the others before me had and I wanted that experience.

Carrying my son, my purse, and my overstuffed diaper bag, I returned to the house. I transferred my foul-smelling son to the changing table and took care of the offensive package that he had delivered me. Additional cleaning was necessary since the explosion had shot up and out of his diaper, covering his back and spoiling his soft footy pajamas.

I pulled another outfit, not nearly as cute as the first, from the laundry room and dressed him again. I looked at the clock to gauge my estimated time of arrival at school. Despite this unexpected incident, there was still enough time to make my appearance before staff members would begin to head home.

I gathered up all my baby items and headed out to the car. By now, the fact that I had taken a shower last night seemed irrelevant. I was sweaty and tired and already overwhelmed, but still determined.

This time we traveled past two exits before I heard the familiar rumbling again. I told myself that everyone knows that a baby poops and I convinced myself that it would be okay to change him once we arrived.

More rumbling and foul smells began to waft through my car. I started to cry. Although no one was expecting me, I felt as though I had let them down. This trip was harder than it should be. I was craving adult companionship but the energy that it required was too much for me that day. If I'm being honest, it was too much for a while.

If any of the other mothers had taken more than one attempt for their visit, they didn't tell. If any of them were tired or overwhelmed, they didn't share. If any of them were experiencing doubt or fear or loneliness, they never said.

It would be six more weeks before I would finally get a fairly clean baby and a somewhat put together mother back to my school. Everyone was so kind and sweet and said all the right things as they admired my beautiful boy.

When I look back, I think about the fact that even *I* didn't tell my friends and colleagues about the multiple attempts it took me to make that visit. I regret that I didn't share the truth. I know that as long as I keep quiet about the unexpected diaper explosions, the tiredness, the days without showers, the fear that you aren't doing it right or that it's harder for you than the others, I'm perpetuating the same high expectations that were created by those that went before me.

Now, when another mother is about to go out on maternity leave, I tell her. I wish that someone would have told me.

My Teflon Birth Plan

Lisa Trank

Yes, I believe that C-section rates are probably too high in this country. But having gone through this experience, and knowing that our child might have died if it had not been for the C-section, I will never sit in judgment over how any woman births her child.

I had it all figured out. The bona fide, iron clad birth plan. I was so certain I was going to deliver vaginally that I skipped over every chapter of every birthing or "what to expect" book. I never even considered it in the realm of possibilities. I had been at my sister-in-law's forty-hour delivery that ended in a C-section and swore on the bible in the waiting room that was not going to be me.

I'd had an easy and uncomplicated pregnancy. I'd taken the right birth class that emphasized movement and breathing during labor. I did pre-natal yoga. I lived in Boulder, Colorado.

The day before I delivered, I went in for a non-stress test, as I was eight days past my due date. Everything looked normal; the baby was big and healthy, in a downward position and ready to go. We talked with our midwife at length about her delivery philosophy, which she compared to a hawk or dove approach. She called herself a dove and told us she was not worried about my being past my date, nor was she interested in taking an aggressive approach. On the way home, we stopped for Indian take-out food and my husband headed off to work, since neither of us thought I would deliver before the weekend. I slept most of the day and ate three bites of something curry or tandoori.

On the fourth bite, I started feeling a little flushed and took my temperature. 100 degrees. I called Jack who told me to call the midwife and to start drinking water. She told me the same thing and said that if it didn't go down, I'd need to come to the hospital. I rested on the couch and drank some water. In another fifteen minutes I took my temperature again. 99 degrees.

Five minutes later my water broke. I called Jack and by the time he arrived my contractions were fairly hard and four minutes apart. We headed off to the hospital.

As soon as we got to the maternity floor I handed the nurses our birth plan, which they tossed onto some side table and then proceeded to immediately hook me up to the fetal monitor, as well as an IV with antibiotics, as my temperature was now 101. Jack called his sisters and our doula was on her way. After twenty minutes, I begged to be unhooked from the monitor and allowed to get into the birthing tub. I was met with a look of concern from the midwife. She told me that the baby's heart rate was not accelerating with the contractions. She bargained with me for a ten minute respite in the tub, but the monitor would have to come with me.

Time is a strange thing in labor. I don't know how long it was, two minutes or two hours, when the midwife told me that she would need to insert an internal fetal monitor to get more accurate readings. I cried at the thought of that piece of wire being inserted into our baby's scalp, but I wanted to know the baby was all right. There was a growing concern about the lack of differentiation in the baby's heart rate, despite some fairly strong and growing stronger contractions. I was worried.

The midwife said to me, "You need to surrender to what's happening right now in the moment. Surrender to the contractions, yield to them. Surrender to how your baby needs to come into this world."

More twilight zone time passed. The fetal monitor was not giving any better readings than the external monitor. The doctor, a slight and calm woman, sat next to me. She told me she would need to take a blood sample from the baby's scalp in order to test the level of white blood cells. More tears. The blood work was taken to the lab and we waited.

The results came back and a C-section was probably not necessary.

All of us took a collective breath. A chance to rest. A small relief.

Or so we thought. I turned to see the doctor and midwife standing by the bed and they told me that we should proceed with a C-section. I heard them say that the baby would not handle a prolonged labor well and would perhaps end up in the neonatal ICU unit. I gripped the bedrails. They asked if we needed some time alone to discuss this decision.

That iron clad birth plan? Teflon.

I looked around the room at the beloved team of people who had been there for the last ten hours. My sweet sisters-in-law, who had been gently putting cold compresses on my forehead and not blinking an eye at my stark refusal to wear any clothing, who smiled at my howling through each painful contraction. I looked at my beloved husband, who stroked my forehead and whispered it was going to be all right. I heard the midwife's words again, telling me to surrender to what was happening in the moment. What was happening in the moment was that my baby needed me to let go of my desire for a different experience than the one that was unfolding.

"No," I replied. "We don't need any time alone."

Thirty minutes later, they wheeled me into the operating room. Jack put on Lyle Lovett. The room was cold and the light bright. The anesthesiologist explained to me the spinal block. *One more contraction.* He told me I needed to roll myself into a ball and laughed with me when I told him I was already one. I curled my spine as best I could and felt a small prick and started to feel a tingling in my toes. I concentrated on Jack's face and the music as the tingling grew to numbness and made its way up my legs to my pelvis. A contraction hit just as my pelvis started to numb and the pain disappeared.

Jack stood by my side as they draped the sheet and started the surgery. I felt a certain pressure, but had no idea what they were doing. I turned to Jack, who was holding my hand and still stroking my forehead, and asked him if they had cut into me yet.

"I see the baby's head. They are suctioning out its mouth."

I asked if it was a boy or girl.

"Can't tell yet, they are working to get the body out."

Through the numbness I could feel a pulling, a lifting.

"You are going to be very happy. We have a baby girl."

I watched as they lifted our daughter in the air and carried her to the warming table.

The next few seconds seemed like a lifetime. Waiting for the cry.

Waiting for the cry. And then there she was, in all her eight pounds, thirteen ounces, and twenty-two inches of glory.

Forty-five minutes later, they wheeled me into the recovery room. She and her father, her aunts, and my mother-in-law were waiting. We unswaddled her and placed her on my chest. She rooted her mouth toward my left nipple, but was too tired to latch at first. She latched on the third try and started sucking. Her body, her warm flesh lay against my breast. I was in love beyond love.

Two weeks later, when we were home, I talked to a pregnancy friend. She'd had a long home birth—forty hours—also a baby girl. She told me about her birth, about feeling her daughter come out between her legs. She quietly asked if it was all right for her to talk to me about her "natural" birth.

"Of course," I said.

I cried when I got off the phone. That is what I had wanted, that is the way I had planned it. Jack reminded me of what our midwife told us the day we left the hospital. She said she believed a woman's body has its own intuition when it comes to birth and that the body will do what is needed for the baby to come into the world as it needs to. My desire for another kind of delivery has nothing to do with our daughter, and everything to do with my own agenda, my own attachment to an idealized birth.

When I would tell people that I had a C-section, I could feel the mixture of judgment and pity. That's all right, I had them as well.

When we met with our doctor, she asked how we felt about the surgery, the birth. Her voice was filled with concern that we were disappointed in the way things turned out. As I held our girl in my arms, I smiled. Our daughter was healthy and thriving and that was all that mattered.

Yes, I believe that C-section rates are probably too high in this country. But having gone through this experience, and knowing that our child might have died if it had not been for the C-section, I will never sit in judgment over how any woman births her child.

Giving birth is part of a long process that begins with conception and continues with the remarkable bond between child and parent.

Having a C-section did not make me less of a mother, or less bonded with my child. I was a mother during the nine months of carrying her, feeling her grow and move and wondering who was this person inside me.

How she arrived into the world was just another part of the journey we're lucky enough to take together.

Every act of childbirth is an act of surrendering. And that act is a great gift, if one is willing to be present for it.

Giving Death

Nora Neill

Giving death is miraculous and magical and full of wonder and
overpowering feeling too—I want to tell her she has to
understand this, this experience must penetrate her too.

The doctor held my arm and told me, "This is not because of anything
you did."

Of course not, I thought, turning to look back at her, watching
the subtle shaking, the twitching heart.

Later, I would repeat that doctor's words, carrying them around
to halt the scolding spoon.

"Do you want to hold her?" the nurse asked.

I tried to imagine what we would see. I pictured unrecognizable
flesh, but then in the weeks to come, after we'd said "yes" and the
doctor said "good," after her delivery, touching the tiny light pink hat
on her head and her perfect small fingers, I couldn't stand to look at my
reflection in the mirror, seeing her there.

"How about Grace?" she asked. Again and again, I looked up
the definition: "elegance, decency, kindness, glorify, enrich . . . the
bestowal of blessings, being favored by someone." I rolled the word
around in my mind, trying to understand, as I lay cradled by a white
and an orange cat.

They say, "I had one too." And at first I don't know what to say,
so I nod. I want to explain how I am different, she was different, we are
different. But there is no use.

In a month, when I am home alone, I will wish to hear every detail
of their losses. Sitting in my chair in front of the window that is as tall
as me and as wide as my arms span, I will hope for each story to come
to me flushed out and messy, reassuring and agonizing. Next, I will
put those thoughts out of my mind, preparing myself to believe this
couldn't happen again. The next one will have no choice but to stay.

A woman tells us that this world is scary and she just wasn't ready.

She chose not to come down, and I can understand that, but my body's diagnosis tells a different story.

"How are you feeling? Physically, I mean," they wonder.

My body has morphed into my enemy. Abruptly shedding all the symptoms of success: the vivid dreams, the fatigue, nausea.

"I'm fine," I say. Because, really, I am. I am alive.

This body loses five pounds quickly and then gains it back when suddenly I am no longer worried about sugar or appropriate weight gain.

Physically? I am rounder and sloppier, falling outside the lines, and angry with my body's "incompetence." Then, I am gentle. Begging it to do this all over again. To stop. Stop bleeding, make the full, tender, aching breasts lose the milk and return to normal. They will never be that old normal again. They are bigger and different. Physically, I am different. Is that what I should say? I'm different everywhere; no part of me will ever be the same.

All the agreements I'd made: to accept the changes that would come, to embrace the shifts, to let go of the old, are gone now, because the thing that made all that change okay will not be here in June.

My therapist asks about my questions for Grace, if I had the chance ask. I tell her no, for the first time ever, it is too hard. Instead of our meetings, I want to drive to a clearing and sit in peace, realizing I could never travel far enough away.

They say nothing to Grace's other mom. At the kitchen table I watch her cry, telling me it was my loss, no one sees that she lost anything at all. I think about this every day, wishing someone would walk up to her, corner her on the phone, in the restaurant, wanting to confess something: you'll get through this; so-and-so wants to talk with you about *what happened*, is it okay? I want you to know that I was just giving you space, not trying to be distant. Why must I temper their feelings and my own? Why have they given this to me and watched her stand alone?

A childhood friend miscarries a few weeks after me. I cry over her loss; I send messages, think of kind gestures, wish to make her okay. Over coffee, together again after twenty years, looking for one more who understands, we talk immediately about the last two months. She asks, "Do you feel like a mom?" Together our eyes well and I don't know.

I am forced to think about what it means to be a mom. The sort of mom I want to be. I think about all the choices we made and I'm still not sure. Someday, I hope, maybe, I think.

A friend tells me now that she's given birth she tears up every time she hears about another woman who has too. I am offended, being excluded from this group. Giving death is miraculous and magical and full of wonder and overpowering feeling too—I want to tell her she has to understand this, this experience must penetrate her too.

Wisely, they do not tell me Grace is my teacher this way too. No one says just wait—there is still so much to learn. I remember when my therapist said, "You deserve to be happy." Over and over I wonder if this is true.

A friend says it will take time, just time. I do not know that one day in April, after the big bold moon has gone away and a new one arrived, I will realize I am good. When they ask, concerned, "how are you?" I will smile and know I am filled with grace.

Little Stranger

Jennie Robertson

The words I really needed, nobody thought to say. It took me a long time to realize that what I knew about romance applied to babies, too: that love isn't just a feeling, it's a commitment and a choice.

I could not feel Angus moving inside of me at any time during my pregnancy. On a pre-dawn summer morning, I gave birth to a stranger after frenzied moments and a hasty episiotomy when his heart rate started dropping. I had used a birthing chair; when I first saw his face lying beneath me on the floor, eyes closed, not breathing, I felt a surge of panic that was not unrelated to love, but was also not at all a warm, comfortable, or happy feeling. He'd had a massive head. The cord was through his legs and wrapped around his neck twice. I'd told God that I felt it was a bad idea to leave the baby alone for nine months with a long rope. How could something so dangerous be so vital to gestation?

"Call his name," said the midwife, as she and her assistant started working over him, sucking out his mouth with a tube, or breathing into it, I'm not sure which. I called to him, "Angus, Angus, Angus," and then I started a holler prayer to God to save my baby.

"Jennie, get a hold of yourself," rebuked the midwife, thinking I was becoming hysterical. This has always bothered me. If you can't cry out to God, loudly, desperately, when your child is lying nearly dead on the floor, when can you? I felt a little gypped. Don't get me wrong . . . when he started breathing, I thanked both God and the midwives in the same breath.

I took the stranger home. He demanded to sleep in my bed. He nursed constantly. I had read great books on nursing, but no one had mentioned that in the early weeks with a new breastfeeding baby, you're basically a nursing machine. Don't plan on doing anything else at all ever. This guy may have been taking it further than the average baby; my midwife said to put my foot down on all this snacking.

A few days after his birth, we went to nearby Wolfeboro on Lake Winnepesaukee. Daniel thought I needed to get out of the house. I sat in back with Angus during the drive and stayed in the car with him while Daniel went to a bookstore. It was probably only a few minutes, but I panicked. I was sure he was too hot; he was dying. Was he breathing? I ripped off his clothes and dashed into a nearby store with air conditioning, a fancy boutique, carrying this skinny, naked, large-nogginned newborn. I'm surprised they didn't call the cops or whoever it is that manages feral mothers.

He did not want to be put down, ever. Attachment parenting was and is popular. Can I be honest? It drove me crazy, all that closeness. We had a swing that was a lifesaver because every so often, he would let me put him there. Every so often, he would nap in it; some of my few good memories from that time are of slow dancing with Daniel to the swing music after Angus finally nodded off. Mostly, he would only briefly nap when I was holding him. When my sister-in-law lamented that her youngest seemed to be done napping, I said, "You've had two-and-a-half good years, Deb. Angus doesn't sleep at all."

Angus was all-consuming. He was consuming all my time, he was consuming me. He was strong-willed and passionate. He was nervous and lonely. I didn't lose myself looking into his sweet blue eyes; I lost myself in his screams, his eyes squeezed shut, and I mean really lost myself. I wanted to be a mother, but I didn't know it was *all* I would be.

There are things people didn't tell me that I wish they had. That the hand sanitizer I used so religiously, trying to keep him healthy, left a terrible tasting residue that got in his mouth every time I stuck a finger in to help him latch. (I'm not sure if newborns have a sense of taste; I cherish only an uncertain guilt on that one.) That earplugs and kitchen timers are priceless and versatile tools for parenting (playing an important supporting role in the sequel to this essay, Angus the Very Naughty Toddler).

There are things they told me that I didn't heed and should have: get lots of help after the baby is born, for example. Accept every single offer.

There are things they told me and continue to tell me that I wish they hadn't: that the kind of carrier I used—sacrificing my sanity and freedom to hold him constantly—probably caused his spine to misalign. That my decision to let him cry it out when he was five months old might have scarred him for life; I was only trying to keep him from suffocating in our bed like a baby we heard about on the news. That I should have gotten him more vaccines; that I should have gotten him fewer vaccines. That I should have been stricter with him; that I should have been more flexible. Sometimes I kinda wish "they" would just shut up.

Before Angus came, a close friend with a baby told me she didn't know why everyone said newborns are so difficult. Her docile infant didn't clue us in, either. I wish she hadn't said that, because it later made me feel there must be something desperately wrong with me if I couldn't handle this "easy" task. Of course, she was a new mother, too; she didn't know how difficult some babies can be.

The advice my father gave me was the most helpful. When I agonized over the fact that I was supposed to enjoy babyhood and I wasn't, Dad said, "Nobody enjoys cranky, angry people. It's not more enjoyable just because the cranky person is a baby." Another time, he allayed my fears by assuring me that he had enjoyed my siblings and I from the beginning, but had enjoyed us more and more the older we grew. I fortified myself with his words every time an old woman at the store said wistfully, "I miss those days."

The words I really needed, nobody thought to say. It took me a long time to realize that what I knew about romance applied to babies, too: that love isn't just a feeling, it's a commitment and a choice. When I am asked for advice to new mothers, this is what I tell them. Someday, you'll realize that the screaming stranger has the world's biggest smile. He's a kindergartner who is still tempestuous, but who genuinely wants to be kind. He loves with his whole heart. He sings a song about his "sweet mummy," despite your frequent rages and other failings. He feels everything deeply. He's a lot like you. You'd be lonely without him. You get lost in his sweet blue eyes; it's okay that it took a while for both of you, that it cost a huge investment in tears and time. Love's like that.

Lessons From The Mothers' Room

Liza Wyles

*Instead of constantly operating from a point of apology, I
committed to normalizing the act of pumping during the
workday.*

She recognized the panting whir of the breast pump from my
bathroom stall.

"You know, there's a room for that. On the 18th floor."

I suppose she was trying to be helpful.

She washed her hands and left. I said nothing. But I mouthed,
"bitch."

I knew all about the Mothers' Room on the 18th floor. In between
having my first and second children, New York had passed a law
that all companies with fifty or more employees had to provide a
"reasonable" dedicated space for nursing mothers to pump. The room
my organization, a publicly traded cable TV network, had set up
was nice enough: it was a tiny lounge with a chair, a lamp, a side
table and one outlet. There was a bulletin board with a few baby
announcements, mine included. I was so grateful for it when I returned
from maternity leave that second time. My department had an open
office floor plan, so it was a challenge to find the privacy for a personal
call, let alone a pumping session. My first time back from leave, I had
to take two different elevators to the studio and hope that no one was
using one of the lockable dressing rooms at 11:00 a.m. and 3:00 p.m.
every day. It didn't always work out, and I occasionally hunted for
other space. Usually an editor, and fellow mom, would take pity on me
if she wasn't on deadline, and give up her room for twenty minutes to
grab coffee while I pumped. I never grabbed coffee.

When I returned from my second maternity leave, the Mothers'
Room was such a gift. It had to be booked in advance, like any of
the conference rooms in our building. And although I tried to stick
to my regular pumping schedule, my job had evolved. So many more

47

meetings, lots of new initiatives. I often had to miss my scheduled pump time, but the booking system needed twenty-four hours notice if you had to change your Mothers' Room reservation.

The nature of the entertainment business was not conducive to consistent pumping schedules, unless I was willing to miss meetings and fade into the background. Not a good career move. We didn't have Sheryl Sandberg's "Lean In" vocabulary at that time, but I had been working long enough to know that if you weren't heard, let alone seen, at network meetings, you were volunteering to be added to the cuts that would eventually be made during the next budget planning season. I had been out of the office twelve weeks already, twenty-four weeks if you counted the first leave, two-and-a-half years prior. I had to make sure people knew I was back and more valuable than ever.

I could never let on how much brain space I was dedicating to finding a private area to make my baby's food. It wasn't so much that I had to be alone, but I had to be relaxed, and I was most relaxed when I could be by myself. Stress never facilitated letdown.

That day, when the voice schooled me on the whereabouts of the Mothers' Room, I had missed my scheduled time and when I had run up from my cubicle on the second floor to the Mothers' Room on the 18th floor a half hour later, it was in use. I couldn't wait another half hour to see if the room would be free, so I went down sixteen floors, pump and Blackberry in tow, and camped out in a bathroom stall. The pump always wheezed more on battery power, and maybe it was the sadness in that sound that caused the woman by the sink to try to make me feel better by broadcasting the Mothers' Room location. Maybe she thought I was new, and didn't know. She had to be acting from a place of compassion, right?

So why did it hurt?

I knew who she was, could tell by her voice. And I knew she had kids. But sitting there on a lidless toilet, business casual and bare-chested, I didn't locate the sympathy in her statement. I only heard her say I was doing this all wrong.

I don't know what she could have said that would have stung less, that wouldn't have made me feel like a fraud as a mom. If she had said nothing, I wouldn't have felt any less self-conscious and small on that toilet, knowing she could hear the grinding gears of my mothering in a tiny stall where she might have changed a tampon just minutes before.

But I know now I should have thanked her. Because after that, I started to ask for meetings to be rescheduled if they fell during my pumping times. I worked at refusing to feel bad about putting life before work when need be, because the work never suffered. I exchanged smiles with the other moms I'd see, their boxy Medela bags dead giveaways in the elevator. Instead of constantly operating from a point of apology, I committed to normalizing the act of pumping during the workday. Like people normalize having lunch or non-work-related chats in the hallway. I found my working mother voice, and I used it to my benefit. My employer noticed. I was promoted.

Two Babies

Janet McNally

*I'm endlessly grateful to have the friends I've had, who've told me
the ways it gets easier and the ways it doesn't, who've given me
grocery bags full of clothes and extra cribs and high chairs. But I
still wish for my grandmothers.*

I never expected to have twins. Let's start with that. Maybe I should
have, since my Grandma Kate had two sets out of her thirteen children,
but none of my aunts had twins, and neither did any of my cousins.
My husband and I had our first daughter, Juno, and a year or so later
thought, *Yes, let's have a second.* That would be it, we decided. We
thought people who had a third baby on purpose were a little bit crazy.

So picture me, ignoring the signs. I hadn't been sick much during
my first pregnancy, but this time I could barely cook a vegetable,
though I could sometimes eat them if someone else did the cooking
and I didn't have to watch or hear about it. Then my belly popped
out almost immediately. "I guess it's different the second time!" I said
gleefully, naively. I hid my bump under scarves and loose dresses
because I thought it was too early to tell my students. I might as well
have been a pregnant sitcom actress whose character wasn't pregnant
in the script, constantly holding bags of groceries in front of me. I
wasn't fooling anyone.

Picture me, going alone to the sonogram clinic. *Jesse went with
me the first time!* I told myself. *It's routine!* I lay down on the table and
waited to see that sweet little baby blob on the screen. I saw something
different. I couldn't make sense of it.

"How do you feel about two?" the sonographer said.

"No," I said, not an exclamation, not a question. Just a statement.
No.

Well, actually, *yes.* Two babies floating like astronauts in their
separate capsules, white against the black of a starless sky. Two babies.

I cried. I have to tell you that. I cried even though I knew how lucky I was to have two healthy-so-far babies in my belly. I said as much to the sonographer, that I felt guilty for my tears since she must sometimes have to reveal to mothers things that were truly sad. Still, I was flat-out overwhelmed, and I cried. How would two babies fit in my body as they grew? I asked. How would we afford it? Are we going to have to get a new car? *A minivan?*

The sonographer was very kind. "Not necessarily," she said. "Maybe a small SUV." She offered me a hug, and I accepted. "You'll figure it out," she said.

But I couldn't really make sense of this news, at least not at first. I'm a novelist and a poet and a literature lover, so I think of everything in terms of stories. I thought I knew the way things were going to go, and this was different. I felt like a fake, like I was playing someone else's role. How could I be a twin mom? I walked out of the office into a crisp fall day, and my story had completely changed.

Let's stop here for a moment so I can tell you what it's like to be pregnant with twins. I don't mean the all-night party of eight tiny limbs pushing from inside your abdomen, or the crazy belly that keeps growing and stretching. Here's what I'm talking about: when people found out I was having twins, everyone wanted to tell me a story. Sometimes it started like, "Oh, my cousin's brother-in-law's mailman's wife had twins," and I'd stand there, waiting for something else, only to be met with a placid smile. That was pretty much the story. *Fascinating.* Sometimes it was a horror story, which shall be reproduced here in all capital letters because that's how I pictured them as they were told. For example: "MY COUSIN HAD TWINS AND SHE HAD TO HAVE A C-SECTION AT SEVEN MONTHS AND THEY WERE SO SMALL THEY BASICALLY FIT INTO DOLL CLOTHES." Or, "MY HIGH SCHOOL FRIEND HAD TWINS AND THEY NEVER SLEPT AT THE SAME TIME SO IT TURNED OUT SHE WAS MORE OR LESS AWAKE FOR SIX MONTHS STRAIGHT."

Thankfully, I had a few friends who had twins of their own, who were honest with me but kept any true horror stories to themselves. First there was my friend Kelly, who is endlessly practical, smart, and fiercely determined. I had once seen her spoon-feed her boys yogurt in matching highchairs, taking turns, working so fast she was practically a blur. It was amazing and a little terrifying.

Still, Kelly was reassuring. "You can handle it," Kelly told me. "You'll be great."

My friend Jen had an older daughter, like me, and three years later identical twins who were born early and dangerously small. She and her kind husband Matt had us over for pizza soon after we found out about our twins, and Juno played with their girls in the pleasant chaos of their family room.

"It's hard," Jen said. "I'm not going to lie to you. But you can do it." She smiled a little. "I named mine after my grandmothers. I figured I needed the strength."

The spoiler alert here is that I didn't end up naming my twins after my grandmothers, but I still thought about them all the time. Grandma Kate, of course, who had had thirteen children (and lost one), including those two sets of twins. She died when I was a child and had a stroke before that, so I don't actually remember her saying much of anything, though I do remember her gentle presence. Now, I found myself wishing for her words. What was it like to have two babies at once? What was it like to have so many children, especially as a woman who had been to college when most women of her generation hadn't? Was she happy? Was this the life she wanted? There was no way to know.

Most of all I thought about my other grandmother, Betty, one of my favorite people who has ever existed in the world. She had four children and lost the eldest to leukemia at fourteen. My first daughter was born a few months before Betty died. She held Juno three times, and I'm so glad they overlapped on Earth. But I guess I'm greedy, because as I sat on my friend Anne Marie's living room floor after my ultrasound visit, our daughters playing on the rug next to us, I cried again, because I couldn't tell Betty that I was going to have twins. I don't know what I wanted, exactly, her advice or just her pure delight. My grandmother loved babies unequivocally. She would have been so happy to hear this, I knew. I was still getting used to her being gone, and I didn't know what to do with the fact that I really wanted to tell someone who wasn't in the world anymore.

But here's the thing: even after a person dies, you still might see her everywhere. Every time I saw a bunch of bellflowers or an African violet in a supermarket it seemed like a waste, because I used to buy them for Betty. When I passed the assisted living facility where she lived near the end of her life I imagined some kind of complicated time travel. I half-believed that if I parked in the lot and went inside I'd find her there, five years before, and I could finally tell her about the twins. And she, I'm sure, would tell me how to do this. Because this pregnancy was harder, especially at the end. Everything about it was different from my first. I had to leave my midwives, whom I loved, because I was now considered high risk. I had to go much more often for monitoring, so often that I thought I might start to recognize the two babies' shadowy sonogram faces on the screen. I would sit in a cloud-like recliner, a machine hooked to my enormous belly, and listen to the hoofbeat sound of two baby hearts at once. It might as well have been the soundtrack to a spaghetti Western, those heartbeats galloping around each other.

I carried the babies until thirty-eight-and-a-half weeks, but by the end my belly measured fifty weeks and my body was a feat of physics. It was a wonder that I could stand up. Crowds parted in the hallway at the college where I teach. My contemporary literature students secretly discussed who would go for help if my water broke during class (they expected a sitcom-style labor, with the baby born five minutes after the first contraction). I had to be induced, again, but this time I gave birth in an operating room (just in case) with thirteen people, rather than a regular hospital room with three. Daphne was born and they held her up to show me, but I had to get right back to work. When Lulu was born (an hour and twenty minutes later), they put her on my belly, slimy with fluid and chalky with vernix. I had expected them to take her away too, I think, so I was completely surprised.

"Hello," I said. "Sure took you a while."

I'm endlessly grateful to have the friends I've had, who've told me the ways it gets easier and the ways it doesn't, who've given me grocery bags full of clothes and extra cribs and high chairs. But I still wish for my grandmothers. I keep buying tiny orchids at the supermarket, and though I can't give them to Betty, I like having them around.

My cousin Megan thought she might be having twins with her second baby, and when she texted me to tell me that it was a single baby, I was a little disappointed. I admit it would have been nice to have company in our big family as a twin mom. There is so much I could tell her about the way it might be for her. The way it was—is—for me. And I would leave out the all-caps, run-on sentence horror stories. But to tell the truth, I was also a little happy that it's just me in our family, so far, who's had twins, just my girls who came in a pair. A few minutes later, Meg texted me again: "I think you got a special gift from Grandma Kate." I think she's right.

Second By Second

Kristin Vanderhey Shaw

Talk to all of the mothers in your life and do not hesitate to ask for help; we all need a village of mothers to look after and love each other.

The clock ticks by slowly. My mind races faster than it can process, and I struggle to focus on anything longer than a sentence. A page in a magazine is too much information all at once. A list of ingredients, impossible. The hamster wheel in my head has broken free of the spindle and is careening around my brain on a harrowing roller coaster ride.

I don't know what's going on yet, but it's about to become very clear: I am in the grip of a vicious bout of postpartum anxiety. I have slept four hours in the last two days, lying in bed tossing and turning with relentless insomnia.

My husband suggests I go to the gym and run it out. So I run, even though it makes me feel even more anxious about being away from my new baby for even minutes at a time. I breathe forcefully through my mouth and nose, trying to push away the out-of-control emotions. My legs move faster than usual, because everything seems faster.

Except for the clock, which is ticking second by second.

I had no idea this would be so difficult; my view on motherhood was shaped by babysitting my nieces as newborns, and I had them for only short periods of time. My sister had relatively easy pregnancies with all three girls, and she never complained. My pregnancy, on the other hand, was wave after wave of the unexpected.

First, the hyperemesis gravidum. My days were spent lying on the couch, cradling my laptop, overcome by nausea and feeling as worthless as a sack of dust. I played lullabies as I worked, and in moments of feeling semi-human, I sang to my unborn child. Subsisting on a diet high in carbs and sugar, the only things I could stomach for the first twenty weeks were cereal, frozen waffles drowning in syrup, toaster strudel, and Pop Tarts. It shouldn't have been a surprise that severe morning sickness morphed into a failed glucose test and a gestational diabetes (GD) diagnosis. Bam. Bam. Two punches to the gut.

When the nurse called with the news that I had GD, I hung up the phone and collapsed in tears, the weight of my guilt crushing me. What had I done to endanger my baby? It was all my fault. I tackled this problem with an obsession I hadn't seen coming. Spreadsheets were created and diabetes experts consulted. Carb counts were tallied and blood sugars measured religiously. Even when the doctor told me I could relax my blood checks, I kept at my rigorous pace, pricking and squeezing a drop of red onto the glucose meter four times a day. I never cheated or cut corners. I scheduled workouts twice a day, and if my test results were very good, I would reward myself with a slowly-savored tablespoon of low-sugar ice cream. I never knew I had so much willpower.

One positive side effect of GD was a referral to a specialist who would conduct a weekly sonogram. The worry threatened to overtake me in those final weeks of my pregnancy; as I neared the 38th week, I started to panic when I didn't feel my son moving enough. I constantly jostled him and risked a small glass of orange juice to get him moving around in my womb. The story of a friend's baby boy who nearly died at birth with the umbilical cord wrapped around his neck gave me nightmares. My eyes were trained intently at the screen during each sonogram as I asked the nurse to show me that the cord was not endangering my son's life. When my OB recommended a scheduled C-section, I agreed easily: that meant my son was coming soon, and I didn't have to worry about labor complications.

When my son was born, I felt relief, but only for a moment. When friends of ours came to visit from out of town, coincidentally at the same time as my in-laws, I felt the room closing in on me. Me: the confirmed extrovert who never met a crowd she didn't like. Me: the one who loves to entertain and has never had a space constraint issue. I could barely breathe and couldn't wait for everyone to leave. My eyes darted around the room like a deer cornered by a hunter; escape was not an option.

Nursing was unexpectedly difficult, too, and I struggled to

produce enough milk out of the gate. In the hospital, the doctors requested that I start a supplemental nursing system with formula. I insisted on soy, terrified that my son was going to have a milk allergy. When our new pediatrician gently suggested that perhaps we start him on milk-based formula, because soy can be a much higher allergen, I dug in my heels and refused to change my mind. I felt frantic, positive that I was doing the right thing. I was the MOTHER.

When the neonatologist on rounds stopped by to check on our new son, she pronounced him slightly jaundiced. I didn't know anything about jaundice, and I asked her to explain what that meant.

She gave me a general definition, and then looked up from her clipboard and snapped, "Lack of bilirubin can cause brain damage." Then she turned her head and started making notes. I sat up in bed, still in pain from my C-section, stunned. When the neonatologist left the room, I was wrecked. I was already failing, I thought. That night, the overnight nurse held me in her arms as I sobbed with fear. The nurse smoothed my hair, murmuring in a beautiful Indian accent, "You're a good mother. He will be fine. The doctor shouldn't have said that to you."

As it turned out, my son didn't require even a minute under the bili lights. He *was* fine.

When I was released to go home, I was afraid. I had maxed out my hospital visit with four days after my C-section, and the doctors pronounced us free to go.

Wait, I screamed inside. *I don't know what I'm doing.*

At two weeks, I called a lactation consultant, went to her office, and spent thirty minutes obsessing about the number of germs to which I could be exposing my son. Then I called for a home visit from one of the hospital consultants. My husband balked at the high price tag, but I held firm. The fear of failure to thrive was hanging over my head, and the consultant gave me some peace of mind as she carefully weighed my son before and after feeding. I pumped around the clock, on a tight schedule to boost my milk production, which I didn't think was nearly enough.

New to Austin, I didn't have many friends at the time, but at that two-week mark, one friend stopped by with a chicken pot pie.

I can picture myself, slumped in the chair, already wearing my pre-pregnancy jeans. I didn't know how to find time to feed myself, and when I did, it was cold food straight from the refrigerator—grilled brisket from the local barbecue, the oatmeal muffins I made every other day for milk production, cheese. I had lost all of my baby weight already, with more to fall off in the weeks ahead.

At one month, the wheels were starting to fall off the wagon. My husband had scheduled a business trip out of town for a week, and his mother came to stay with me. I was scared out of my mind, but afraid to tell my husband that I couldn't handle it. If I couldn't be Supermom, I wanted everyone to believe I could.

My mother-in-law is a retired OB nurse, so I knew I was in good hands, but I still told her what to do as if she had never seen a baby before. I had done the same with my own mother a couple of weeks before. It was that weekend that I started to lose control of my sleep, and I went to bed from nine p.m. to midnight as my mother-in-law stayed up on the couch, well past her usual bedtime. I got up at midnight with my son, and struggled to fall asleep again after that. The sleep deprivation began to loom like a monster in the dark.

It was an email to an old friend that saved my life.

My friend had seven children of her own at that time, and we had known each other since we were sixteen. I felt that I could ask her anything, and I fired off a long email message to her with a litany of questions, trying desperately to be casual but wishing someone would come and tell me how to do all of this. Within hours, she called me and said, without preamble, "Kristin, I think you're suffering from a postpartum disorder, and I think you should call your doctor. Trust me, I know."

In all honesty, I didn't take her admonition all that seriously. This was normal for new mothers, surely, I thought. I figured it wouldn't hurt to check in with my OB, and I made the appointment for the following Monday.

That weekend following my friend's call was the worst yet. I was beyond exhausted; I was a walking zombie. I cooed and smiled and fed my son, but as soon as he fell asleep, I fell apart.

Arriving at my doctor's office alone, with my husband watching our son, I waited ninety minutes for her to finish a C-section for another patient. By the time she arrived, I was a shaking, crying, pacing mess.

"Help me," I said, as she walked in the door, tears streaking my cheeks.

She took one look at my face and prescribed Zoloft. She warned me that we might need to adjust the dose, and I drove off to pick it up from the pharmacy. The next two weeks were a blur of calls back and forth to the nurse; she was my lifeline as I waited for the drugs to kick in. She prescribed Ambien and Tylenol PM for sleep, and I agonized over the potential loss of milk supply with the latter and the side effects of the former.

One night, not long after my appointment with the doctor, I was still suffering from insomnia, and lying in bed was torture. I took a whole Ambien, and clenching my teeth, I contemplated waking my husband and telling him to lock me in the car in the garage in case the side effects on the warning label happened to me. I imagined sleepwalking and dropping my son on the floor, or forgetting to wake and feed him. Even a full Ambien only gave me three hours of sleep, and the deprivation was almost too much to bear.

I Googled in-patient PPD programs and fantasized about driving myself to the hospital and begging them to just allow me to sleep there. After two weeks of alternating sleep aids, the Ambien prescription ran out, and the nurse told me that I could not get any more. I was going cold turkey, and that night I prayed to God for assistance, over and over.

I can do this, I told myself. *I am going to do this.*

The only thing that held me together was my son. My sweet, easy baby was the joy and the light I had waited for my whole life, and looking into his eyes made toughing it out possible. I desperately wanted to nurse him and didn't want anyone else to be responsible for feeding my baby. I worried that I would lose connection with him if I went to the hospital. The tenuous hold I had on my mind was driven by that tiny little boy, and nothing could have torn me from him.

After my son was born, I started to feel more like myself again. The Zoloft regulated my sleeping patterns so that I could fall asleep easily and get back to normal. Or, at least, as normal a life as I could have with a newborn baby.

My anxiety wasn't finished with me yet. There was the problem of going back to work, and I begged my husband on a daily basis to let me quit my job. Pleading, in tears, I asked to stay home with my son. The pain on his face when he was forced to tell me no is forever etched in my memory. We had agreed that he would build his business, and I had to work a few more years. I had picked out a perfectly lovely bilingual immersion daycare for our son, and before he was born, it seemed like the ideal choice.

Now, it sounded like hell on Earth.

We agreed to find a nanny and move to a house during my last few weeks of maternity leave. When we found a place, my husband moved nearly everything by himself, taking the burden on his own, knowing I was not strong enough to take on one more thing.

At twelve weeks, I returned to work from my home office. I had run the gauntlet and made it through to the other side, but not without severe scarring. Within months, my husband and I had decided that we could never go through that again. He had suffered alone, too. He finally admitted how lonely it had been for him while I was lying in bed, unable to function, and how frustrating it was that he could not cure me of postpartum anxiety. Neither of us had known what was coming, and it hit us hard.

We let go of our dream to have two children, which was, and still is, difficult. I can't help feeling that postpartum anxiety stole something from me: my desire to have a second pregnancy.

Even now, the voice in my head whispers, "Have another one" and my memory says, "Absolutely not." It's a chance I am not willing to take.

So here we are, with one wonderful and sweet boy standing beside us. We have walked through fire, our little family, and I'm not going to tell you that we're better for it. I was one of the lucky ones, with a friend who saw what was going on and wasn't afraid to speak up. She was watching over me like the guardian angel I needed, just in the nick of time. Talk to all of the mothers in your life and do not hesitate to ask for help; we all need a village of mothers to look after and love each other.

I'm here to tell my story so that somewhere, someone will read it and find the strength to go one more day until help arrives. You can make it too.

The Curse of the Working Mother

Gargi Mehra

*Most working mothers feel secretly relieved at the prospect of a
workday stretching out before them, because at least that way
they get a little time to themselves.*

About three years into my career, I got my first female reporting
manager. She followed a strict work ethic, never smiled, and as Mr.
Kipling suggested, she treated the impostors Triumph and Disaster
just the same. In short, she was never one I'd associate with surging
maternal instincts.

So it was with some surprise that I noticed her burgeoning baby
bump. She had already entered her second trimester when she shared
the good news with me and devised her succession plans. Her
pregnancy cast a glow over her and she even deigned to smile
occasionally. I found her much happier than I'd seen her before.

Workaholic that she was, she drove to the office and clocked in
her eight hours every day until her due date. After that, thankfully we
did not see her for another six months.

She returned to the office having negotiated shortened hours with
her boss. Maternity had not dimmed her firmness in handling the
work, but in one of the coffee sessions where it was just the two of us,
I took the plunge and asked her how she was feeling.

She sipped her latte. "I'm so tired. In fact, I'm glad to be in the
office for a while!"

I must have looked scandalized, for she laughed. Keep in mind that
I hadn't even hit my quarter-life crisis yet, and though I was married
I didn't plan on starting my family any time soon. But her words
shocked me, because until then I had only thought of mothers wanting
to cuddle with their babies all the time. Even my staunch sister had
dissolved into a puddle of mush on beholding her little girl, so I had
assumed all mothers wouldn't want to stay away for even a moment.

I said, "Really? Why is that?"

She glanced out the window at a greying overcast sky. "I'm not sure. I love my son so much, but sometimes it feels nice to be in the office, among adults. I have a little time to myself. I can read the news online in peace rather than in five-minute increments when I can barely make sense of the words."

I nodded, but I didn't really understand. To me it was still baffling. Babies were so cute—how was it possible that anyone, let alone the mother, would want even a five-minute break from their adorable globs of chubbiness?

Two years later, a checkup by my ob-gyn confirmed the presence of fibroids in my uterus. This discovery accelerated my progress to motherhood, as the doctor gave me an ultimatum—now or never. I chose now, as I knew I'd always regret never.

The fibroids did not trouble me during my pregnancy and I eventually gave birth to a baby girl. When she turned five months old, I rejoined work. My former manager had left the company, preferring to settle somewhere in Europe with her husband and son. We had fallen out of touch but recently reconnected on social media.

One day I was standing around the water cooler with my colleagues. Someone cracked a joke, and we burst into laughter. As I walked back to my seat, one of the young girls in my team said, "You are enjoying being in the office without your daughter."

Her words cast me back to my earlier conversation. The epiphany struck me with a force it hadn't earlier.

"You know," I said, "you're right. I am. And you should know that, too. Most working mothers feel secretly relieved at the prospect of a workday stretching out before them, because at least that way they get a little time to themselves."

She looked aghast, and in her eyes I saw a reflection of the question I had asked many years ago. But I didn't feel like elaborating any further. I just knew that unwittingly, my boss had shared a critical insight into the mind of the mother who worked outside her home, and it had taken me a few years to truly appreciate it.

I measured my words carefully, and told my young friend the truth: "When you have a child you will understand."

Having Twins Will Be Okay

Nina Garcia

*The positive testimonials reassured me that having twins would
be okay, that I could handle it.*

I entered the doctor's office assuming I'd see the little embryo growing
in my womb. Instead, I saw two. Amid congratulations, I did my best
to seem excited while inside I crumbled, trying to absorb the news and
its implications.

Twins.

It didn't feel real, not when I saw the sonogram, nor when I
returned home later to face these new changes in our lives. I had *plans*.
This was supposed to be my second child—a girl, I just knew.

Except it wasn't a girl (it was, I would learn later, two boys).
I cried, then felt guilty for crying. The worries began to yammer:
How will I carry twins, me, so tiny? How will we afford them, with
childcare and education costs through the roof? And, perhaps oddly, I
didn't want to be *different*. I didn't want people "ooh-ing" over the fact
that I was a mom to twins.

I thought I had this pregnancy in the bag, it being my second time
around. I was once again in new territory.

Online searches for images of twin bellies didn't help (note: new
soon-to-be twin moms, don't *ever* Google images of twin bellies). I
literally threw my phone across the room.

I needed information and support. I wanted practical how-to
tips as well as advice to assuage my fears and doubts. And since I
didn't know any twin moms in my "real life," I found support online,
on a twin mom board. Women from all pregnancy stages
participated—those like me just learning about their twins to those
further along encouraging us to hang in there. I also found reassurance
from moms who'd already birthed their twins, from those somehow
surviving the newborn stages to those with much older twins.

And the photos! Moms posted photos left and right of their

adorable twins, and videos of twins babbling and laughing with each other in ways only twins can. Whenever I'd feel scared, I'd find photo threads of twin babies. The positive testimonials reassured me that having twins would be okay, that I could handle it.

Once I gave birth, I relied on these nameless women for support once again. My questions ("How am I supposed to feed them at the same time? How will I put them to sleep?") were met with practical advice and a reassuring "You can do it."

And when things seemed downright impossible, when I was ready to throw my hands in the air, and I asked them, "How did you all do this?!" these ladies simply said, "You just do." There were women who did things I never thought I could (like taking their twins to the grocery store—why don't grocery stores make their shopping carts like Costco?), inspiring me to challenge myself and believe in my capabilities.

My twins are now two years old, and I'm still active on those twin boards, hoping my own journey thus far can be a lifeline to those who were once in my shoes.

If I hadn't received that support from the beginning, I'd have a lot more self-doubt. I'd feel alone. I'd have to learn the hard way to take care of twins. But I did find support; I'm so glad they told me having twins would be okay. Two years later, I learned they were right.

To Be Enough

Jennifer Berney

"Breastfeeding is mysterious," she said. "It's not like bottle feeding where you can see ounce-for-ounce what your baby's drinking. It takes a leap of faith. If your baby is happy and growing, you've got to trust that your milk is enough."

Two weeks before my first baby was due I sat in a room full of pregnant women for a two-hour class about breastfeeding. I was skeptical. What could I learn about nursing without a live baby or breasts full of milk? But, like most first-time mothers, I wanted to be ready. I was naïve enough then to think that readiness was possible.

The class met in the waiting area of the midwives' office where I got my prenatal care. The other mothers and I, all of us with enormous third-trimester bellies, sat awkwardly in wooden chairs, shifting our lower backs every few minutes.

Our teacher was a certified lactation consultant named Polly who looked like she belonged to an earlier century. I could imagine her, with her freckled face and broad smile, wearing a bonnet and apron, churning butter with a baby at her waist and two older children in the kitchen.

Despite her appearance, Polly was all business, all data and posters. She wanted us to know that a baby's stomach is only the size of a marble when he's born, and she explained why colostrum—the extra concentrated milk that our bodies were already producing—was the perfect substance to fill those small bellies. The best time to establish the nursing relationship, Polly said, was in the quiet but wakeful moments after our babies were first born. They would be ready, hungry, looking for a breast.

She told us to avoid washing our nipples with soap so that we'd always smell faintly of milk, and demonstrated how to offer a breast so that our babies could more easily latch. She did this holding her own breast beneath layers of cotton, and we all craned our heads to see.

None of us had brought paper to take notes on, and even if we had, we wouldn't have known what to write. Then, before leaving the rest of the class time for questions, she imparted this closing thought.

"Breastfeeding is mysterious," she said. "It's not like bottle feeding where you can see ounce-for-ounce what your baby's drinking. It takes a leap of faith. If your baby is happy and growing, you've got to trust that your milk is enough."

When my son was born three weeks later, I was surprised by how lucid he was. From my limited experience with newborns, I expected him to be half-there, not fully present—larval, almost. But as the nurse placed him against my body, I was stunned by the warmth and the heft of him, and even more surprised by his wide-open eyes. He was a person already, a being quite separate from me.

Just moments after we greeted each other, as Polly had predicted, he seemed to squirm and root for something, and so I guided him toward my breast. His latch was weak, and he only lasted a few minutes, but still I took this as success. My labor had been hard on him—his heart rate had slowed with each contraction—and so I let him drift to sleep against my chest. Both of us were tired. He slept and I watched him. It was five in the evening.

He slept into the night, waking only when the nurses roused him for tests. At two in the morning, he returned to our room, crying in my partner's arms. When she handed him to me, I had already removed my breast from the hospital gown. This was my moment to really feed him, I thought, to fill his marble-sized belly with colostrum.

But instead of suckling, my baby stopped crying and promptly fell asleep. I stayed awake the rest of the night watching him tucked beside my partner. The room was only half-dark, and the quiet was constantly interrupted with hospital buzzes and beeps. I lay there wondering when he would wake up, when he would latch, when he would nurse for longer than a minute. Weren't newborns supposed to keep their mamas up all night?

When morning finally came, I spoke to the nurse, a large woman in her forties named Brenda who wore her hair in tight curls. "He's been sleeping all night," I told her, trying to hide the desperation in my voice. "Should I be waking him to feed?"

"I would," she said. Her answer struck me as casual, tentative, as if I'd asked for a personal opinion rather than a professional one. Didn't she know for sure what I should do?

My partner had left the hospital in search of decent coffee and Brenda watched me as I roused my son and offered him my breast. His latch was as weak as it had been before. As he drifted back to sleep, she tickled his chin and then his armpits. He wriggled and then sucked with more vigor. "Just see if you can get him to stay awake a little longer," she said, and then she left us alone in the room.

For the next twenty-four hours, I tried Brenda's tricks every time my son nursed, but they didn't help much. He'd rouse a bit, and suckle a few moments longer before his lips loosened and the weight of his tired head pulled his mouth away from my nipple.

On the morning they were sending me home, I confessed to Brenda that I was worried. "I'm not sure that I'm making anything," I said. Perhaps my baby wasn't nursing well because I was dry. As usual, he had just fallen asleep against my arm, leaving my left breast exposed. Without warning, Brenda reached over and pinched my nipple, hard. For a moment I felt offended, but when I looked down and saw the drop of bright yellow colostrum, my indignation gave way to relief. "See that?" she said, "You're fine."

But my relief didn't last long. I didn't know what I would do at home, where there would be no one but my partner to assist me, and she knew less than I did. My baby had been in the world for nearly three days and he still wasn't eating. The nurses and doctors who surrounded me, they seemed so concerned about every detail—my blood pressure, my bowel movements, his heart rate, his blood tests—but no one seemed the least bit worried that he languish for want of milk.

When we did arrive home, the house felt stark and empty. The fridge contained a near-empty carton of half-and-half and some leftovers that were too old to eat. My partner offered to get takeout, but I didn't want to be alone. When I sat down to nurse, the living room couch seemed expansive, like it might swallow my baby and me. I had this growing feeling that I would fail at all of this, that my failure to feed my child would be the first of an endless string of parenting failures, that I would fail to keep him clean and safe and loved.

Over the next three days, I hovered over him as he slept, waiting for him to wake so that I could press him to my breast. Though we managed now to nurse regularly, we still hadn't found our groove. I gauged our progress by comparing to the first two days in the hospital. I took comfort in noting that latch was undeniably stronger, and sometimes he lasted up to twenty minutes.

When friends dropped by with casseroles, they asked, "Has your milk come in yet?"

I would answer: "I'm not sure." *How would I know?* I wondered. Sometimes I noticed what looked like a drop of milk in the corner of his mouth, but other than that I had no evidence.

And then, on the fourth night, my baby woke up. He woke at eleven and I carried him to the living room couch and turned on the light. (It would be another month before I could nurse lying down, and two more before he could find my nipple in the dark.) His eyes opened wide as he nursed. He kept at it, steadily, for nearly an hour before drifting off to sleep, and then he woke again only twenty minutes later.

By morning, my milk had come in. It was suddenly clear to me how I would know. My breasts were at least twice their usual size, ridiculously round and firm. Naked, in front of the mirror, I could see gray veins below the surface of my skin. When my son pulled away in the middle of a feeding, milk shot from my nipples in an arc that could reach the books on the coffee table.

In the days that followed I would nickname my son Piggy Ravenous because he nursed constantly, often with those wide-open eyes and a slight grin. He looked like he was scheming as he suckled, like he was plotting to conquer the world one breast at a time.

But not even Piggy Ravenous could keep up with my milk flow. Even after a long feeding, my breasts still felt uncomfortably full. I took to pumping twice a day to relieve the pressure.

One day a friend dropped in while I was pumping at the kitchen table. Her own baby was now six months old; she had just passed this phase and so she laughed at me in recognition. "Looks like your milk came in," she said. The bottle beneath each breast was nearly full—four ounces per bottle, enough to feed a newborn for several days.

"You don't even realize," I told her. "I've been pumping for less than five minutes."

The condition of my over-full breasts was temporary. Some weeks later, I'd squeeze each breast to gauge its softness and wonder if I could possibly be making enough. Where had the milk gone? But Piggy Ravenous didn't seem bothered. He nursed at the same pace he always had, and every day he grew more wakeful.

It turned out that Polly was right. Only in those few days of over-supply could I measure my product in ounces. For the rest of our nursing days, I had to trust measurements that were less precise, harder to define: was my son happy, bright, growing? Did he seem satisfied after feedings? The answers were yes, but they required me to trust myself. Could I do that? Here was a human who couldn't speak or walk, or even roll over on his own. I had to communicate with him at every hour of the day, but our only common language was a language of the body. He'd been assigned to me, and it seemed that he trusted me: to be there the moment he woke up, to carry him from place to place, to rock him and nurse him and love him. My face, my voice, my smell, these were the things he'd quickly come to know, to need, to trust.

That I was an inadequate parent was an idea that had never occurred to my baby, and in the end I had to trust his judgment: I was, and am, enough.

Six Weeks

Amy Dillon

Neither choice is perfect, and there's probably no such thing.

Take me with you.

From the window of the second-floor bedroom, I watched my husband, Pat, leave for work: off to his air-conditioned office, where he'd make small talk with co-workers, take breaks to stretch his legs or use the bathroom, walk down the street to buy a sandwich for lunch.

"Crash me, Mommy!" my four-year-old, Noah, exclaimed, running a Hot Wheels car across the blue and red plaid bedspread. I picked up a car and ran it into his.

"Boom!" I said with all the enthusiasm I could muster.

It was 10:00 on my first day as a stay at home mom, and I already wanted to quit.

Before I had kids, I was sure I would stay home with them. It wasn't ideological; staying home presented an escape from work. I liked my job in advertising, which I had fallen into a few years after college, but I wasn't passionate about it.

My first maternity leave—twelve gray winter weeks spent inside pacing and rocking the baby I thought would be my sole purpose in life—gave me a newfound will to work. I missed interacting with adults. I missed solving problems other than how to make the crying stop. Noah was a good baby, sleeping through the night by three months and nursing well. But I found the quiet hours of his naps almost as unnerving as his inconsolable wails.

Even so, I fell apart the night before I returned to work. I slept two hours and spent the rest of the night crying. What was I doing? How could I leave my tiny baby with a virtual stranger? I dropped Noah off at the babysitter's with puffy eyes and cried the whole way to work. My co-workers welcomed me with freshly brewed coffee, a monogrammed lunch bag for my pumped milk, and pictures of Noah at my desk. It felt good to be back.

Getting out of the house had been my initial goal, but getting home to Noah each day was what focused me. With this new motivation, my career started to blossom. By the time Noah was one, I was traveling monthly, packing heels and jackets and presenting to clients, going on commercial shoots.

It wasn't all good: there were bad bosses and frustrating clients and assignments that seemed pointless. There were days that I wanted to quit. Lonely nights in hotel rooms when I wondered if staying home with Noah might be the better option after all. But there were also good bosses who encouraged me, colleagues who coached me through the infant stage, and the satisfaction of doing my job well. I was home most nights for dinner and bedtime. Noah liked his childcare providers and was growing up to be a smart and funny boy. Three years later, I embarked on my second maternity leave with no doubt that I'd return to work.

If my first maternity leave was a prison sentence, my second one was parole. The weather was warm. I was more relaxed. While there was still plenty of crying, I felt confident enough with a newborn to enjoy myself. Noah continued to go to daycare. Meanwhile, I took Rory on walks and pointed out birds; we'd drive to the mall, where Rory would sleep in his stroller while I tried on nursing bras and shirts to cover my still-distended belly.

I was sad for our time together to end, but I looked forward to going back to work. I slept the night before. I did not cry when I handed Rory over to our new babysitter, Kelly. Back at work, I greeted a first-time mom also newly returned from maternity leave. She was frazzled, eyes puffy.

"How are you so calm?" she asked me.

"I've done this once before," I told her. "I know that it will be okay."

And it was. It was harder to get out of the house with two kids—nursing Rory, answering emergency emails while Noah threw a temper tantrum—but with Pat's support and help from Kelly, not impossible.

Work wasn't as simple. Upon my return, I was offered a promotion, but turned it down with the hope of easing back in after maternity leave. When no other opportunities opened up, I languished in limbo. Then the agency lost accounts. Shortly after Rory's first birthday, the CEO called everyone to the auditorium and announced the worst: layoffs. My name was on the list.

The agency asked me to stay on for six more weeks to wrap up some projects. It was a gift. I had time to give Kelly notice, to get my files in order, to say goodbye to my co-workers. I had time to find another job, too. But instead, I decided to try the thing I had always wondered about: staying home with the kids. Though it would be tighter financially, Pat and I hoped it would make our lives a little less frantic. The layoff was the push I needed.

On Kelly's last day, we stood barefoot on the hot driveway saying goodbye. I picked up Rory as we watched her white sedan back out to the street. The car paused for a moment as she shifted into drive.

"Bye, Kelly!" yelled Noah, waving frantically. Kelly waved back. I felt a lump rise in my throat, my eyes start to well.

I pulled myself together for dinner and bedtime. But once the house was quiet, I leaned against the frame of the bathroom door and cried. It was a big cry: a mascara running, snot-bubbling, hiccuping cry. It was a dumped-by-my-high-school-boyfriend cry. And what was I even crying about? A babysitter we had known for a year? A job that I had considered quitting hundreds of times?

"You should be grateful," my mother told me. "So many women wish they could stay home with their kids. I would've loved to stay home with you girls."

It only made me feel worse.

Because most of the time, I was not feeling grateful. I felt like an outmatched amateur, experiencing an even harder version of my first maternity leave. There were good moments: building forts and parking garages out of diaper boxes, throwing water balloons in the driveway. But more often, I was climbing the walls. Even the outings that were supposed to be fun were exhausting: squeezing squirming bodies into bathing suits and rash guards, battles over sunblock and swim diapers, meltdowns over snacks, missing pool toys and musty towels.

When Pat got home from work each day, I was shell-shocked, ready to run screaming from the house.

"I'm a terrible mom," I told him. "I hate this."

"Do you want to go back to work?" he asked. "I want you to do what makes you happy."

I believed him, but I wasn't even sure what that was. Did I miss work, or did I just want to get away from my kids? And what did that say about me as a mother?

I decided to give it a year. It was a hard year. Some afternoons I took the kids to the playground. Other afternoons I let them watch TV in their pajamas. Some days I was relaxed, not worried about spilled milk and Play-Doh messes. Other days I was tense, barking orders and rolling my eyes at the kids' whining.

But by the end of the year, we were finding our routine. We moved to a house on a quiet street with three boys next door and adults who stopped by to chat, restoring my sanity. Noah started all-day kindergarten and Rory went to preschool three mornings a week. I chaperoned field trips and subbed at Rory's school. I wrote and went to the gym. There were still moments I wanted to escape, but the highs had started to outweigh the lows.

"I could get used to this," I thought.

Then, one month into the school year, my old agency called. They had a freelance opportunity, a six-week project they wanted me to work on. I found a new babysitter and said yes.

I loved being back. I felt rusty at first, squinting over Excel spreadsheets and fumbling through discussions with clients. There were nights when I rushed home, kissed the kids as they sat at the table with Pat eating macaroni and cheese, and ran upstairs to take a call. I stopped working out. I caught a virus from Rory just before flying to LA for a shoot, and met my clients and the celebrity stars of the commercial with double pink eye and a croaking voice. The days were long, but I liked the challenge. I felt invigorated.

I worried about how the kids would adjust, but they seemed happy. They liked the attention they got from the babysitter, Sarah. They liked coming to my company's Halloween party, they liked watching the rough cuts of the commercials I was working on.

Halfway through the six weeks, Pat and I took the kids out for burgers and fries.

"Mom," Noah asked during dinner, "how much longer are you working?"

I tensed up. Here was the conversation I had been dreading.

"Only a few more weeks," I told him cheerfully.

"Aww," Noah said. "I'm going to miss Sarah."

My shoulders relaxed.

The six weeks ended, and I had to pack my desk and say goodbye to my coworkers all over again. But this time, there were no tears. I returned home with a renewed appreciation for things I had missed: hugging Noah as he dropped his backpack inside the front door after school; taking Rory to storytime at the library on Tuesday mornings; going to Target by myself.

Those six weeks reminded me that I like to work, and that's okay. They reminded me that I'm lucky to stay home, but if I don't always love it, that's okay, too. Those six weeks reminded me that neither choice is perfect, and that there's probably no such thing. And either way, I'll be okay.

Motherhood, Writerhood

Ashley Roth

*You want to be an active mother, and you hope you can write
and create again. These thoughts stay internal—you don't want
others to think you're a bad mother only focused on your
ambitions.*

Pregnancy is clairvoyant, swollen with prophecies of your future as a
writer and a mother. A rosy-cheeked, sleeping cherub sits on one side
of your future self and a purring cat on the other. Your writing is in the
center, masterpieces churned out effortlessly with the muses cheering
you on. This will be during your three-month sabbatical from your
draining retail job, a job you hope to write yourself out of. A writer
at the Southern Festival of Books once told a story about writing her
bestseller during maternity leave. You can do it, too. You'll be just like
Didion, Angelou, and Plath. They were mothers. They were writers.

Your daughter arrives seven weeks early, an unexpected event that
pregnancy didn't predict. She slides out from between your quivering
legs and is whisked away by strangers to the NICU. They leave you
alone with your hollow womb. Down the hall you hear other babies.
These babies stay with their mothers, probably snuggled skin-to-skin
as your childbirth class had promised. Your baby is four floors below,
inside a heated plastic box and hooked up to screeching machines.
A tube gags her pink throat. The nurses wheel you to see her. In a
broken voice, you ask to hold your baby. You have to ask someone
else's permission to hold your own child. Two days later you're sent
home with balloons and stuffed animals and a rented hospital grade
breast pump—and without your baby. You forget you're a writer and
just want to be a mother.

You visit your baby several times a day, toting the breast milk you
dutifully pump every two hours in a thermal Whole Foods bag. This
duty extends to the middle of the night when you watch *SVU* reruns to
stay awake. Nurses in the NICU appreciate the milk deliveries but tell

81

you not to come so often. It isn't healthy, they tell you. Get rest while you can. You protest and tell them this is where you're needed. It's comforting to watch her under the photosynthesis lights, her puckered mouth open. You pump in a closet-like room, tucked in an unused part of the NICU. The pump heaves rhythmically, the only sound in the room. Code blue, someone hacks over the intercom, ruining the quiet. *Twenty-four weeks old. Triplets.* The intercom voice is stoic, a crackling sound over the heave and ho of the hospital's pump. Your mind and breasts empty and you hear an idea turning itself into a disjointed paragraph. Quickly, you type some words into your phone's notepad. Something about NICUs and natal tragedies. After twenty minutes pumping, you return to gaze at your inert, bionic baby. You tell her, silently, that you finally feel inspired. You start writing while you pump, composing unintelligible chunks. One day you revisit the novel, which you abandoned when you rushed to the hospital with blood clotting between your legs.

Your daughter spends a total of nineteen days in the NICU. When she comes home, she weighs less than five pounds.

Alfred Prufrock measured his life in coffee spoons; you measure yours in baby feedings. The routine is pumping every three hours, then attempting to nurse your premature baby with a messy, bulky piece of plastic, and then offering a bottle of breast milk. She mostly sleeps, between her swing and vintage bassinet. You bring your computer to her, where you write while listening to her soft, whistling breath. Between words and sentences you stop to stare at her, to marvel at her narcoleptic expressions and the rise and fall of her tiny chest. You write flash fiction and discover an interest in children's literature. Smaller word counts are your forte, the scope aligning with your ephemeral bouts of writing. On occasion, you return to your novel for one paragraph at a time. You write a lot about pregnancy and tragic experiences of motherhood. While watching your baby stretch, her fists raised above her squishy face, you wonder what it would be like to have your water break in public or to keep an appointment for a prenatal massage. You had one scheduled for your thirty-third week, the week she was born.

You learn to wrap the Moby from YouTube, practicing with a

teddy bear first. Trembling, you fold your malleable baby between the stretchy fabric. She's curled as if inside the womb, her ear pressed against your chest. Together, you climb the stairs to your writing room. She sleeps and you write. You write for hours, stopping only to feed and change her. During a pause, you take a picture of yourself on your phone—being successful as a mother and writer. You devise a silly hashtag for this moment: #motherhoodwriterhood.

You've established a plentiful supply of milk. She latches sometimes without the plastic nipple-shield. You write every day. You're living your aspiration.

Your maternity leave is almost over.

Your first publication happens when you return to work. It's a flash-fiction piece centered on pregnancy and motherhood, the ubiquitous theme of your recent writings. You're accomplished and think you've mastered the balance. That thought dissolves when you return to your role as a cashier. Between an erratic retail schedule and nighttime feedings, there isn't time to write. An open laptop glows in front of you after work. Nothing happens, and you'd rather zone out in front of the television. You're so tired. You ask your retail job to be flexible, lessen your hours. You miss your daughter while listening to the repetitive beeps of the cash register. You don't want to ask a million people how their day is going, if they found everything okay. You want to be an active mother, and you hope you can write and create again. These thoughts stay internal—you don't want others to think you're a bad mother only focused on your ambitions.

Baby develops and doesn't want to be restrained, immobile. She prefers flailing her arms and kicking her dimpled legs on the floor. You dangle jingling foxes and musical owls above her wide eyes. You think about stories while doing this, constructing sentences in your head like you do when driving to work. Inspiration is rampant. An attached recorder could be a blessing, because these sentences are almost always forgotten. Fragmented thoughts clog your phone's notes. Writing is dormant, heavy in the air and waiting while you stretch out on the floor beside your daughter on the cushioned mat, cooing back at her. It's liberating to speak her language. She's eager to absorb everything. You show her the texture of cat fur and the twinkling of a sequin dress.

You teach her the pauses of conversation and you sing the ABCs in English and French. Writing waits. You won't be a passive mother.

Your creative-self is antsy. You plot in the shower, her panicked wail blaring through the monitor. Half-covered in sudsy soap, you rush to her. You'll fit in some time after the shower, maybe for another nap. That doesn't happen. You bring her to your writing space, beneath her hanging toys. She doesn't want to lie there. She doesn't want to be wrapped against your chest. Days go by. Weeks go by. You wonder if you can just have an hour to write. You just need one hour.

You're resentful of fathers, of men. Resentful of their freedom, of the sleep they never lose, of the time that appears to be all theirs. They write their daily song and invite their friends over for recording and jam times. You bristle in the rocking chair, a wiggling baby on your shoulder. You only asked for that hour of writing, in your writing space. There are many days you're glued to this rocking chair, her suckling and doing what you worked so hard to achieve. You rarely see old friends and have found new camaraderie with other mothers. You bond over the concentric cycle of motherhood and how you never get a break. You hear him plug in his guitar while his friend tickles the piano. You want to go yell at them that it isn't fair, that you only asked for an hour. One hour. Instead, you say nothing. You already know that yelling doesn't yield results.

Your daughter is six months old, four months adjusted. Most days, she has a predictable routine. You eat, shower, pump, and write during the morning nap. The children's book becomes a revisited file, and there's planning for illustrations. You muse about publications and write a paragraph here and there. Occasionally, you get your hour in the writing space. Even if that means letting dishes pile up, wearing the same pants for days, and skipping your own naps. Even if that means being assertive and interrupting band rehearsals. If you aren't completely exhausted at night, you write then, too. It isn't a fluid trajectory, motherhood and writerhood. One day she'll plop beside you with her own creative effort; you'll be artists together. You're grateful for moments of writing; you appreciate efficient time management. Sometimes, motherhood trumps writerhood and you don't write because you want to nap next to your daughter. You never regret that choice. She's the greatest inspiration, connected to you while you collect fodder and a heightened perception of the human condition.

You find a new rhythm daily.

You are a writer. You are a mother. They're not always disparate.

It's Not All About The Baby

Vicky Willenberg

"The biggest mistake your generation has made is convincing
young mothers that their needs don't matter. All that does is
breed resentment and grow martyrs."

"Do you need to cry?" she quietly asked from her place at the head of
the table.

And with those five seemingly simple words, the tears were
unleashed. Silent rivulets slid down my cheeks, dripped from my nose
. . . into my Rubio's chicken salad.

The chicken salad I didn't even want but felt I had no choice but
to order. The tasteless chicken salad devoid of cheese and dressing and
cabbage. The chicken salad that was *not* the salty, garlic-laced Chinese
food everyone around me was enjoying.

But I knew I couldn't have what I really wanted. After forty-
five hours of labor, I was now a mother. This tiny, fragile baby boy
was counting on me to protect him from a world full of
dangers—beginning with gassy foods.

"Look at me," she whispered. Her volume was soft, but her tone
left me no option but to comply. "It's okay to cry. It's okay to have no
idea *why* you're crying. And it's most certainly okay to eat the egg roll
you're not so subtly eyeing."

My husband and father quietly watched our exchange, wide-eyed,
having no idea how we went from a peaceful dinner for four-and-
a-half to this madness. Of course they thought we were crazy. Who
could blame them? I was inexplicably sobbing into a dry salad. What
sane person does that?

"Let's get something straight right now," she continued, her eyes
unblinking. *"It's not all about the baby.* Do you hear me?"

My red-rimmed eyes, underlined with the deep purple circles of
a postpartum mother, stared back at her with confusion. Both the idea
and the words seemed foreign, as if she were speaking the language of

the people who invented the egg roll I so desperately wanted to shove into my mouth.

"The biggest mistake your generation has made is convincing young mothers that their needs don't matter. All that does is breed resentment and grow martyrs. The world has enough of those. It's okay to have needs, voice them, and fill them. Cry if you need to. Eat that egg roll or five for that matter. No one will die if you do. Not you," she pointed her finger at me, and then toward my newborn son, "and not him. *It's not all about the baby.*"

Since that day, those words have remained difficult to swallow. They lodge themselves in my throat every time I have to answer the question: What do *I* need in this moment? They are counterintuitive and counterculture. This generation of motherhood is defined by time spent, classes attended, books read, and routines established.

By the time my son was seven weeks old, my abysmal milk supply was attributed to his sleeping through the night so early. "You should feed him every two hours to increase your milk supply—even at night," the pediatrician scolded. When I called my mom, tears of exhaustion and frustration clogging my nose, again she was the voice of reason, stopping my incoherent ramblings about fruitless pumping and hourly feedings. "Is he thriving?" she asked.

"Of course he is. He gained back all his birthweight plus," I replied, mildly offended that she would question her grandson's perfection.

"Then why on earth would you put yourself through the torture of waking him up to feed every two hours? *It's not all about the baby.*"

Since those foggy early days after my first child entered the world, I have been walking the tightrope generations of mothers before me have struggled to navigate, precariously trying to find the balance between being "theirs" while still being "mine." It's a tricky path we dare to tread, weaving around the peaks and valleys of being everything to so many while still retaining something for ourselves.

My mother's words have woven their way into my everyday vocabulary. They're a whisper when I contemplate skipping coffee with a friend because I'll miss the bedtime routine. Other times they are a roar laced with resentment when I debate whether or not it's okay to leave for the weekend or miss a football game. Mostly, though, it's the gentle reminder that releases me from the stronghold of guilt when I choose me over them.

We Don't Have an Option For You

Sarah Hosseini

I've been told I can "have it all," but they forgot to tell me—I can't have it all at the same time.

Walking down the familiar halls, sweat seeps from my skin and soaks my dress. In between each office, a co-worker comes out to admire my new baby. I struggle to use my arm strength without looking like I'm dying from the weight of the car seat. My arm shakes and aches. After all, you don't move a sleeping baby. I hold it steady, and twirl my newborn baby in her car seat so my work friends can coo and *"ooh"* and *"ahh."*

I'm visiting the newsroom for the first time since I gave birth. The chaotic, noisy place I call home for eight to ten hours a day is suddenly foreign to me. I want to go back and crawl into my baby bunker—my house—a place that I haven't left in weeks. A place that is currently piled high with dirty onesies and breast-milk-caked bottles. But instead I'm at my job, draped in the only dress that fits. I'm here to talk business with my boss. Six weeks have swiftly passed, but I feel removed from my co-workers. Separate. Other.

When you work in TV news, you stay in a state of persistent panic. Our bodies are always at the ready for flight—and faster flight. Breaking news is in our blood. We seek it, the stories it generates, every second of the day. It's an unhealthy hunger for a human narrative. This narrative is my very nature.

But, for now, my journalism adrenaline is replaced by a new narrative: a newborn.

This baby has formed a wedge in between me and the world I knew, a world I was wondering if I could ever leave.

I'm jilted by motherhood, and the transition, and now I have to smile to my peers and pretend I'm fine. Pretend as if this "Act" in my life was indeed just that—an "Act," not the final curtain.

My pinnacle performance after pregnancy hinged on whether or

91

not my boss would grant me a more fluid version of my job with a more flexible form.

Sweat pools in my nursing bra and wet spots speckle my upper lip. The sogginess stains my armpits in the shape of a half-moon. Carrying that car seat, my five-pound boobs (each, I swear), extra baby weight—oh yes, and the weight of my professional future—I indeed perspired.

I approach my boss's office. I suck down a deep breath and let it out. There's a dull ache in the bottom of my belly. I could pass out. Or throw up. I feel so small standing in that doorway. A change has occurred over the past six weeks. Am I still a mega-driven career woman? Do I still have the vigor? The edge? I don't feel the same professional passion anymore.

My metamorphosis to motherhood made me question everything I've ever done in the past, and will do in the future. Maybe it was hormones? Oxytocin is tanking every day. Maybe I was just tired? I average three-four hours of interrupted sleep every night. Maybe I knew that keeping up with a baby like I wanted to—and having this job—wasn't going to work. I've been told I can "have it all," but they forgot to tell me—I can't have it all at the same time.

A fellow co-worker offered to watch my baby while I chat with my boss. I step softly into my boss's office and sit down in front of him. Despite dropping the weight of that car seat—and the baby in it—I feel heavy sitting in that chair.

My boss begins.

"So, I got your email about wanting to talk about transitioning back into your job, but I'm unsure what you mean by that."

Almost apologetically I say, "Yes, I was thinking if it was available, I'd like to ask for a more flexible arrangement. Something that helps me divide my time up more—so I can spend more time caring for my newborn."

"Yeah, I'm not sure we have an option like that for you. It would be impossible. Your job doesn't have a flexible option."

I pause. I am ready for this response. I just didn't think it was going to *be* his response. Plan B, for me, it is.

My chest is tight, but I say, "I will be resigning then, effective today."

My boss barely bats an eyelash. He hardly looks surprised.

"I'm sorry to hear that. We'll miss you. You have a place back here anytime. Of course, with technology changing such as it is, I'm not sure we could put you right back in your job. You'd have to work your way up again."

"Thank you. I understand. I really appreciate it."

I stand, shake hands, and leave.

Like that, I quit. I quit everything I had known for the past five years. I walked away from my work like it was nothing. The very thing that defined who I was. My character was so deeply intertwined with my career—who am I now?

Television news—the hustle, bustle, the insane schedules and deadlines, demands—done. I am done. I am no longer a working woman. I retrieve my baby, say a few goodbyes to the co-workers I care most about, and walk out.

I feel like bursting into tears walking that same hallway I just entered through.

How could I be given no option? None? Was I valued as an employee? Didn't I do a good job during my tenure? I feel the money I earned was too little to justify time away from my child. My income only covered daycare, and that didn't seem worth it to me. I mean, was I supposed to simply work for peanuts, pay for full-time daycare, and say it was all in the name of career climbing?

I was just forced out of my job. I had no choice. Keep my job—as it was—and never see my kid. Or, leave it all behind.

I need time—but not forever. I just need more time than my company is willing to wait.

Wasn't I worth it?

I'm so glad my boss told me I wasn't worth it . . . to him.

Admittedly, at first I was bitter over losing the only thing I had known. I went through an identity crisis of epic career proportions. I stared at all those suits and high heels in my closet wondering if I'd ever wear them again. Wondering if I'd ever feel important and powerful to another adult human being again.

The next six months were filled with busy-bored days with my newborn. I was exhausted, and sick of baby activities. Tummy time, feedings, naps, baby story times, etc. I hated it—I was bored constantly. I resented everyone. I blamed myself, my baby, my boss, and my husband for this supposedly sub-par life of baby puke and Mommy-and-me yoga. Again, I'm not saying I wasn't busy. I could barely wash my hair or dishes that whole first year of motherhood. I was inflicted with the ennui of motherhood. My tenure track was derailed. My career cart crashed because of a kid. My soul was being sucked away, one mind-numbing task at a time.

I couldn't take it anymore. When my baby turned six months old, I accepted a job. I could mostly work from home while the baby slept or played independently. I didn't care about burning the candle at both ends. I didn't care that I was exhausted. I was simply tired of being bored. I was depressed that I didn't have direction outside of child-rearing. I loathed being labeled "just a housewife." That job started to save my soul one project at a time.

My career has since evolved into a path that serves every single passion I have. It fulfills my family, my love of literature and language and creativity.

I spend quality time with my kids. I get lost in beautiful words when I write. And I don't sacrifice a dime for it. I get paid, for the first time in my life, fairly. I get paid what I am worth, based on my skills and talents. I don't get screwed in my finances because I demand flexibility for my family.

I'm so glad my boss told me that he didn't have a job for me at my old TV station. If he didn't, I wouldn't have fallen and created a new future. A future that is filled with family time, funds, and enough ideas to write non-fiction forever. Some of my stories even have a fairy-tale ending.

Careful on the Stairs

Katie Coppens

I know because I now know what it means to be a mom. The love you feel is so strong that you will do anything to protect your child.

As a child, the only other person I knew who had to wear a bike helmet was my sister. Each time I would get ready for a bike ride, my mom would check my helmet to make sure it was on properly by having me quickly nod my head up and down and side to side. As I rode off, I always envisioned myself turning the corner and hiding the helmet in a bush, but I never did. I knew my mom was slightly neurotic about safety, but I also knew that, more than anything, she loved me.

Our friends' moms also loved us; they just showed it in different ways. They would give us spare change and let us walk to the corner store to buy ice cream or let us sit on their laps and turn the steering wheel as they slowly drove around the block. My mom was not like them—she was the mom who called my new friends' parents, before a sleepover, and had them reassure her that I would wear a seatbelt if I were in their car. I tried many times to explain how embarrassing her fixation on injury prevention was, but I knew there was no point: She was steadfast in her role of keeping me safe.

This continued for over two decades, right up until my mom's death. She had done everything possible to keep everyone she loved safe, but she ultimately died of cancer. When my mom passed away, she was an RN, had a PhD in psychology, and was a dean at a university. But perhaps the thing that mattered most to her was that, seventeen days before she died, she became a grandmother.

My husband and I left the hospital with our newborn baby girl and drove straight to my mom, who was on in-home hospice. Cradled in the comfort of my mother's arms, my daughter spent day after day lulled to sleep by the sound of her labored breathing. It was the most heartbreakingly profound period of my life. I was learning how to be a mom, but the person I needed to teach me the most was dying. I wanted to ask questions, get advice, and seek approval, but no grand words were said to me in the days before my mom died, except for four that will always stay with me.

One night, my daughter wouldn't sleep and I could see the exhaustion on my husband's face, so I brought her to the room where my mom lay in her hospital bed. My mom immediately mumbled to me asking for the baby. For a few hours, my daughter slept in her arms as I lay a few feet away and also got the sleep that I so desperately needed. Late that night, as I moved to bring my daughter back downstairs to the pullout couch we had been sleeping on, my mom reached for my arm and looked me straight in the eyes. She held my arm with her shaking hand and said in a strong, but tired voice, "Careful on the stairs."

She died three days after that and now, over two years later, those words still echo in my head. She was dying, but she still thought about the safety of my daughter and me. I know she listened as I turned on the light and walked down the stairs, and breathed a sigh of relief once I had closed the door. I know because I now know what it means to be a mom. The love you feel is so strong that you will do anything to protect your child.

Now, as I hold my two-year-old daughter's hand, I too say "Careful on the stairs." My mom is gone, but I understand her better than I ever did before. I wish I could tell my mom that I get it now: I understand. But she knew. She knew that having a child would help me see just how much she loved me.

Motherhood Is Hard

Mimi Sager Yoskowitz

"You're not a failure. Try to be okay with how hard it is to be a mom. Babies are cute, yes, but they're also really tough. Don't put pressure on yourself to do everything right all the time."

One hand on the stroller, the other clutching my newborn son to me, I plow my way up Third Avenue. Caleb's wails drown out the loud din that is Manhattan. The usual cacophony of bus brakes hissing, taxi cabs honking, and people hurrying is lost on me. All I hear are his cries and my shushing. I've never been the type who sweats a lot, but pregnancy changed that. Right now I'm drenched in a perspiration that smells acrid and peppery, the stench of hormones. My breasts, once small and perky, now heave with the milk I'm producing to feed this screaming creature. His fierce cries cause them to tingle, and I can feel the let-down starting. Tears, sweat, and breast milk seem to be the main ingredients in the cocktail of my life these days. I'm every mixologist's dream.

This reality is so different than what I imagined motherhood to be. I pictured blissful walks with my baby in the buggy. People would admire his chubby cheeks, oohing and ahhing while I smiled and glowed in my postpartum glory. We'd stop on a park bench, and he would quietly nurse, while I hummed a little tune to cultivate his brain development. But none of that happens. Instead, I find myself day after day pushing an empty stroller, clutching a screaming Caleb to my chest, and wishing I were back at my desk at work.

Not too long ago, I escaped the grind of producing for a primetime newscast by daydreaming of a baby. Now I find myself fondly reminiscing about daily deadlines, last minute rundown changes, or canceling guests I'd victoriously snagged for our show. Never did I imagine during my pregnancy, as I counted down the days until my baby's arrival, that I would be yearning to return to the newsroom so soon after becoming a mother.

Yet I miss the collaboration that comes with putting together a nightly broadcast. I miss commiserating with my colleagues when something didn't go right. And I miss having executive and senior producers around to help guide me in my editorial decisions. Motherhood often feels like I'm stranded on a deserted island with an untamed wild animal as my boss.

Today is no different. Only for some reason, Caleb's cries seem louder, and my grip on him, on the stroller, on life, seems more fragile. I need salvation, and I need it fast. I know it won't come from any of the many faces passing by me. My attempts thus far at finding another mom in my predicament have been futile, and my other friends with kids are busy making their own way. On top of everything else, I find myself lonely. So I reach for my cell phone.

I stop the buggy in the middle of the sidewalk and press the parking brake. I don't even care that I'm blocking the pedestrian traffic. Caleb remains hysterical, and I need to hear the voice I think will bring me the most comfort right at this moment. I tighten my grip on him in my right arm, and dial with my left hand. Good thing I'm semi-ambidextrous. The ringing purrs in my ear, sounding almost symphonic compared to Caleb's non-stop cries. "Please pick up," I say, rocking him side to side. I bite my lip as the tears start to pool in my eyes.

"Hello?" my cousin Ellen answers.

"WHY DIDN'T YOU TELL ME THIS WAS GOING TO BE SO HARD?" I bellow into the phone.

There are times when I'm grateful that New Yorkers walk around with blinders. This is one of them. I must look like a lunatic.

"I know. I know. It's so hard, Mimi. It's *so* hard. Especially in the beginning. But it gets better. I promise," Ellen says, trying to soothe me from halfway across the country.

Ellen is my cousin, but she's also the closest thing I have to an older sister. We grew up at each other's homes and took family vacations together. She was my matron of honor. Now she serves as my go-to for all things baby. She has two kids of her own with one more on the way, and she's been my savior since Caleb arrived.

"He's hysterical. And now I'm hysterical. He won't calm down.

He won't go in the stroller. I can't figure out that fucking Baby Bjorn thing. What. Is. Going. On?" At this point, Caleb and I are going head to head on who can scream the loudest. He at least has the good excuse of being a baby. What's mine? I'm starting to wonder if maybe I *am* a lunatic.

Ellen's voice brings some relief. Hearing the familiar sound of someone who loves me is a salve for my postpartum wounds. "Where are you right now?" she asks.

"In the middle of the sidewalk."

"You have to get home. You'll feel better once you're there," she says.

Given how overwhelmed I feel at that moment, I'm not sure how I manage to process what Ellen tells me. But thankfully her words compute. I cradle the phone between my ear and my shoulder, hoist the still screaming Caleb up on my chest, release the stroller brake, and start walking.

"You should see what I look like right now. And can you hear that he's still crying? How am I supposed to get him to stop?" I wail into the phone.

"Babies aren't robots. You can't program them to do exactly as you wish. But you should trust yourself and your own maternal instincts. It is hard to figure things out with a newborn, but you have a better sense of what to do than you think," Ellen says.

Hearing her tell me that motherhood is hard helps me regain some sense of composure. I had been starting to think that I was the only struggling mom in the world. On the Upper East Side of New York that sweltering summer, Bugaboo carriages abound, pushed by perfectly coiffed and tanned young mothers. Unlike me, they don't have sweat stains under their arms or circles of breast milk on their chests. It's like that old game on "Sesame Street," when they would sing, "One of These Things is Not Like the Other." That is how I feel every time I step outside of my building to take a walk with Caleb. I'm the "other" amidst a sea of motherhood perfection. Or at least what looks like it.

"So the fact that I feel like a total failure these days is normal?" I say between sobs. At this point I'm calmer, but the tears still come.

"You're not a failure. Try to be okay with how hard it is to be a mom. Babies are cute, yes, but they're also really tough. Don't put pressure on yourself to do everything right all the time," Ellen says.

Her continuous comfort is essential for me to complete this journey home. Before having a baby, I wasn't the type who needed constant reassurance that everything would be fine, but these days I can't get enough of it. Hearing that motherhood is difficult is therapeutic. Ellen's words grant me permission to embrace myself as a mama and all that I'm feeling in this new chapter of my life.

Caleb and I finally arrive back at our building. The air conditioning blasts us, a welcome relief to my sweaty self. Baby boy whimpers still, but it's nothing like the shrieking I encountered just a few long minutes ago.

"I'm going to lose you. I have to get in the elevator to go up," I say. "But thank you. Thank you for being there for me when I really needed you."

"Of course. Remember how I said that being a mom is harder than it seems. But you're okay. What you're feeling is totally normal. Don't forget that. Love you," Ellen says.

After I reluctantly press "end" on my phone, Caleb and I head upstairs.

We enter our apartment where the cushy brown sofa beckons. I park the stroller behind the couch, grateful to be rid of it for now.

With both hands free, I pull Caleb toward me and inhale his newborn scent. It's a relief to finally have him peaceful in my arms. We have miles to walk together before I'll adjust to how hard motherhood can be. But these cuddles amidst the struggles, at least those are easy.

Don't Look Down

Kimberly Zapata

*Being a new mom, sleep deprived and essentially strung out on
cup after cup of half-drunk coffee, I didn't give sex another
thought—at least not until my six-week checkup.*

I was horny during my pregnancy. I don't know why, nothing says
sexy quite like nausea, constipation, and excessive sweating, but chock
it up to hormones or a healthy body image and I wanted to bone
all day, everyday. My husband, however, did not feel the same way.
While he constantly told me I was beautiful, sex became foreign to
him, and increasingly so after we found out we were having a girl. I
told him, in the kindest way possible, that he wouldn't hurt her—he
wasn't that, um, big. But it wasn't that. It was something else, and by
the end of that ten-month incubation period known as pregnancy, I
could count the number of times we had sex on one hand. So I couldn't
wait to give birth and resume "normal" sexual activity.

Yet sometime after birth, after passing the placenta and lochia and
receiving innumerable stitches for a second-degree tear, that changed.
(For those unacquainted, lochia is just a super sexy word for your
revenge period, i.e. two months of mucus and postpartum bleeding.)
Being a new mom, sleep deprived and essentially strung out on cup
after cup of half-drunk coffee, I didn't give sex another thought—at
least not until my six-week checkup.

Six weeks.

My ob-gyn rested his large hand on my shoulder. With a slight
squeeze and a smile he let me know we were done. "All right,
Kimberly. Everything looks great. You can go ahead and get dressed
and then come back to my office." He paused, "No rush, though; take
your time."

I lay still for a few moments, my unshaven legs still raised and
separated—a thin, white strip of medical paper covering my crotch. I
took in the sterilized silence and let my eyes dart around the room. This

was one of those rare moments that was mine and I decided to protect it. I decided I was more comfortable naked from the waist down in a strange room than I was anywhere else. I decided I would in fact take my time.

I scanned the room. My eyes shifted from the sink to the red sharps container above it. I glanced at a poster for tubal ligations and long-term birth control, giving it a second thought and then a third. Eventually my gaze settled on an unused ultrasound machine across the room, and then between my legs. I didn't look down. I was okay looking past my knees. I was okay overlooking my soft and still swollen stomach and ignoring the fading bruise on my upper thigh, but I didn't dare look between them. I was too scared and too ashamed.

The truth is I was relieved the appointment was over. It was the longest anyone had looked at my vagina in six weeks, and to say I was self-conscious after pushing a seven pound human being from my one-hundred pound frame, and after ripping open, would be an understatement. I couldn't be sure what he saw but I knew it wasn't me—or at least the me I used to be. (I made the mistake of sneaking a peek hours after my daughter was born, when the stitches were still bloody and the skin was puffy, taut, and bruised.)

As I lay there, a slick patch of medical-grade lubricant began to pool between my labia and upper thigh, that small line of skin where a properly fitted pair of underwear is supposed to sit— where my underwear used to sit, when I wore bikini briefs that weren't two sizes too big. I stepped into my mint green Hanes Her Way's. As the cotton came in contact with my unshaven lips I could feel it absorb every moist, sticky bit. I felt disgusting. I could have slipped on one of those super absorbent maxi pads I was still wearing to soak up the errant bits of afterbirth. I could have scavenged through my purse, also known as my daughter's diaper bag, for a tissue or baby wipe but I didn't because I didn't want to. I wanted to stay lost in that room and hidden behind ill-fitting clothes forever.

I wondered how long I could linger alone in the exam room. Would they allow me to take a nap? Could I use the time to connect with Facebook friends? Could I sit and simply enjoy the silence?

I was stalling, but I was scared. I was scared of what the doctor would say and more terrified of what he wouldn't.

After a few moments I gave up and pulled on my dark blue jeans. I fought with the zipper, yanking it up in half-inch increments before I reached that fucking brass button. It wouldn't close. I knew it wouldn't close—it didn't on the way here—but I still couldn't come to terms with the fact that my life, my breasts, and my battered vagina were not the same.

I entered my doctor's office and fell into the oversized brown leather chair beside his desk, the type of chair you see in movies, with a high broad back and brass studs. "Everything looks great. You can go ahead and resume normal activity and, if everything stays the same, I don't need to see you for another year. Do you have any questions?"

"So," I paused, "the stitches have healed?"

"The stitches look great. There's no bleeding or infection and no scar. In fact, you can't even tell you tore."

He smiled but I cringed. I could tell. I could tell every time I wiped myself. I could tell every time I caught my naked reflection, and saw the full forest of overgrown hair shrouding my lips, in the mirror. I could tell when my husband tried to touch me. I could tell; I couldn't forget.

"And sex?" I didn't want to ask. I knew what the answer was, but I was hoping he overlooked something. While I didn't pop any stitches, maybe there was a yeast infection he'd forgotten to tell me about? I was hoping to buy more time, begging to buy more time. I was grasping at straws.

"You can resume normal sexual activity."

There they were. The six words I didn't want to hear; the six words I hoped he wouldn't say.

I was a dead woman walking.

That night, when my daughter went down for bed (or the four straight hours of sleep which distinguished this nap from every other), I felt my husband's hands wrap around my waist as I was boiling breast pump parts. He kissed my neck and moved up my stomach and toward my engorged breasts, which he freed—one at a time—from the yellow nursing nightgown I was wearing. I wanted to stop him. I wanted to tell him the thought of being penetrated where I had just ripped apart terrified me. I wanted to tell him I didn't feel sexy, that there was nothing sexy about my "pouch," leaking breasts (which were bound to shoot him in the eye with errant milk), or war-torn vagina. But instead I stood there with my eyes closed fighting the urge to flee, fighting the urge to push him away.

I focused on his touch and his breath, as my own breathing was far too erratic and my mind too cluttered with self-loathing. I listened. I could hear the anticipation building with each inhale; I could feel the lust on my neck with every exhale.

I could have lied. I could have said I had a headache or was still bleeding, but I stayed. I stayed. I slipped out of my granny panties, and let him slip inside. It wasn't pain-free—hell, it fucking hurt—but I stayed. I felt. I listened. And that was a start.

Work–Life Balance

Jeanne Bonner

*I remembered I liked work, and I liked interviewing people, and
considering proposal ideas, and synthesizing large amounts of
information into digestible stories for my audience. I liked having
a specialty. I liked living in the world of ideas.*

As with so many things said in conversation, what I remember first
about her comment is the tone. The quick way she interrupted me,
almost as though she were upbraiding me. Which wouldn't have been
out of the question—she is, after all, my older sister, and a "Type A"
person. Plus, she was the expert. As we spoke, I was pregnant for the
first time, while she was running after four children, ages five to fifteen.

"You probably don't want to quit your job now or tell them that
you may not come back after maternity leave," she said that day on the
phone. I was sitting on the futon upstairs in our bedroom, looking at
items we'd bought for the nursery. "You may want to go back to work
after you have the baby."

I immediately thought she was channeling her guilt as a working
mother and trying to steer me away from becoming a stay-at-home
mom. That she had forgotten what it was like to be pregnant and have
a newborn. How would I ever bring myself to leave my child for hours
a day with strangers?

Plus, I had tried so hard, and for so long, to become pregnant.
What would be the point of leaving the child, after such effort, such
anguish? Didn't I want to be a mother? Besides, I wasn't crazy about
my job, and considered motherhood a pretty good excuse to finally
leave it.

On the phone that day, I silently dismissed what she said and we
moved onto other topics. But her small, offhand comment lodged in
my head. I heard it replay over and over. Nagging at me. *Thankfully.*

A few months later, I was in the throes of my maternity leave. And
while I was humbled and amazed by the experience of pregnancy and

childbirth, I was also overwhelmed by the demands of being a first-time mom.

My maternity leave days, in the full heat of an Atlanta summer, were often just a series of failed, desperate attempts to coax a nap out of my infant son, Leo. I'd embark on long walks in the stroller in the hopes of inducing sleep. Or I'd walk him around his room for what felt like forever.

I even consulted a sleep specialist. I knew establishing solid sleep routines would be key for his development. But I also needed time alone to think, to be me, to use my brain in different ways.

I quickly found most days I longed for any kind of a break. When my partner came home from work some nights, I would go swim laps in our neighborhood pool, and then drive around the park, practically in a trance, as I blasted a Bruce Springsteen song about desperate love.

In other words, I was beginning to realize I could bear being away from my child.

Nonetheless, as the days of maternity leave dwindled and the date of my first day back at work loomed, I began to panic. How would I marry the two sides of my life? My mother was no help. "Can't you take a year off and then go back to your job?" Um, no, Mom. It doesn't work that way.

Other young mothers I knew warned me I would cry when I left three-month-old Leo at daycare for the first time. Many said they dissolved into tears when they climbed into their cars in the parking lot of their children's daycare.

You know what? I didn't cry. Not at all. I was too exhausted to cry. I couldn't sleep the night before my first day back at work. And maybe my frustrations had built up, because I was fine with letting someone else put him down for a nap.

When I arrived in the office, all of my colleagues were gracious and full of questions about Leo. They wanted to see pictures, they wanted to catch me up on news and kvetch about office-place gossip. Good colleagues that they were, they were glad I was back.

Me? I was stiff and awkward. I barely remembered how to make chit-chat or sit in a desk chair for hours. Plus, I felt tired, jittery, and hungry. And I needed to figure out how I would fit in breast-pumping sessions with the demands of my job as a public radio station reporter. Indeed, before long, I would be pumping milk in a tiny bathroom in the state Capitol as I covered the legislature.

But then something happened, in the first few weeks after returning to my job.

I remembered I liked work, and I liked interviewing people, and considering proposal ideas, and synthesizing large amounts of information into digestible stories for my audience. I liked having a specialty. I liked living in the world of ideas.

In short, after three months of doing no work, of barely looking at my work email, and avoiding news updates about anything I might have covered, I realized I'm not someone who could stay at home. I'm not someone who can be fulfilled without working for pay. And a big part of being me consists of writing, ruminating, and reflecting—on something other than diaper rash.

It was as if my personality was suddenly, instantly crystallized—for me. One of those moments where all you can do is slap yourself on the forehead, and go, "Duh."

Back in the office, I was also thrilled to be in a different part of the city. There was more to life than my bedroom, my kitchen, the front porch and our neighborhood park. Yay! I could read the newspaper while I pumped breast milk, and maybe even stop at a shop on my way home.

Was it possible the best week of maternity leave (after the initial week where you're walking on stars and the baby is too shell-shocked to do much but sleep) was the week mine ended?

To be sure, I've had my doubts about how long I'm away from my son each day and the vagaries of American daycare. At times, I find it amazing that we are so quick to leave our children with strangers. For hours. Every day. When you look at your schedule, it becomes as though *you* are babysitting your own children when you only spend three or four hours a day with them before and after daycare.

There were also days in the early months back on the job when I'd suddenly think, "Where is Leo? What have I done with Leo?" One day, I was covering an important talk by the Speaker of Georgia's General Assembly when suddenly I felt a sharp pain in my chest. I thought to myself, "Leo is with strangers. How can I be here covering this event, laughing at the Speaker's comments, when my baby is across town, without me?"

Another day I noticed myself running through a mental checklist as I drove out of the parking lot of Leo's daycare. The top item on the list was: should my son be in full-time daycare? The thought took on a particular urgency that day because Leo had entered the stage of lavishing affection on his parents and giggling effusively at any attention we gave him. That morning, he stared into my eyes as if dazzled by me. "My God," I thought, "the last time someone looked at me this way, it was his father and we were in a bar in Italy, about to embark on an epic romance! Why am I leaving this beautiful boy to go to a job I don't even like?"

But luckily I never got too far in the whirlwind of post-daycare anxiety, if for no other reason than I decided professional, accomplished men didn't have these thoughts. Or at least they weren't paralyzed by them. More importantly, I'd already gleaned what my sister, a lawyer, might have been hinting at: I love working. I love thinking. I love the intellectual debate about ideas that my field of journalism affords me to indulge. And if I stop working, I'm unhappy.

Of course, it's ironic. I spent most of my maternity leave lamenting how few months I had off from work. Commiserating with other mothers that it would never be enough. And yet the moment it was over, I went back to being me. The old me. The journalist, the colleague, the news buff.

I was also the new me—a mom. But that didn't mean forsaking everything meaningful that had come before.

My sister and I didn't talk much more about my post-maternity leave plans. It was just an off-hand comment she made. But I still remember the exact tone she used to warn me about leaving my job. I can feel myself flinch, and my heart race a bit, in remembrance. Now I realize the tone was really just the voice of experience. Just a flag from someone who had had the same misgivings, the same trepidations, and had learned the lessons for herself. And she was trying to help prevent me from making any decisions I would later regret.

I also like to think she considers me a hard worker and a

consummate writer. But that's just the little sister in me. Or does she know me better than I know myself? Who knows? All I can say is that one line she tossed off on the phone tossed me a lifeline.

Milking It

Ann K. Howley

*Now I might even be one of those random strangers on the street
who approaches pregnant ladies and gives unwanted advice. So if
you're pregnant and I ever run into you, I'm still going to give it
to you straight.*

Ladies, I'm going to give it to you straight.

Breastfeeding sucks.

But I don't want to say that too loud or I might pick a fight with
the American Academy of Pediatrics, The World Health Organization,
the Centers for Disease Control and Prevention, UNICEF and, quite
possibly, Maxim magazine subscribers.

When I was pregnant with my first son, doctors, nurses, relatives,
friends, and random strangers on the street bombarded me with
warnings that if I didn't breastfeed, my baby was going to be at risk for
a plethora of ills from diarrhea to leukemia. And if that didn't convince
me, they dangled the ultimate carrot.

"Did you know that breastfeeding burns 500 calories a day?" they
asked.

No fair. What pudgy, postpartum mama would rather run five
miles if she can sit in a rocking chair and lactate to burn off baby
blubber that looked way cuter when it was still a bump?

Warning: just because it's good for you and your baby doesn't
mean that breastfeeding is going to be easy.

"He's still not latching on," I said, using the nursing vernacular for
what I thought meant "sufficient suction to extract a drop of milk from
my tender boobs."

"Just keep trying," the nurse said, not caring that I was in as much
agony as if my breast was being attacked by a piranha.

The truth is, a baby can gnaw and chomp uselessly for days until
he figures out how to suckle efficiently, and in the meantime, some

mothers just give up and beg to use the bottle, thinking that only Similac will end her torment.

This isn't accurate, though, because whether or not a new mother breastfeeds, her milk will still "come in," and when it does, she's in for a big surprise.

Just imagine you're sitting there, minding your own business, and all of a sudden you feel a strange tingling and pressure in your breasts, and when you look down, you can practically see your boobs growing, just like "in Whoville, they say, when the Grinch's small heart grew three sizes that day."

My milk "came in" shortly after I came home from the hospital after giving birth to my first son. I had just stepped out of the shower when I felt an odd, stinging sensation in my chest and did a double take when I glanced in the mirror and saw that my normally modest-sized boobs suddenly looked pumped up like double-D balloons that were about to burst. I only had time to gasp at this shocking miracle when milk suddenly began shooting at the bathroom walls and mirror as if two garden hose nozzles with precision spray settings were attached to my chest.

This was only the beginning of what became the focal point of my existence as the mother of a newborn. Day and night, my breasts expanded and contracted at regular intervals in an unending enterprise to feed my baby. At the slightest provocation, like hearing him whimper, or even thinking of him whimpering, my body would fly into a frenzy of uncontrollable milk production that could only be relieved by attaching a hearty, hungry infant to each breast.

Between feedings, I stuffed cloth diapers into my nursing bra to try to soak up the excess milk, and I even tried those pancake-sized nursing pads that promised more protection from public embarrassment than they were able to provide. Many times, I came home from the market with two wet circles on my chest that looked like I just filched two slices of bologna from the deli and hid them under my shirt.

All this was quite unsettling, but it helped me understand one of the great dairy mysteries of my life. When I was a girl, I used to watch Little House on the Prairie and The Waltons, and noticed that milking the cow was always the first task that farm folks did when they got up at the crack of dawn. In fact, I was always curious as to why milking a cow was such an urgent matter that it could not be delayed or avoided. I didn't see why Half Pint or Jim Bob couldn't milk the cow before lunch, or after they had finished some of their other chores.

It wasn't until I was a milk producer myself that I began to understand how important it was for a cow's personal health and well-being to be milked first thing in the morning before her udders stretched to the breaking point. I even wondered how serious the consequences could be if a cow wasn't milked. However, when I Googled the question, "can a cow explode if it's not milked," I landed in the middle of a series of heated posts by vegans who complain that this is the Number One Stupidest Question they are regularly asked.

I do not disrespect bottle feeding mothers. I know that there are medical and personal reasons why a mom chooses bottle feeding over breastfeeding. I can only imagine how painful and difficult it must be for a non-nursing mother to wean herself. Bottle feeding is not a cheap way out.

Actually, I often felt jealous of mothers with bottle fed babies. As easy and convenient as it was to whip out a ready-made milk feast for my babies any time, any place, I sometimes wished I could take a break.

So why didn't I just pump my milk?

I did. But unfortunately, both of my sons *hated* bottles. Even if I had just pumped fresh, sweet breast milk and put it in a bottle, still warm, both of them would scream and writhe, outraged that somebody dared to insert latex into their mouths. My infants clearly conveyed the message that they would rather starve than suck a bottle. In fact, they acted upon this threat by spitting out the nipple, turning their heads to avoid it, and screaming until they were red in the face. When they finally had to accept the bottle, it was only long enough to obtain enough sustenance to survive.

My maternal guilt started with the bottle.

I didn't have much of a choice, though. Eventually I had to go back to work, which always caused me even greater angst.

"Don't worry, he'll take the bottle when he's hungry enough," my mother first said about Son #1, then repeated four years later with Son #2.

It never made me feel better, not at the moment my mother said it, nor when I had to leave for work and accept the unsavory truth that I was forced to call my baby's bluff.

"Yeah, go ahead . . . starve," I felt like I was saying.

Tough love sucks.

Like breastfeeding.

This, however, highlights another unpleasant task that is unique to lactating women—pumping breast milk at work.

All experts agree that a state of relaxed calm is best for mothers to successfully express breast milk. However, I could be sitting in a chaise lounge on the warm deck of an exclusive beachfront property, listening to the ocean and sipping a cool drink while a professional masseuse massaged my shoulders, and I would still have a hard time relaxing enough to let a small machine squeeze the living daylights out of my boobs.

Never underestimate the magnitude of chivalry a mother displays by pumping breast milk at work.

In many work venues, it's hard to find a private place to pump and, in my opinion, the ladies room isn't the most satisfying option. I don't care if we're "all girls," I would never want anyone to walk in and witness the sight of my boob being held hostage by an electronic suction machine.

Although my boss generously said I could "do whatever I needed to do" after my son was born, I faced two key dilemmas. First, all the private offices where I could take a "pump break" had glass windows and doors, which offered zero privacy. I solved this by taping a flannel baby blanket across the window and door, positioning it so that it would be impossible for anyone to sneak a peek unless they deliberately tried (which I trusted nobody would do at the risk of seeing me in a delicate position that might permanently alter their perception of the female anatomy.)

The second obstacle was that my mostly young, twenty-something, professional male co-workers looked confused and terrified every time I hid behind the baby blanket to do some mysterious woman thing that involved the constant drone of a whirring motor. My colleagues sensed the indelicacy of the situation, and every time I exited my makeshift pumping station, the boys kept their heads down and avoided making eye contact with me. Even the pre-children, married guys were as brainless about babies as the younger guys, who were barely beyond the college beer bong stage of life. As I walked past their work stations, they sat still as statues, pretending to be concentrating, when, in reality, I knew my daily lactation schedule was terrorizing the bejeebers out of them.

It became an unending cycle of embarrassment for me, as the longer they kept silent and avoided me, the more uncomfortable I felt. The only person who seemed completely oblivious was the boss, who remained steadfastly unaware of everything. Once, as I stood at the kitchen sink, he approached and engaged me in a chatty conversation without even noticing that I was washing my breast pump. Then one day, he absentmindedly wondered why a flannel blanket was taped up and tried to open the door while I was inside pumping. Fortunately, I screamed loudly enough to dissuade him from entering, but after that near disaster, the boys outside practically quivered in fear at the sight of me.

That's when I knew I had to do something to clear the air. I couldn't live with this awkward discomfort anymore. The more my co-workers ignored me, the worse I felt. I had no idea what I was going to do or say, but I knew I had to be brutally honest and forthright with them. They, too, had been silently suffering for months. They deserved the truth.

So the next day, as I walked past the boys, who instinctively dropped their heads as if they had the sudden urge to pray, I gathered my courage.

"Well," I said loudly, "it's time to take Bessie to the barn."

Instinctively they froze, startled that I would actually speak to them. Then, one guy's lips twitched and slowly bent into a grin. One by one, they all started to laugh.

Thank goodness, it broke the ice.

Unexpectedly, the youngest guy, who looked like he was barely old enough to drive, looked me straight in the eye and asked what all the guys were probably wondering all along:

"Does it hurt?" he asked.

"Yeah," I said.

I didn't go into detail. As a working mother, I appreciated that a twenty-four-year old, baby-faced boy had just found the inner strength to bridge the nearly insurmountable divide between young males and lactating females.

That was enough.

So I survived the ordeal of breastfeeding and my kids are all grown up. Now I might even be one of those random strangers on the street who approaches pregnant ladies and gives unwanted advice. So if you're pregnant and I ever run into you, I'm still going to give it to you straight.

Breastfeeding sucks.

But now I have to run five miles.

Full Circle

Yvonne Spence

*She said mothers of premature babies felt that it was their fault,
mothers felt robbed of their pregnancies, mothers felt angry and
ashamed, mothers felt like walking away from their babies. "And
yet," she said, "they come, day after day, to spend hours by their
babies' side because they cannot bear to not come."*

I could only hear one side of the phone conversation, but that was
enough to know it wasn't good. I could hear it in the tone of my
husband's voice and in the words he said: words like *critical* and *stable*. I
could see it in the droop of his shoulders, in the grip of his hand on the
receiver. He put down the phone, and stood, not speaking. Fear filled
the space between us.

"It's a lung infection. She's on a ventilator. They're giving her
antibiotics for the infection and morphine to make her comfortable."

I sat down. In my mind's eye, I saw our baby in her incubator,
her tiny body punctured by yet more needles, morphine pumping into
her veins. I imagined her pain and fear. I imagined her permanently
damaged by this illness and for one horrible moment, I wondered if it
might be better for her if she died.

***

Just over a week earlier, when I was desperately trying not to give
birth, a doctor came into the room, and warned, "Your baby has a fifty
percent chance of survival, and a ten percent chance of being normal."

That was before my waters broke, when I was still clinging to a
shred of hope that the contractions would stop, that my baby would
not be born over three months early.

Sometime in the first hours after her birth, a doctor used the words
"emotional roller coaster." He had no idea what he was talking about.
Roller coasters are thrilling; people willingly go on them to have fun.

Some other time in those first blurred hours, I saw my baby.

117

Through the glass walls of an incubator, I saw her bruised face and closed eyes. I saw the wires and tubes that criss-crossed her body and tangled around her. I saw the splints on her arms and legs, splints that held in place drip needles in both her hands, hands the size of my thumbnail. A nurse told me they didn't hurt. I didn't believe her.

The drip needle in my own hand throbbed.

The nurse said I could touch my baby. I washed my hands with Hibiscrub for the recommended minute, and the nurse opened one of the incubator windows.

"You can stroke her back," she said.

My baby's skin felt dry and fragile, as if it could tear as easily as tissue paper. I didn't want to stroke her the way you might a cat. I wanted her where she should be, safely inside me.

"I'm so sorry," I whispered, "so sorry."

Sorry, sorry.

Guilt was a coat I wore, fear a blanket I pulled over at night and wrapped tight. They twisted around me in the darkness until I jerked awake, breathless and soaked with sweat.

In daylight, I shrugged off the blanket and, trying to be normal, went to eat breakfast in the dining room.

I sat alone.

At another table, women with huge bellies moaned about being stuck in hospital. One complained she'd been on bed rest for two weeks and nothing had happened. She said she was going home, that she had a life to lead and a family who needed her.

I wanted to yell at her, to say that I would gladly have stayed a month or more in the hospital if it could have kept my baby safe inside me. I wanted to tell these women to stop being so complacent, so cavalier. But all I could do was rush from the room in tears.

A friend came to visit me. She had driven over a hundred miles, and I thought she was stopping off on a journey somewhere else. It didn't occur to me that she had driven all that way just to see me. She gave me flowers and a card that said, "Congratulations on the birth of your baby."

I felt embarrassed at her mistake. I had done nothing to deserve congratulations.

That evening, I shuffled along the corridors to the Newborn Unit. Intensive Care Level 1 was filled with nurses. One explained it was shift change time.

"I'm sorry," I said, and stood helplessly, trying to think what to do next.

"It's okay," she said. "You weren't to know."

Yet, from somewhere in the fog of fear and confusion that surrounded me, a memory came of a nurse explaining their twelve-hour shift patterns. I should have remembered, should not have been a nuisance.

The nurse showed me a little waiting room. I wanted to leave, to run away back to my room, but I stayed. I stayed because the nurse had shown me where to sit, and I didn't want to upset her even more. Mostly I did what the nurses said, because I had no clue what else to do.

Other mothers somehow figured things out. The premature births of their babies didn't make them into idiots, didn't render them incapable of retaining information like nurses' changeover time. The mother in the denim dress, whose baby had been five hundred and eighteen grams at birth wasn't standing over him. My baby was over a kilo, so I should be able to cope like she did. No other mother was here, bothering the nurses, getting in the way. I was an idiot, a fool, an imbecile.

As my thoughts spiraled deeper and darker, a woman appeared in the doorway. She wasn't in uniform, but a skirt and blouse.

"You're Louise's mum aren't you?"

"Yes."

Her name was Teresa, and she was a nurse who specialized in the babies' emotional care. She told me that in the past, although premature babies had all their physical needs met in intensive care, their emotional needs were not. She said, "Because of all the medical interventions, they come to associate touch with pain. Babies were often bad tempered when they came home." Teresa said that now there were ways to help premature babies learn that touch didn't always mean pain, that it could soothe.

She talked about containment holding. I listened in the dazed way

I listened to most explanations then, struggling to comprehend her words through the fog. I understood that containment holding didn't mean getting to take my baby from the incubator, but I would get to touch her more than I had the day before, that placing my hands on her head and back would somehow help her feel calmer. It was hard for me to believe that I could do anything to help my baby feel calmer, since mostly I wanted to cry when I saw her.

Then Teresa talked about massage.

"Oh, yes," I replied. "I did that with my first daughter."

Teresa explained that it would be a few weeks yet until Louise would be ready, and that it was quite different than massaging a full-term baby. "I come in on Tuesdays and Thursdays and will show you how when it's time."

I felt embarrassed again, my stupidity exposed. My baby's tissue paper skin was far too fragile for massage.

Teresa spoke about something called kangaroo care. This was skin-to-skin contact, and you held the baby high up on your chest. She explained that to do it I would need to wear a shirt that buttoned down the front, so that my baby would stay warm inside it.

"Would you like to hold your baby?" she asked.

I was wearing a t-shirt rather than a button-down shirt, so I thought she meant containment holding, and said yes. But Teresa told me to sit in the chair near Louise's incubator and then she put screens around. She told me to take off my top, and that she would give me a blanket.

As Teresa opened the nearside of the incubator, my heart was thudding. As much as I longed to hold my baby, I was terrified of hurting her, of crushing her fragile body or breaking her tiny bones.

Teresa and another nurse took Louise out. They laughed. "She's been knitting again."

Teresa looked over to me. "We'll just need to straighten out these wires. There are so many they've got tangled. Are you okay for a moment?"

I tried to smile. My heart went on thudding.

They positioned Louise upright on my chest, and Teresa showed me where to place one hand under her bottom and another across her back.

I was scared to move in case I hurt her.

From the shelf above my head came a loud and insistent beep. The nurses paid no heed.

"Why is the monitor doing that?" I asked, trying not show my panic.

"It's okay," Teresa replied. "Her oxygen probe will have come off when we moved her. I'll put it back on in a moment." She reached up and pressed a button, silencing the monitor.

I didn't feel reassured.

"Her color is more important," Teresa said. "And she looks fine."

She laid a white cotton cellular blanket over us to keep Louise warm. Then she replaced the probe, taping it back onto a tiny foot.

She looked up. "Yes, she's fine."

The other nurse went to attend to a different baby and Teresa closed up the incubator.

I could see no more of my baby than the top of her head and the tube for the CPAP, a machine that used air pressure to help her breathe. But I could smell her. Among all the hospital smells, her own scent came through— that baby sweetness. I could feel her bird-like body nestling into mine, the feathery movements of her tiny arms and hands. I could feel her heartbeat, fluttering so fast it seemed it might break out of her body.

Teresa returned, and looked up at the monitor. "Her oxygen saturation has gone up. That's because she's relaxing."

Teresa smiled and went home, her shift having finished almost an hour before. She had stayed late for us.

Monitors beeped and nurses bustled around, yet I was alone with my baby. I mattered to her, enough that a monitor showed she was calming. And she was almost back where she should be, back with me. I was her mother again.

Tears escaped from my eyes, taking with them a trickle of the tension that had been building inside me for days.

Yet in the middle of the night, I woke sweating.

For a moment, I was still pregnant; my baby was still due in

November and it was only the heat of a fever in August that had woken me. Then I remembered that fever had torn away my baby too early, and I shivered as the sweat on my back turned cold.

I thought about my poor baby in her incubator, with all the drip needles piercing her skin, the tubes and wires.

I got out of bed and shuffled along the fluorescent-lit corridor to the nurse's station.

The nurse sitting behind the desk was a mass of curly brown hair and a smile. "Couldn't you sleep?"

When I'd met her the previous evening, she had invited me to come to see her any time I needed to.

"Sorry for bothering you…" I stammered, worried that she hadn't meant it.

"That's what I'm here for." Her eyes were soft as she gestured toward the seat in front of the desk.

I kept standing. "You said that if I needed to know how my baby was…" I trailed off again.

"Would you like me to ring over to the Newborn Unit to see how your baby is doing?"

"I'm sorry for being a nuisance." Now I would annoy her with my incessant apologizing. I was annoying myself.

"It's no trouble," she said, smiling. "You can sit while I ring."

I sat. My heart pounded.

The nurse dialed. My baby was fine, was sleeping.

"I'm sorry." I wanted to stand up, but my body wouldn't move.

"It wasn't your fault."

"How did you know what I was thinking?" My eyes filled, my vision blurred.

She smiled again.

For three weeks before her sister was born, my toddler had been ill. I had been up with her night after night, until the virus hit me too. I explained to the nurse that I should have taken better care, should have realized what to do.

"You had to look after your little girl," she said.

My eyes brimmed over.

My little girl, Melissa, came to the hospital every day with my husband. We took her to see the fish tank halfway down the ward. We said, "Fish; swish, swish."

She repeated, "Fish; swish, swish."

We took her over to the Newborn Unit. The first time, my husband held Melissa in his arms as we said, "See the baby."

She looked at a little boy in a nearby cot. He had been in hospital for six months and looked like a baby. Louise, with her red face, half-covered by tubes, shut away behind glass, did not.

Five days after Louise's birth, Melissa followed me out of my hospital room when I went to the bathroom. "Daddy," she said.

That was when I knew it was time to go home.

Two days later, while my husband held her in kangaroo care, our baby breathed without the CPAP. That could have been one of the highs on the doctor's imaginary emotional roller coaster, but he and others had told us again and again to expect setbacks until the words rang in my ears and stole my joy. Expect setbacks, expect setbacks.

The first came that same night.

***

By morning, when my husband called the hospital, our baby was seriously ill.

That terrible moment when I thought she might be better off dead felt like death to me. As my flickering heartbeat restarted, I couldn't bear to think Melissa might never remember her sister. I wanted our baby to survive no matter what; I wanted us to be a family.

I felt ashamed even then—it wasn't instant burning love that made me want Louise to live, but selfish desire.

As we drove to the hospital, I knew, without a doubt, that I was a terrible, awful mother. I grasped my new mobile phone, willing it to stay silent until we reached the hospital, willing it never to ring.

In the intensive care room, we understood less than half of what the doctor told us, but enough to know that the worst was far from over. As well as the lung infection, the blood tests they ran several times a day indicated another infection was brewing.

The nursing sister, Dee, came to speak to me. She said it was hard, seeing my baby so ill. She said mothers of premature babies felt that it was their fault, mothers felt robbed of their pregnancies, mothers felt angry and ashamed, mothers felt like walking away from their babies. "And yet," she said, "they come, day after day, to spend hours by their babies' side because they cannot bear to not come."

She described everything I was feeling. Slowly I realized I wasn't a monster. I wasn't a terrible mother, but a normal one. It was like being wrapped up, loved.

Dee's words came back to me again and again in my daughter's early years. They were what got me through the months that followed; they eased the fear of that first doctor's warning, a warning that didn't come true. The kindness of Dee and Teresa, and the gentle words and smile of a nurse whose name I can no longer remember, stayed with me.

Louise eventually moved from intensive care to our local hospital. There I met a mother who was in the same state of shock I'd been in a few months before. One day, I told her all the things Dee had told me.

"Oh," she said, just as I had done. "I thought it was just me."

To everything I said, she repeated those words. I could see her relax, as I had done.

Our baby came home, but after only two weeks both her lungs collapsed. The night we rushed her back to hospital, that mother was in the ward. As doctors and nurses worked to save my daughter's life, that mother came to talk to me. She told me how happy she had been when my daughter got home. How sorry she felt for me right now. How much she was rooting for us. She told me that what I'd said to her had saved her life.

I was so glad she told me. Her words gave myself back to me.

What I Wanted

M.K. Martin

We talk. He admits he, too, feels overwhelmed. He's been trying to seem strong for me.

I sit in the glider, head down, tears cool on my hot, humiliated cheeks. I tell myself, "This is what I wanted, what we wanted." I remind myself that I would have given anything to save Annika.

It's late, sometime after 2:00 a.m. Varya's been fussing since around 8:00 p.m. I don't know how much more I can take. My husband and I take turns walking her up and down the hall, in an effort to keep her quiet enough for the other to grab fifteen-twenty minute naps.

This is what I wanted.

I struggle with the SNS (supplemental nursing system). A woman on a blog described it as requiring the precision of a surgeon to place the tiny, flexible tube properly. Too far over the nipple and the baby chokes. Too far back, and she doesn't suck the tube in. Precious pumped milk goes everywhere, covers me, her tiny face and hands. She wails.

This is what I wanted.

The baby cries and my husband scoops her up, takes her away, cooing softly to her. We're all exhausted. She was sleeping, and I dozed off. I heard her waking. Please, go back to sleep. Please, just five more minutes. But no, now she's crying in earnest. "What's wrong with her?" Is it my imagination, or is his tone accusatory? What kind of mother sleeps while her baby cries? What kind of mother doesn't know what's wrong with her own child?

Ever since she was born, he only has eyes for her. Does he even know how hard this is for me? Does he still care?

What kind of mother is jealous of a father's love for his daughter? A monster mother, that's who.

This is what I wanted.

125

"Incompatible with life." This is how the doctor describes Annika's heart defect. Incompatible is a term for computer games and graphics cards, for two people on a date, for my mother's religious beliefs and my lack thereof. Incompatible can't apply to Annika and life.

How do you say goodbye to someone you never met? How do you have closure on a life that never opened?

After she's gone the house is full of flowers and my belly is empty.

Eventually we try again. I'm advised, "Don't be stressed. Stress is bad for the baby." I spend the whole nine months terrified.

This is what I wanted.

"I don't know how we're going to make it." I try to keep my tone light, joking, play it off as an exaggeration, not a desperate glimpse of my truth. I'm drowning in the sea of motherhood. Varya has lost too much weight and I'm still not producing enough milk for her. Yet another sign I'm not cut out to be a mother. With the SNS and her slow feeding rate, each session drags on between forty-five and sixty minutes. She needs to eat every two hours, round the clock. All I do is feed her.

This is what I wanted.

"We're just going to have to make it work," he says with grim determination. He takes the baby while I pump. I'm trapped here for fifteen minutes, watching the drops slowly fall, trying to coax every bit of milk out of me.

My lap blurs through my tears. I hang my head, hide behind my hair. *This is what . . .*

"What's the matter?"

"Nothing." My voice trembles.

He bends down, sees the tears. He insists I tell him what's wrong. We talk. He admits he, too, feels overwhelmed. He's been trying to seem strong for me, for Varya. He, too, is drowning. I'm not alone. I'm part of a family.

This is what I wanted.

Regret

Vanessa Hua

Each time I looked ahead to my next parenting mission, I forgot the present.

Holding the bottle to my son's lips for the first time, I sobbed. In their first month, I'd tried to nurse my twins, but Didi, the smaller one, the younger one, wasn't gaining weight quickly enough. His latch was shallow and his suck weak.

Cradling him awkwardly, I looked into his watermelon seed eyes as he swallowed. I'd failed to bond with him as I'd imagined, failed to give what he deserved. My preparations–the books, classes, and videos on breastfeeding—had led me to believe I had control where I had none. All my life, I'd achieved through effort and sacrifice, and I'd taken pride in, been defined by my accomplishments as a journalist. My ambition to nurse was no different than what drove me to expose a political fundraising scandal and report stories from around the globe.

My pregnancy had been charmed. Feeling healthy and hopeful, I swam daily until a week before I delivered, surely alarming gym-goers who thought they were going to witness a water birth. Doctors induced three weeks early, because I'd developed pre-eclampsia, a life-threatening rapid rise in blood pressure.

Gege arrived first, around 7:00 a.m., and Didi twenty-six minutes later, with the help of an extractor that gripped onto his head while I pushed. "He looks like your father," my husband said. Didi shared my father's elfin ears and squat nose. Holding him to my bare chest, I noticed the raised red mark from the vacuum, as though he'd escaped the clutches of a lamprey.

Later that morning, I fainted the first time I stood up. Dizzy and weak, I hadn't eaten or slept for more than 24 hours, and my blood pressure remained high. Doctors put me on medication that set my body afire. I was trapped in bed, on a catheter, unable to use my arms, with an IV in one and a blood pressure monitor on the other, which made breastfeeding near impossible.

Gege would learn to nurse with enthusiasm, his jaw pumping like a piranha's, but we had to wake Didi by rubbing his scrawny limbs with a wet washcloth, stripping him to his diaper, and tickling his feet. A borderline case of jaundice left him sleepy, and when feeding, he'd scream, take a few sucks, and fall asleep, overwhelmed.

I was just as overwhelmed. Late one night, a nurse performed breast compressions on me while Didi suckled. "Hold it like a sandwich," she said, milking me by a monitor's pale glow. I asked my husband to continue—we desperately wanted Didi to eat—and he squeezed so hard he left bruises in the shape of his fingers.

Because Didi's condition wasn't improving, doctors wanted to keep him at the hospital overnight. My insurance only covered a stay of 48 hours, the nurse said briskly, and we had discharge paperwork to complete.

"I don't want to leave him," I bawled. I didn't want him alone under the light box while the rest of his family went home. Born second, born small, he shouldn't be abandoned. If the nurses introduced bottles of formula to him, the nipple's faster flow might deter him from learning to breastfeed. Doctors decided to let us take Didi home, where he'd receive portable phototherapy.

I'd been told to enjoy the newborn period, when the babies slept all the time and wouldn't move from the spot where we placed them. Instead, I tormented myself, attempting to nurse up to a dozen times a day. I'd clasp a twin to me, then the other, sometimes both at the same time on the giant foam nursing pillow, awkward and bulky as a life preserver. The twins nursed for twenty, forty, sixty minutes or more in each session. Then my husband or his mother would give expressed breast milk and formula in a bottle while I pumped for the next feeding.

I'd been formula fed, as had many of my friends, and though I'd told myself I shouldn't be ashamed if I had to do the same, I didn't realize how much I'd want to nurse until after the twins arrived. For their nutrition, for our bonding, and I must admit, to reach my goal in my usual Type-A fashion. As much as I wanted to start a family, I'd feared losing my identity and the sense of control central to it.

To encourage abundant flow, I swallowed grassy teas and fenugreek pills, ate oatmeal, drank gallons of water, cranked up rain sounds, and visualized waterfalls, advice I'd found online in the wee hours, while pumping or nursing. I'd always found answers, with enough research, but I became more frantic, not less, and felt farther, not closer, to my twins.

One morning, Didi wailed in the bouncer while I was hooked to the pump, unable to travel beyond the length of the plug. The bottles collecting breast milk protruded from my hands-free pumping bra like pasties. As I knelt before Didi, milk spilled, splashing onto my feet. Cursing, I unhooked myself and scooped him up, tightened his swaddle and shushed him. Cuddling him, but not for long, because I had to finish filling out an elaborate feeding chart, with its mocking promise of order, whose columns of numbers seemed like a secret code whose mystery I would never solve. I staggered off topless, to air dry my chest, while I stored and labeled the breast milk and washed the pump equipment.

I dreamt my nipples fell off, leaving breasts smooth as a mannequin's. "Should I put it on ice?" I asked my doctor. "Will I still be able to breastfeed?" In short, I had lost my mind.

Often in or near tears, I had no patience for myself, or the people around me. If drops of breast milk spilled during a feeding, I turned so sullen that Marc and his mother began treating it like radioactive uranium ore.

A month after their birth, Marc and I took the twins for a walk around the park. Steering our long double-stroller was like piloting a battleship or herding a wiener dog. Running alongside, I adjusted the shade every time sunlight fell upon the sleeping babies. I tucked in the burp cloth coming loose around Didi's head, to keep him in position. His head was flaky and pink with cradle cap, and he had the receding hairline and flyaway tufts of Bozo the clown. His head was egg-shaped, not round, because he'd been squashed to the side of my uterus, crowded by his brother. I felt like I'd neglected Didi, even in utero. To even out the shape, we had to keep his head turned to the right while he slept.

We discussed whether I should nurse Gege and bottle feed Didi, if I could handle two kinds of feeding. It didn't seem fair to Didi, who had setbacks from the beginning, to deny him the emotional connection I had with his brother. But could he survive by breast alone?

The next day, Didi thrashed naked, howling on the digital scale. The numbers jumped around, up, down, up, down until he calmed down. The same: he weighed the same as he did before the weekend, when we'd stopped bottle-feeding the twins with formula and breast milk.

I dipped a refrigerated bottle of breast milk into bowl of warm water, gently swirling the cream layer. Taking Didi into my arms, I tipped the nipple into his rosebud mouth. I cried again, more tears in the last month than in the last five years of my life. I thought I'd have to stop nursing and pumping for both twins, because I couldn't keep up the punishing routine. It felt like nothing I'd planned for him had worked out, and nothing ever would. A day passed, and I questioned my decision, unwilling to give up. This time, Didi gained weight, without bottle supplementation.

As the months passed, we found our footing as parents, and I grew adept enough to feed the twins at the same time. "Both! At once! You're like a woman in National Geographic," a friend marveled at a party. I couldn't help but savor my accomplishment, even though I knew that my goal-oriented focus had undone me early on. Each time I looked ahead to my next parenting mission, I forgot the present. To help the twins nap, I read sleep-training books and blogs, and strapped them on, taking hour-long walks or bouncing on a yoga ball. To make their food, I peeled, diced, steamed, mashed, and pureed on an industrial scale. If only I'd spent more time touching the nub of their noses, kissing their tiny fingers, and stroking their velvet skin. If only I lived as my sons did and do: in the moment.

In the nursery, Didi and Gege are stirring, giggling awake from their morning nap. Their first year has been like watching a time-lapse film of evolution, as they emerged from the muck to roll over, crawl, stand, and take their first steps. Didi yelps and Gege babbles and soon they will pull themselves to their feet, waiting for me.

It's Okay

Elaine Alguire

She placed her hand upon mine, "You know, it is okay that you came back to work."

"You want to go grab a bite to eat?" my co-worker asked as she casually leaned into my office door. My eyes were almost crossing from staring at a spreadsheet full of product numbers, so her familiar face and the potential for a break were welcomed distractions.

"Yes!" I exclaimed. "Just give me a few minutes to finish inputting these numbers. Where do you want to go?"

Lunch breaks were part of my daily sanity efforts once I returned to work after my first son was born. My colleagues were my saving grace, listening as I talked about his latest infant feats—such as saying "dah" for Dad—and appeasing me by smiling and complimenting the photos I presented of him.

Many months before, I admired my baby belly constantly as my husband and I made decisions about the baby's birth and what color swaddling blankets to scan while registering at the baby store. Still, one final decision lingered—whether or not I would return to work once the time came.

After reviewing our finances and agreeing that we wanted to purchase a home in the near future, we decided together that I would to return to my job. We found a reputable home daycare run by a single mother who employed two ladies to help her with ten babies from six weeks to twelve months old. Her set-up was nice: a converted garage that she made into a large daycare room and plenty of toys and love to go around from the sweet, adoring Hispanic ladies who worked for her. I felt it was the best place for my baby to be.

Everything was set—the only thing unsettled and remaining was my "mommy guilt." A large part of me was eager to return to work. Even though I wanted to start a family more than anything, having a baby turned my world upside down. From the moment my baby son entered the world, becoming a mother was not what I expected, so I was quite relieved when my husband and I agreed that going back to work was best.

After my twelve-week maternity leave was over, I placed my little baby in Elsa's cradling arms, and tried to make myself cry. But I could not. I felt like I should be mourning the loss of our days alone together but inside I was silently celebrating. I felt strangled during many of those days, the clock slowly ticking away while this little being and I tried to figure each other out with the television as our only companion. I fretted over breastfeeding and nap times and counted the minutes until my husband returned home.

Now, spending each weekday away from my baby boy, my guilt was two-fold because I was a working mom who truly *enjoyed* being a working mom.

One day I had lunch with that same co-worker and she asked me if I was thinking about quitting. There were changes in our company and the shifts were making us all uneasy. I took her question the wrong way though, and told her that yes, I felt guilty every day for leaving my baby, but I wasn't sure I could stay home and care for him.

The conversation took a turn, and since she was older and wiser, she knew things that I did not because of her own life experience. I knew she could see in my eyes that I loved my son, but she was a good friend and also knew that the best thing for both of us at this point was being separated during the day.

"Elaine," she placed her hand upon mine, "You know, it is okay that you came back to work."

Her words were like a hand turning on a faucet and the tears immediately started to flow from my eyes.

"Oh, Hon."

"I just needed someone to say that to me," I said.

We sat there together while I cried and let out the many feelings I had been pushing deep down inside. As I tried to wipe away my tears, she held onto my hand and then we started laughing about the fact that it would be really nice to order a margarita at lunch time, just this once.

After our lunch I still carried guilt. It was impossible to get rid of those feelings completely. However, I knew my friend's words were true. It *was* okay that I had decided to go back to work. I reminded myself that many mothers do the same every day for a myriad of reasons. And though it wasn't gone, the guilt did diminish somewhat.

What I realized that day was that I needed someone else to validate my choice. I longed for an outsider (someone outside of my brain and family) to tell me that what I was doing—leaving my son five days a week—was all right and that it did not mean I loved him any less or that I was a bad mother. Thankfully, she did just that.

Eventually, I did leave the work place, after my second son was born. Things were different that time around though, as I was more accustomed to motherhood and knew what to expect. It was time for our family to change and adapt in a new way. Being home full time with my boys was definitely an adjustment, but as a second time mother I was much more comfortable in my own skin and choices.

There were days however, once I became a "SAHM," when I missed those lunches immensely. Guaranteed daily conversations with adults and time to myself were things I greatly cherished in those early days of new motherhood. I believe those times and my friend's words were a catalyst for other choices I made down the line for my family and myself.

All someone had to say was "It's okay." And often in motherhood, those two words are all we need to hear.

Seventy-Five Percent

Meghan Moravcik Walbert

*If you want to like your kids, and you want your kids to like
you, give parenting 75 percent of your effort.*

I was a perfect mother. For eight days.

For eight painful, exhausting days, I thought of nothing but my
newborn son's happiness and wellbeing.

Each day, I allowed him to feed from my breast at ninety-minute
intervals, despite the terrible latch, the cracking, and the bleeding.

"It's okay," the lactation consultant reassured me over the phone
on Day 3. "If he gets a little blood with your milk, it won't hurt him."

"*It hurts ME!*" I wanted to scream.

But mothers aren't supposed to scream about their own needs, so
I gulped hard and croaked out, "Really? Oh. Okay. Good."

In my best attempt at a compromise between his needs and my
pain, I hooked myself up to a torturous manual pump each night as
soon as he fell asleep. It still hurt, although not quite as sharply, and it
enabled me to extract enough milk so that when he woke in the middle
of the night, I could feed him a nutritious meal without biting back
tears of pain in the dark.

Of course, when I did feed him milk from a bottle, I chose the
most complicated kind. The one with approximately twenty-three
parts in each bottle—all of which I hand washed to save them from
harsh dishwasher temperatures—because they promised to limit the gas
in my precious baby's tummy.

My perfection didn't end there.

Each day and each night, I diapered his tiny newborn bottom with
the softest of cloth diapers. My starter stash of orange, green, and blue
diapers had cost us hundreds of dollars, but that was a small price to pay
to protect his delicate skin from evil disposable diaper chemicals.

Sure, I didn't anticipate the full extent of the leaks and the overall
mess. Nor was I prepared for the way it added to the laundry that was

already collecting in endless piles throughout our small condo each day.

A new mother doesn't complain about laundry, though. She expects to drown in dirty garments. She accepts that the joy of motherhood comes with a side of suffocation.

I had other grand plans, too. Screen time would be strictly limited. He would eat only homemade, organic food—no preservative-laced purees from a jar and definitely none of that kid food garbage like frozen chicken nuggets.

I was tired, I was aching, and the years ahead of me seemed to stretch on infinitely. It felt like it might be centuries before my mind and my body were my own again.

How daunting all of my perfection suddenly seemed.

On the afternoon of the eighth day, my baby mercifully fell asleep in my arms. I cradled him, dreading the moment when he would awaken, hungry. I stared across the room at the day's growing pile of laundry, knowing there was little I could do to battle it at the moment.

I plucked a forgotten magazine from the coffee table with my one free hand and began to flip through it in zombie-like fashion, barely recognizing the faces of celebrities in fancy gowns.

I flipped past blurry articles and photo spreads until a series of large, bold words jumped out at me. It was a piece of parenting advice from someone with a name I've long since forgotten, but the words practically glowed on the page:

If you want to like your kids, and you want your kids to like you, give parenting 75 percent of your effort.

Not 100 percent, it said. Not 150 percent, it said. *75 percent.*

I blinked to clear my vision, to clear my mind.

I . . . couldn't possibly . . .

. . . could I?

I looked down at Ryan, peacefully asleep in the crook of my left arm. For the first time, I considered him for what he truly was—not just *my baby* but an individual.

I thought of all the things I wanted for him in life—love, happiness, friendship, success.

I thought of how I would always want him to be true to himself.

How I would never want him to be completely eclipsed by another person. Not even his own child.

I pictured my own mother cradling me as an infant, how she might have sat, rocking back and forth, wishing all the same things for me.

And I realized: I'm important, too. I matter. My pain *matters*. My exhaustion *matters*.

I heard the locks on the front door click open and turned to my husband as he walked through the doorway.

"I'm done breastfeeding. We're switching to formula," I announced.

"Okay, sounds good," he nodded.

Encouraged, I rushed on: "And I know I spent all that money on cloth diapers, but I hate them. The laundry, it's too much. I'm tired, and the diapers are gross, and I just want to be able to throw the mess away. I know, cloth is better, but—"

"It's okay. I hate them, too," he nodded again. "Don't worry about it; we'll sell them."

Decisions made, I looked down at Ryan again. I studied the way his upper lip jutted out just slightly from his lower lip as he slept. Did he look a little sweeter than he had a few minutes earlier?

The moment Ryan was born, he made me happier than I had ever been. But the sustainment of that happiness was not on him; it was on me.

I wanted to be the best mother I could, but that would only happen if I was content with myself. I had to relax my standards for him, and ultimately for me.

In the years that followed, that meant letting a baby watch Sponge Bob while my husband and I gulped down quick, peaceful dinners.

It meant frozen chicken nuggets stocked continuously in my freezer for those nights when we craved an easy solution.

It meant babysitters for regular date nights and a toddler who could navigate an iPad better than an adult.

It meant throwing all twenty-three bottle parts in the dishwasher for harsh-temperature cleansing.

Since that moment, I have given parenting exactly 75 percent of my effort, and we're all 100 percent happier for it.

Second Thoughts

Marie Holmes

For a while, I had myself convinced that having endured the
psychological pain of infertility would enable me to gracefully
handle the physical pain of labor and the exhaustion of caring for
an infant. On both counts, I was totally wrong.

It was a long day. A beautiful, warm summer Saturday, and not the
slightest hope of rest or relaxation was in sight for us. My partner and
I took turns pushing our adorable, newly toothy, almost one-year-
old son through the shady paths of Inwood Hill Park in his stroller.
A year earlier, I had been heavily pregnant. Our talks then were all
about what our lives would be like when Max was here, our voices
giddy with excitement. Twelve months later, we spoke longingly of
exercise, books, the newspaper, the theater, sex, and sleep, sleep, sleep.
Our voices were gravelly with exhaustion. We shuffled along, envying
the new new parents, the old-hat parents, and any parent who could
count on help from family nearby. Everyone, it seemed, had it better
than us.

What were we thinking? What had gone wrong? And why on
earth weren't we happy?

I recalled a Maureen Dowd column that I'd read way back when
we measured Max's age in weeks and before he was dexterous enough
to wrest the paper from my hands. The subject was women and why
they are unhappier today than in decades past, and Dowd quoted
a researcher as saying that data showed a strong correlation, across
population groups, between having children and being unhappy. It
was just one sentence in the entire column, but my heart stopped the
moment I read it, and it has remained with me since. Nonsense! I had
tried to tell myself. Nothing could make me feel more fulfilled than
nursing my precious baby to sleep. My other immediate thought was
that the only thing that more reliably led to unhappiness than having
children was wanting children and not being able to have them.

Infertility was a land I visited first by dint of being a lesbian, my visa extended after numerous failed fertility treatments. Max was our second IVF cycle. He was embryo number eighteen. And if you had told me, during the two weeks that we waited with bated breath to see if he was in there, or the full night in early pregnancy that I spent staring at the ceiling because I had spotted pink blood, that the day would come when I would wonder what we had been thinking when we decided to have a baby—well, I might have just shot a syringe full of hormones into *your* stomach. What I would give, I would have said, to have *those* problems.

And, oh my, there were problems. I hadn't slept a full night in three hundred and fifty-some days, and it was starting to catch up with me. My old trick of moving my wedding ring from my left to my right hand to remind me of something, for example, just left me staring down at my fingers in the evening and asking my partner Sarah, "What was I supposed to remember?"

Max's sleep had recently taken a turn for the even worse. His addiction to the breast was threatening to tear us apart—at least during the night. When I brought him into the bed with us, he squirmed around so much that Sarah often gave up and slept out on the couch. The night before, she had held Max for twenty minutes as he screamed and kicked and thrashed after having woken up while I was in the shower—at eleven at night. I was bathing with unhygienic infrequency, and the fact that I had made it in there at all was a victory.

Oh, and he had begun to bite. My nipples, that is. With his brand-new, razor-sharp teeth

He is downright gorgeous, our Max, with his fine blonde hair and his great blue eyes and his incessant, dimply grin. But sometimes, we called him a maniac. Other times, we called him a monster.

I would like to think that parents who struggle long and hard to bring children into their lives have a special perspective that allows us to deal more effectively with the challenges of childrearing. I want to think that my suffering earned me something. But it's hard to define gradations in something as incomprehensibly immense as a parent's love for a child. And there are too many factors that make us into the parents we are to bestow special powers on those of us who worked hardest to get there, much as I might wish it so. For a while, I had myself convinced that having endured the psychological pain of infertility would enable me to gracefully handle the physical pain of labor and the exhaustion of caring for an infant. On both counts, I was totally wrong.

Just like any of the other parents whose strollers passed ours that Saturday afternoon, Sarah and I were sometimes in over our heads, and on that day in particular we were desperate for a break.

Sarah had a tennis date, with my blessing and deep resentment, and I walked Max up and down the streets, hoping he would nap. He chose not to. After carrying him in his stroller up four flights of stairs and finally getting him down in his crib, my reward was to clean mouse urine and excrement that had been building up in our stove. I had known for days what the smell was. I had gone out and bought steel wool and duct tape to keep the vermin from getting in, but even a project as urgent as this had been languishing, our entire nights and evenings taken up with trying to get Max to sleep.

So I cleaned up after the mouse, cursing my apartment and the city, certain that if only we were rich and lived in a doorman elevator building I would never have to sponge up mouse pee. Then Max was up again. I nursed him, then went to go take the dog out while Sarah gave him his bath. It was getting late, he showed no signs of tiredness after his late nap, and we had decided to just order a pizza for dinner. The usual scene.

"Stick a fork in me," Sarah likes to say around this time of day. "I'm done."

I loaded up e-mails and articles on my phone as the dog trotted down the stairs. I was determined to engage in some adult communication during my five-minute reprieve. And what I read was an article about a six month-old baby who had been killed that morning by a falling tree branch in Central Park. The mother was seriously hurt. The father, said witnesses, was out of his mind.

I went back upstairs and told Sarah what had happened, and we both sat there silently for a moment next to the tub, relieved to see him splashing water across the floor, and terrified that we had created something we could love this much.

Max was not going to bed, of course, and as I played with him and read him books, much more present than I had been all day, I thought about how when he was tiny I had both spent a lot of time staring at him googly-eyed, falling in love, and worrying about his death. There was the ritual checking to see that he was breathing, and, every day, moments when I would be struck by just how helpless he was. How I could just toss him out onto the train tracks or drop him from the window and he wouldn't even know to fight. My therapist said the fact that I was afraid of doing these things was pretty good assurance that I wouldn't, but I kept my distance from the edge of the platform and open windows during those months nonetheless. And now, having heard about this other family's tragedy, he seemed mortal once more and I was in love with him all over again.

I shouldn't need to think about a child dying to feel the depth of my love for my son, but on that Saturday, in the hard, thick exhaustion of parenting, that was what happened. There was something about his newness months earlier, his proximity to the place before, that made him seem closer to death, or as though his stay here among us were less certain. I held him close, then, and wouldn't set him down. Now I leave him on the floor and tell him he's okay when he hits his head. It seems as though he's always been with us, and I can't fathom his absence. Except when I can, again, and I don't think for a moment of yoga classes and runs along the water and lazy Sunday mornings with the paper, but of that raw yearning that I had when we were trying, doggedly pushing me from one procedure to the next, and how it is but a hint of the chasm of longing I would feel if I were to lose him. Singing with him on the floor late into that long night, I felt again very lucky, and, yes, happy.

Just Wait

Meredith Samuelson

*I wish someone had told me parenting would become more
manageable. So I've made it my mission to reassure. It's going to
get better. It's going to get easier.*

He crawled across the playground, all shapeless knees and round
cheeks, his blue eyes wide and searching. The wood chips, jagged-
edged and still damp from an overnight rain, pressed into his soft palms
but he hardly seemed to notice. He stopped, lifted a chip for inspection,
then popped it into his mouth. I sighed, then heaved myself off the
bench. Again. Hadn't I just sat down a moment before? Had I sat down
for more than a moment in the last eight months? The mom next to
me glanced over knowingly. "Just wait until he's walking."

As soon as Ben could sit on his own the warnings began. "Just
wait until he's crawling." When I would steel myself against his defiant
wails it was "Just wait until he's a teenager." Did this playground mom
mean it was going to get harder? It already felt really, really hard.

An unexpected paradox about the infant stage is that no single task
is truly very difficult. Not diapering, not feeding, not swaddling. Yet
all of it together can be just short of impossible. For me, the physical
responsibility was crushingly relentless while the mental numbness
was liquefying my brain into slop. It was lonely and repetitive and
exhausting. Was my baby's walking going to make it worse? Every
experienced mom seemed to agree it would.

And yet for me, Ben learning to walk had an immediate and
thrilling payoff. He could get toys on his own. He could grab books
off a shelf. Sure, he immediately threw them at the cat. But for the first
time in over a year I felt a little bit freer. I could carry an armful of
groceries into the house while he toddled behind. He learned to grab
his own apple from the fridge. He learned to take care of business on
his own. I finally had my arms back.

It was the same when he started talking. It would be all whines and

145

incessant demands, the other moms cautioned me. And to be fair, there was (is) a lot of whining and incessant demanding. But now instead of crying, Ben could tell me he was hungry, he was tired, he wanted to throw something at the cat.

Some moms profess to love the infant years. There's an unparalleled pleasure in being relied upon. In being wanted all the time. Maybe in being the only one who can soothe, or for some, can feed. For me, life has gotten better, easier, and more pleasurable as Ben, and then his brother Eliot, have grown. Cautious first steps have evolved into 100 cumulative pounds of boy running and leaping onto me as I walk in the door from work, like two puppies wrestling me onto the ground, their oversized paws flattening me onto my back. Slurry first words have given way to harrowing tales of pirates and birthday wish lists. And "I love you," miraculously reciprocated.

I think those playground moms mean well. You bond over tales of war. And for some moms it truly is the ideal as sports practice and school meetings and tween attitudes loom in the future. But it was never helpful to me. I wish someone had told me parenting would become more manageable. So I've made it my mission to reassure. It's going to get better. It's going to get easier. You will marvel as these little nuggets turn into real people who can do things. Your little boys will brush your hair. Your little girls will build a Lego Castle/Swamp Prison hybrid. You will sit and read a newspaper. And drink coffee. At the same time. Your trips will become vacations. They will walk. They will run. They will speak. They will sing. It will be better. It will be wonderful.

And yes, there's a profound sadness, an uneasiness in watching their faces thin out, in imagining the day when they're too heavy to lift. But that worry is a blessing. It's a worry that comes with having made it past the stage when every day is a struggle. We'll save that sadness for when we've had a good night's sleep.

++++++++

"Nevergreen trees lose their pineapples in the Spring," says Eliot, now three and speaking without pause. An absolutely terrible understanding of botany. But from his honeyed voice, cuter words were never spoken. I will immediately post them on Facebook, then sit down and have a cup of coffee.

More Than Sleepless Nights

Navarre Overton

"Motherhood is hard," they told me. "Say goodbye to your youth; you've grown up too fast." When you're a pregnant teen, people talk to you about motherhood differently than they do to your counterparts in their twenties and thirties.

We ran through the grass today, holding hands and laughing the whole time. When she glanced at me, her wide eyes transferred her enthusiasm straight into my nerves, extinguishing all the worries of adult life. Her giggles silenced the everyday sounds in our neighborhood—the birds no longer chirped, the traffic was at peace, and the dogs stopped yelling at us to get off their lawn. It was just me, my baby girl, the grass, and her laughter. She turned the air into pure happiness and I felt it brush my skin as I ran through it. For a moment I enjoyed being a mom.

"Motherhood is hard," they told me. "Say goodbye to your youth; you've grown up too fast."

I was only sixteen when I found out I was pregnant with my first child. When you're a pregnant teen, people talk to you about motherhood differently than they do to your counterparts in their twenties and thirties. They don't mislead you into believing that motherhood is a blissfully easy job. Nor do they conveniently omit details that might lead you to second guess becoming a parent. Instead, those details are mostly all you hear. They don't tell you that you'll love every minute of it. They tell you everything they can think of to convince you that mothering is the most difficult thing you will ever do and that you'll hate it.

I was told about the sleepless nights and days, the spit-up and poop that would cover every outfit in my closet, being worn down by the energy of a child, the expenses that I would never really be able to afford, the terrible twos, the grocery store tantrums, and the picky eating. I was also told I would hate it. They told me that motherhood meant sacrificing parts of myself and my life, that I'd barely see the few friends who would actually stick with me through it all, that it would be the hardest thing I would ever have to do. I was told all of this not once or twice, but over and over again for the entirety of my pregnancy. But I was never told that I could find happiness being a mom. I was supposed to be miserable. Motherhood was supposed to be my punishment for having unprotected sex too young.

And I believed it all. Motherhood felt like a prison. For too many years I focused on what I lost instead of what there was to gain, missing out on all the moments that make the stress and sleep deprivation worth enduring. I never ran through the grass with my first born when he was a toddler. I wanted to, but I didn't. I suffocated any spark of happiness inside me, like a kid having fun while grounded, afraid the punishment would get worse if I let it out and smiled.

When I was pregnant I had no baby shower. Nor did I have a nursery to decorate. I was a high school dropout with no job and no money; I was in no position to take care of a child. I didn't deserve to celebrate the life I carried inside of me. Motherhood was supposed to be a source of shame instead of celebration. Forever my baby was to be a reminder that I made a mistake and ruined my life.

"You could put it up for adoption," I remember a counselor saying as if I had never heard of adoption before.

"No, I've already decided I'm going to keep it," I nervously replied, knowing that a lecture on the difficulties of teen motherhood was to follow; it was a plea for me to take this get out of jail free card. And again the list of things I would miss out on was repeated; I had it memorized by then and just nodded, "I understand." And I did understand: motherhood was supposed to make me miserable—it was my punishment after all.

Whenever I was completely alone, I would find myself getting excited about what motherhood could be for me. I'd dream about meeting my baby for the first time, my whole being bursting with love. I would imagine the seemingly endless stares back and forth as I waited for my baby's first smile. I thought about the pride I would feel watching my baby take his first steps toward me. I envisioned all of this and more, thinking that there had to be more to motherhood than just eighteen years of servitude. Secretly smiling to myself, I was hoping that I would get a happy ending.

I tried to build up the courage to share my excitement with someone, anyone, but I was always swiftly reminded of the part others wanted me to play: a miserable teen mom, an example of what will happen if you don't play it safe. Being a teen mom was far from something to be proud of, or happy in spite of. My potential happiness ran the risk of encouraging other young girls to start their own families too early.

"You had your whole life ahead of you," they'd say, as if motherhood was a death sentence. I was so sick of the disappointment, in their voice, their words, and their eyes. It felt as though their whole being was screaming violently at me, "you stupid whore!" If congratulations ever came it was after the obligatory shaming.

I wish someone would've just celebrated with me, without the lectures or shaming. Whatever they thought they were going to teach me came too late anyway. Where were they when I needed to learn how to assert myself and make the guy I was with wear a condom, or when I needed birth control? I was already going to be a teen mom. There was no going back.

I just read a friend's Facebook post. She's excited because she just heard her baby's heartbeat for the first time. She is rewarded for sharing her happiness with likes and congratulatory comments. Her friends are truly happy for her. Me included. But for myself I feel a mixture of guilt and heartbreak. Posts like these remind me of the love and support I missed. Memories of all the things I didn't share when I was pregnant with my first child are reawakened.

The day I got my ultrasound and found out that my baby was a boy is one of those memories. I didn't share my excitement with anyone. Other moms are encouraged to have elaborate parties where they revel the sex of their unborn child, but as a pregnant teen the sex of my baby didn't matter as much as him being a mistake. I told a handful of friends who didn't seem to care much. And I didn't blame them; they were teenagers and their world didn't include thoughts of babies and nurseries yet. Their world was parties, boyfriends, and planning their lives after high school— all the things people kept reminding me I was missing out on.

Most of the time I longed to enjoy the life my other friends had. But there was a part of me that wanted to move forward. The truth was I was looking forward to being a mom as much as I was nervous about it.

It was a spring day and I was in the last trimester of my pregnancy. I couldn't afford baby clothes because I was focusing my efforts on getting my GED at the time and didn't have a job. My mother drove me to the local crisis pregnancy center to look through their donation bins. I remember reading in some old worn pregnancy book I got from a thrift store that I would need a going home outfit. So, as I was grabbing all the staples—the onesies, the blankets, etc.—I was also in search of a decent outfit to take my baby home in. Something without stains, that looked almost new. I found a pair of blue and white Winnie the Pooh footed pajamas and stuffed them in my bag, telling no one what my plans were for them. I thought I could dress my baby up and be proud for a moment, even if I didn't let anyone else know.

Keeping my secret was easy. I knew how to play the part of a mother who hates motherhood because this illusion of motherhood as a joyless endeavor was only a reiteration of the messages I received as a child. Since the days of being mothered myself, motherhood was misrepresented to me.

My mother taught me more about motherhood than anyone else. "I never even wanted kids!" she'd scream when frustrated with our childish behavior. I know very well the sting of feeling unwanted.

But there were good times. I remember all the things she would do with my siblings and me that our father wouldn't. She'd sit down and finish a coloring page with us, showing us how to stay in the lines. I even remember the many times she would yell at my dad, "you can't even take them to the park!" And then she'd take us herself. But I never remember her enjoying it. She rarely laughed, or smiled. Motherhood was doing a bunch of stuff you hated doing for your kids. Love was something done out of obligation.

As I got older those moments with my mom faded away. She stopped taking us places, and participating in our lives.

"All I have to do is feed you, clothe you, and keep a roof over your head," my mom would tell me. I now wonder if maybe she felt like me. If she also felt she had to hate motherhood. Perhaps she too received messages about her choice to become a mother. Was she too young? Did she make getting a professional degree too hard on herself? Did she feel the constant pull between living for her children and living for herself? Was she ever told that she could have it all and enjoy it at the same time? Did she ever regret the happy moments she missed? I'll never know; she died of cancer last year, before I could ask her.

I still have those footed pajamas I picked out from the donation bin, the ones my firstborn wore home from the hospital. I have no pictures of him wearing them. But I know he did; they still faintly hold his newborn smell in their fibers, or perhaps the memories are so strong that the scent is only a phantom imprinted on my brain. When no one was around I used to take them out and inhale the memories, feeling the happiness I hid from the world. They now sit in a box with all of my other secrets from when motherhood was new to me. Memories of his toddlerhood that are held in the scuffs on his first pair of shoes, a novelty birth certificate from the hospital reminds me of kissing his tiny feet, and his first photos from before my arms held him when I first learned he was a boy. Memories of little moments when I let the shame hold back my joy. Reminders that I failed him, as well as myself.

When I became pregnant with my last child a few years ago I decided that I needed to escape this illusion of motherhood that caused me to miss out on so much. I needed to start ignoring the messages that didn't feel right to me and accept the happy moments that motherhood was offering me, openly and without shame this time around. Liberation was in my future; I had another chance.

And this time I wasn't up against a society wanting to shame and make an example out of me. People treated me differently. Motherhood is acceptable when you're thirty, even if the pregnancy is unexpected. Many of my friends had their own children by then and could offer a little bit of the support they couldn't before. But our experiences are still vastly different. While they're all caught off guard by how difficult motherhood is and just how much they hate it at times, I'm slowing down and trying to take it all in, finally letting myself enjoy the moments that make it all worthwhile.

I'm still learning that motherhood is something I can love. Sometimes I find myself walking right back into my cell. Like a commuter mindlessly driving to work on their day off, I am on autopilot. I watch as I act out scripts from my past, complaining about motherhood more than I am enjoying it. The shame and guilt still surface after all these years. But it is no longer all that is there.

Today I held my toddler in my arms and sang her to sleep: a made-up lullaby from me to her. She fought her sleep as I fought the expiration of my patience; we struggled together. When she finally closed her eyes, I looked down at her and let her peacefulness overcome me. This peacefulness is freedom and, for this moment at least, I have escaped my prison.

To Do: Declutter Mom's Head

Sharon Holbrook

We are swimming in small choices, and for someone like me who can't even declutter the house without a full-scale analysis of every paper and item, we can get buried in overwhelm.

"Sick, sick," my sixteen-month old cries plaintively, standing up in his crib. He's just learned this new word, because this is the sixth or seventh time tonight he's thrown up all over himself and his bed. I haul him out, wash him, change his clothes, and put new sheets on. I run out of clean sheets. I tuck twin-size bedding around the crib mattress, like Gulliver sheets on a Lilliputian bed. My husband is out of town. I'm pregnant. By 4:00 a.m., I'm vomiting too.

Somehow, it's all okay.

I'm not Supermom. I don't even want to be Supermom. It's too much, trying to be and do everything and meet someone else's Pinterested idea of perfect. No, I want things to be simpler, to follow a path I know is right through my ordinary everydays.

It sounds crazy, but the sick days can be easier. I know just what to do, without thinking or second-guessing. Everything else falls away, demoted to the second tier of life, and I soothe and watch over a retching or feverish or broken child. I *mother*, and I know exactly what that loaded term requires in the clarity of those hard moments. It doesn't matter if it's 3:00 a.m. and I'm washing vomit sheets—I do it, and gladly, to the extent one can be glad while near vomit. My child needs me.

Clarity is harder to find in the ordinary days of motherhood, and self-interrogation is its enemy. It starts in the protracted days of mothering an infant who doesn't yet talk or, frankly, do a huge amount of anything. How much was I supposed to be talking to him? Reading to him? Singing? If he was awake, could I turn my back on him and get something done without feeling guilty? Maybe I should be engaging with him more? (Or was it less? "You talk to him so much," my mother said, when my son was one and I was growing ever more pregnant with my daughter. "I mean, it's wonderful! But I just wonder how he'll adjust when there's another baby.") And let's not even talk about sleep training and breastfeeding choices.

The answers to my little everyday dilemmas weren't in any book. Or, rather, maybe they were in too many books and on too many tongues and in too many Facebook statuses, all with differing conclusions. Like a growing pile of mail and papers on the kitchen counter, these questions and many others waited for me to sift through them, nagging at me even when I tried to ignore them. We're expected to decide *how* to mother, when our mothers and grandmothers could just mother.

All this angst? We're both spoiled and punished with too many shoulds, and not enough musts.

This is the classic First World Problem, Modern Parenting Edition. We don't (generally speaking) have to worry about storing away enough food for winter, keeping the house warm, or fending off bears or deadly child-stealing diseases. We are swimming in small choices, and for someone like me who can't even declutter the house without a full-scale analysis of every paper and item, we can get buried in overwhelm. I'm not wishing for illness, or for a fire to consume the kitchen, papers and all, but if it happened I'd know what to do. That carries its own kind of peace.

I can't stop asking what the "best" decisions are for my children. It's how I'm wired, and I'll keep seeking answers, as tiring as it is. Someone has to figure out how to get this kid to pitch in around the house, whether to let that kid quit soccer, and how to get them all to eat a vegetable or two.

After ten years of parenting, though, I realize I need to keep the parenting decision monologue running in the background, and not give it center stage.

There are clear things in front of me, things I need to focus on and savor. These are the things I'm sure of, the ones that work for our family, that don't require a lot of thought or gnashing of teeth. They are different for every family.

What works for my family is what matters. And, no less

important, what works for me. I get to be a whole person, with my own interests and foibles and faults and quirks and talents, not a cardboard cutout of birthday-party-throwing motherly perfection.

Elementary school ends next week. We're keeping summer ambitions and expectations small—that's my clarity, at least this year. I don't have to do amusement parks or daily crafts or piles of math worksheets. No, I'll leave that to Supermom—or any parent who actually *likes* those things. At my house, it'll be berry-picking, lots of reading, eating on the screened-in porch, biking, and some sacred time alone for Mom to write—that's what looks clear, simple, and beautiful to me. The rest will take care of itself, and I won't (I *won't*, darn it!) let the Mommy-shoulds take over.

And, oh, one more thing. Fingers crossed, there'll be no sick kids this summer. But if there are, I'll drop everything, and happily.

Sometimes You Don't Know

Dana Schwartz

It took several more years to accept what has been the hardest lesson for me about parenting: Not only can I not prevent my children's suffering, but sometimes I will be the cause of it.

My three-year-old son watched a show on the iPad while I took a shower. He sprawled on a towel in the bathroom, his little chin propped up in his hands, perfectly content to enjoy an extra episode of My Little Pony.

A few moments later I heard him say, "Look at that, mommy. Look at Emma's belly."

Even before I pulled aside the curtain, I knew exactly what he was talking about.

He pushed a finger on his sister's naked torso, smudging the screen. "Emma's belly when she had gluten," he said, glancing up at me for confirmation. I nodded, not needing to look.

A bulging stomach on a stick figure girl, her chin pointing down as she peered at her roundness. My husband took those pictures to document her illness and for some reason they still exist. Neither one of us has deleted them.

My son is the same age as his sister when she was diagnosed with celiac disease. He doesn't know exactly what gluten is except that it makes her sick. Since he hasn't shown any symptoms, he eats gluten free at home, but enjoys the illicit pleasures of Goldfish crackers and Fruit Loops at preschool.

I can't help but worry about him. Every time he complains of a "stummy ache" my heart races. I lift up his shirt and feel his belly. Is it soft or hard? Does it look bloated? Every time he spends twenty minutes on the toilet with his face in a grimace of pain, I feel the curtain of my panic rising. Could he have it too? Should I have him tested?

Vigilance for him because of how much I missed with her.

After Emma's diagnosis I met a woman online whose college-aged daughter had celiac. She pointed me in the right direction for the best gluten free brands and websites, but one day she gave me a shocking piece of advice.

She said, "There will come a time when you'll accidentally gluten your daughter. Don't be too hard on yourself."

I thanked her, but was secretly appalled. I'd done enough damage by not noticing my daughter's illness. Surely, I would never be that careless again.

The details leading up to Emma's diagnosis remained vivid and shameful. The two of us running into public bathrooms all over our Brooklyn neighborhood because I thought she had a stomach bug. For almost a month. How I carried around extra pairs of pants and plastic bags for emergencies.

When we arrived at the hospital the day before her third birthday, I held her while my husband took care of the paperwork. "Mommy," she said weakly, "it's happening again."

I rushed into the bathroom in time for her to have an accident all over the scuffed black and white tile floor. The stench was unbearable, the mess obscene. I mopped it up with fistfuls of paper towels as best I could, apologizing in tears to the nurse at the front desk. "It's okay," she said, trying to reassure me.

But it wasn't. I was in the emergency room with my little girl who had a beach ball belly and spindly limbs. I missed all the signs of her drawn out distress. The significant weight loss, her distended stomach, how the light had evaporated from her big blue eyes. Somehow, despite my around-the-clock care, I never noticed that my daughter was wasting away.

Six months earlier, she had been a picture of health. A robust two and a half year old, always in the top percentiles of the growth charts. Sure, she slept like crap, had severe separation anxiety, and hung off my boob most of the day and night, but she was thriving physically, and I had the stats to prove it.

However, under the radar—mine, at least—things began to change. She started to lose weight. When my husband expressed concern earlier that winter, I dismissed his fears.

"She's thinning out," I told him.

"What about her stomach?" She was splashing around in the bath as we stood whispering above her. "Is it supposed to look like that?"

I nodded, all breezy confidence. "It's just her toddler belly." Secretly, I was a little relieved she was thinning out. Though I never expressed my fears to him, I had worried about our shared genetics. My husband and I were lean, but we both had family members who struggled with weight.

People used words like sturdy and solid to describe Emma. Words that had been compliments when she was a baby suddenly sounded barbed. *Did they mean fat?* I wondered. Emma towered over her friends and it probably didn't help that they happened to be wispy little things, but the fact that you could fit at least two of them inside my daughter's silhouette unnerved me.

I didn't want her to suffer with the burden of extra weight as my mother had, always telling me how lucky I was to inherit my father's skinny genes. But these thoughts made me feel petty and ashamed, so I shut them down and reminded myself to feel grateful for my healthy, beautiful girl.

That spring Emma came down with a stomach virus. She had painful diarrhea for days. Just when we thought she had recovered, it returned. A couple weeks in, my husband suggested we take her to the pediatrician. I scoffed.

"The doctor is just going to say it's a stomach bug. All the kids have it."

One of the reasons we loved our pediatric practice was how laid-back they were, preferring a hands-off approach whenever possible. We used to joke about how no matter what we told our doctor, an Indian woman with big liquid brown eyes, she would almost always respond the same way, her voice a soothing sing-song: "It's normal."

"Dr. Tholany will just send us home. We'll drag her there for nothing."

Reluctantly, he agreed. That week I took her to play group and play dates, strolling through slushy melting snow, bumping up and down crooked sidewalks. One day, after leaving music class early, I strapped her slumped body into the stroller and pushed her down Sixth Avenue, trying to think of what else we could do to fill our time.

"How about the bookstore?" I chirped, swinging my head around to look at her as we walked. "Want to try the playground?"

She looked right at me, holding her stomach. When she spoke her voice was small, almost a whisper. "Mommy, I feel sad."

I stopped the stroller with a jerk and crouched down beside her. For the first time I saw how sunken her eyes were, how her face was twisted in pain. My little girl was trying to tell me something important. Finally, I was listening.

Not long afterward the three of us were in an exam room with Dr. Tholany. She slid up our daughter's shirt and stared at her hard swollen belly. Pressing her palm softly against it, she asked, does this hurt? Our daughter nodded, tears in her eyes.

Turning to us, her voice gentle but firm, she told us we needed to go to the hospital. Now.

My whole body froze with fear while my husband wrote down the address. We rushed to the car in a daze. On the way I called my father, breaking down as I choked out the words: "We're going to the emergency room. Something is wrong with Emma."

In many ways, we were lucky. Our daughter's celiac symptoms presented as typical. Some babies, young children, and even adults flounder in medical limbo for years. The day after we visited the ER, we went to a pediatric gastroenterologist where Emma was diagnosed via blood test.

We cleansed our pantry, and our lives, of gluten. After she went to bed, my husband and I stayed up late researching. Within days of removing gluten from her diet the light returned to her eyes, and soon after her body began to heal.

I was relieved and grateful for her returning health, but I couldn't shake off my guilt. My husband had known something was wrong. He tried to tell me. But I dismissed his worries, feeling secret shameful relief that our daughter was thinning out, when in fact she was starving.

I should have known. I was her mother. Aren't mothers supposed to know these things?

A quick scan of Facebook will tell you "yes." Many mothers write beautiful and moving essays about how they had to convince skeptical family members and doctors that there was something wrong with their child, because they *just knew*. I admired these mothers for their sharp instincts and the fierce battles they fought.

But I felt like a fraud. I was the mother who didn't know.

The term "mother's intuition" is an old wives' tale that still circulates in our modern world, suggesting that only mothers, not fathers, are bestowed with some kind of sixth sense about their children. This notion is false, of course. Intuition has nothing to do with gender; it's the animal part of our brain that resides beneath the rational. Sometimes we hear its low hum and can help our children navigate around bumps in the road, in life, but other times we can't, and they fall.

There will come a time when you'll accidentally gluten your daughter. Don't be too hard on yourself.

Of course she was right. People make mistakes. *Mothers* make mistakes. One day, not long into our gluten free journey, it happened and my heart ached watching my daughter clutch her stomach, knowing it was my fault. I heard the woman's words echo in my mind, but dismissed them. I wasn't ready to grant myself any compassion. My wounds, and my daughter's, were too raw.

It took several more years to accept what has been the hardest lesson for me about parenting: Not only can I not prevent my children's suffering, but sometimes I will be the cause of it.

Emma is now a healthy eight-year-old girl. She is strong, dangling upside down on the monkey bars, scaling tall play structures with ease. I see her muscles moving beneath her skin and I'm proud. We've got the gluten free thing down, pretty seamlessly, though that doesn't cover the social exclusion element and other factors like her anxiety about food and illness. Physically she's thriving again, and it's wonderful to see.

The images of her belly on the iPad are a permanent part of my motherhood experience, whether I delete them or not.

Becoming a parent, being a mother, does not heighten our

intuition or make us omniscient, but it does broaden our definition of empathy and forgiveness, both for our children and ourselves.

How I Learned It's Okay To Go 5000 Miles Away

Chantal Panozzo

*When I'm away from my daughter, all the things I love about
her are magnified and appreciated.*

When my daughter was ten months old, I left her for Paris. My
husband agreed to babysit (funny how dads "babysit" their own
children) so I could meet my sister for the weekend. But even if I felt
like I deserved a break, society told me otherwise.

Friends did too.

When I confided in another mother friend about my trip, she
confirmed my guilt by telling me: "Oh, I could never leave my baby
like that."

So I went to Paris. I already had the ticket, after all. But I felt
like such a bad mother for leaving my daughter that I spent the entire
two days dragging my feet from one Parisian park chair to another.
Traveling to Paris as a guilt-ridden zombie was not recommended and
upon return, I told all my friends who were also new mothers to forget
even thinking about travel.

So naturally, two months later, I went to China.

"You need to go to Beijing too," said my mother over the phone,
when I told her my husband was going to a conference there.

The voice of my friend saying she could never leave her baby
echoed in my mind.

"I can't," I said.

"Nonsense. You have airline miles. I have time. I'm coming to
babysit and you're going," she said.

I cried when I left my daughter, even though I knew my mother
would take good care of her. Sadly, my tears made me feel better. A
good mother should feel bad when leaving her daughter. Was I a good
mother?

I wheeled my doubts and guilty mother baggage all the way to

165

and through the Beijing airport, but finally, in my efforts to take the Beijing subway to the Westin, where my husband's conference was, I got distracted. One cannot figure out Chinese public transport and be a guilty mother at the same time—there is no room in the mind for both activities.

Thank goodness for Chinese public transport.

As a mother, I gave life but lost part of my own in the process. Society and other moms told me to accept this, but China (and my own mother) taught me otherwise. All I needed to do to free my all-consuming mothering mind was to do something equally all consuming—to make my way across a Chinese city via public transport. Who knew?

Now I travel to find me—and to rediscover my toddler too. Because when I leave my daughter—the "go to China" kind of leave—I'm more present upon return. Otherwise, I can be in the same room with her yet not be there—weeks and weeks of being served the same plastic cookie can do this to a person. And what's worse—to be there and not be present or to leave in order to be present again?

When I'm away from my daughter, all the things I love about her are magnified and appreciated. The way more blue marker gets on her hands than on the paper when she writes the word "mom." The way she directs me at the piano while she plays the only note she can play on the recorder over and over. The way she packs her plastic iron and diaper cream along with her stuffed reindeer for her vacation with Grandma. The way she runs to me after I haven't seen her for two weeks.

Which brings me to another airfare sale and another offer to care for my daughter from my mom.

So here I am again, saying good-bye to my daughter. As I'm thanking my mother with a big hug, my daughter pushes between us.

"Go, Mommy!" says my daughter, practically shoving me out the door.

This is the best thing a toddler can say and do to a mother sometimes.

I crouch to hug my daughter, but she laughs and runs the other way, leaving my arms open to nothing but the big wide wonderful world.

Flood

Jackie Pick

*"You should write it all down while they're asleep," the nurse
told me, tilting her chin to indicate my two sleeping babies.*

"I'm sure I'll remember."

*"You will. The big moments. Some odd details. But not
everything. Your days are going to get very busy and you'll forget
things."*

Water is the most destructive force on earth. It doesn't need to rage
like fire to damage, or be accompanied by thunder to threaten. Water
is patient. It feeds on itself. In full fury or quiet persistence, it takes
everything.

The torrential rains came and went quickly, leaving behind cool
beauty and bathing the outdoors in greens and crisp blues. It took a day
for us to learn that local infrastructure work had been miscalculated,
leaving the temporary sewer pipes unable to handle the cloudburst
and our basement soaked. My office suffered more damage than the
adjacent play area, as noted by the watermarks darkening my walls,
threatening mold and promising upheaval.

The movers hired by the utility company keep a reverential silence
as I pretend to be too engrossed in playing with my kids to see them
bringing up boxes of soggy papers. They lug soaked items that had
been hastily thrown on the floor into two piles I could have labeled
"Once" and "Someday." "Now" items are on my desk, untouched by
water. The "Now" pile doesn't hold the academic respectability of my
past career or the seductive creativity of the future career I will fling
myself into once early parenting is done. It is the survival pile of Get It
Done. The Endless Same. The Pile of Parenting.

I ignore the pristine blank journals next to the good pens.

This is what it is.

The workers relocate stacks of my books to the garage. The

margins of the older books are filled with my young, confident, curious voice conversing with the authors. Newer books, just yesterday an imperious mountain of must-reads, are untouched. All are now waterlogged, edges curling.

I am ashamed of the mess. I have not made or been given the time to organize and protect past and future. My office, pre-flood, was a museum. Now it is a mausoleum. I brood.

My sons interrupt my reverie. Although this is a regular occurrence, it is still startling to sink into my own thoughts only to be yanked out by little hands and voices. The boys are a wonderful, sweet sensory assault. They are almost three. From the time they floated and swam in my body, they were roaring rapids. They drew me into their eddy by sheer conjunction of body space. Now they squeal and yell and slam and drum and sing and cry and laugh and spill. Since having them, there is a fullness to my life that, despite the chaos and lack of what is crudely called "me time," is quite welcome. The fullness of time, however, is the toll.

This is what it is.

The movers stand and wait for me to notice them while I bring the boys' rough and tumble to a halt. The one I expect they voted to deal with me because it was likely I'd burst into tears shows me the brown paper bag of photographs all matted together.

"You may want to go through these to see if there's any you can keep. Sorry."

While most of the photos are still digitally accessible, some are from other people and I've not scanned them. I see the boys' ultrasound picture, warped and ruined. The movers instinctively lower their eyes as I finger the edges of the picture that once used to be meaningful blobs.

The ultrasound had been ordered because I measured large by my ninth week. Moments before the technician spoke, she paused dramatically. She'd given this kind of news before and was going for drama. "Here's a baby . . . and here's another baby!"

My husband and I laughed. We, who shouldn't have been able to have kids, who certainly hadn't planned for them, who hadn't even felt strongly about them suddenly were a family of four, and it felt right. My husband's eyes gleamed. Mine were dry, but happy.

We bumped into my doctor in the hallway, spilling over with the news, not bothering to keep it private. Our words cascaded over each other, tumbling around the way the boys soon would be in my belly. The doctor gave us quick advice for dealing with a multiples pregnancy. More rest, more calories, more exercise, more appointments, more risks. There would be many "mores" for twins once they arrived: mess, love, tears, hugs, time, needs, loss, heartache, joy, tiny toys to step on, feedings, diapers, juggling. The only thing reduced was sleep.

Throughout the pregnancy, I felt invincible, able to sustain multiple lives in a single womb. *I am Giver of Life! Behold and please excuse my mighty gas!* I navigated the grey area between public and private as my growing belly took up space and encouraged strangers to offer advice and ask questions, usually unwelcome, often inappropriate, always hilarious when later recounted.

The workmen smile sadly at me as they remove the remaining strips of the boys' art work from the wet wall. The sweet masterpieces had been hung at the boys' eye level, an exhibition of finger paint and feathers. I spy a twist of cotton between the stacks of construction paper and flush as I realize these are the newborn baby beanies that I'd been meaning to pack away. I take the little caps and inhale, smelling only earth. The beanies are set aside to put in the attic. The men continue their liturgical removal of everything.

My boys' appearance in this world, like so many other babies, was preceded by a flood. The gush of amniotic fluid came so violently I could hear the pop and felt the pressure in my body change as what felt like gallons of water poured out of me. We laughed on the way to the hospital, ignoring the rain and the slick pavement, laughing because he wanted to drive fast and I was puffing in the passenger's seat. We were so cliché all of a sudden.

There was urgency once we arrived at the hospital, as feet emerged before heads or tushies. I remember the icy anesthesia circulating in my body. I remember seeing my husband hold one son.

I remember the terrible long minutes of the other child being whisked away because he'd swallowed fluid.

I didn't cry. Not when they showed me my children. Not when my husband cried. Not when my son finally took a breath and wailed at the indignity of the entire birthing process. Not when I finally held two tiny babies only hours old. I blamed the trauma and the anesthesia.

Nurses brought me water in various forms and vessels to provide relief from burning pain, thirst, and my own body emptying itself.

"You should write it all down while they're asleep," the nurse told me, tilting her chin to indicate my two sleeping babies.

"I'm sure I'll remember."

"You will. The big moments. Some odd details. But not everything. Your days are going to get very busy and you'll forget things."

I painstakingly wrote my birth story during the five days I was at the hospital and sent it to the ether. I had the time, then.

There is an unremarkable wet spiral notebook stacked in a pile of unremarkable wet things. In it are dozens of pages of charts and checkmarks. Eating. Diapers. Baths. Naps. I was so careful to track everything and no one ever looked at it. I toss the notebook in the recycling.

The boys are out of my body now, but we are inextricably linked through powerful forces: love, chemistry, senses. They are in my head and my heart and my ears. We hold hands or hug or tickle, our electrons dancing with one another. Sometimes I forget to remember that. There is little time for savoring when your first babies are twins. It's fast and simultaneous and full of doubt. Lightspeed. Godspeed. Childspeed. I often limp behind them, wondering at their energy. They move and it's as though their feet don't touch the ground. My job is to keep up now, reflect later.

One of the movers goes to throw out some of my old Day Planners. I stop him, explaining I will try to salvage those.

Time in early parenthood stretches and contracts. Old calendars and to-do lists are breadcrumbs, reminders of reality and dreams, proof I am alive and functioning. Everything races with young kids—hands, mouth, legs, heart—everything but the brain, which grows thick and sluggish. I write it down because paper is more reliable than my own thought process and memory.

"Where should we put these?" The movers hand me baby books that I haven't filled in since their birth day.

"I'll take them. They need . . . updating." Yes. Three years' worth.

The movers finish. We thank them, and the boys offer a sweet sing-song goodbye. I feel tetchy and close the door to my office. The carpet will be unceremoniously ripped up in a few days. The room will be laid bare to dry out.

After a year of hushed consideration, we decided to take the plunge and have another. Two weeks later I was pregnant. There is little mystery and ample knowledge with a second pregnancy. I worried some about the exhaustion and the feasibility, but thrilled to the idea that soon there would be more rippling in my body, more tiny fingers to kiss, more giggles in the house. My husband, moments after learning the news, began preparing a list of supplies and wrangling that rivaled Doomsday prep. "All hands on deck," he would say.

A few weeks later the bleeding started. I was fortunate enough to get my tests scheduled quickly, and my doctor always returned my calls promptly. After the second round of tests, I called and asked, without much preface, "Am I miscarrying?"

There was a pause, and I realized she was on the phone in the reception area. I heard the voices of expectant families in the background, giggling, giving information for forms, carrying on. Maybe one of them was bubbling over about being pregnant with twins.

She was careful and deliberate with her choice of words.

"Yes, this is what it is."

The wording was odd and stilted and important. This was no trivial "It is what it is" tautology. *This* is what it is. Accept it. Ground yourself in it. There is no ambiguity.

My husband let me crumble into him. He didn't have the words I needed. He didn't have any words. Few people did. Whereas my pregnancy and motherhood occupied public spaces in anonymous and personal ways, my miscarriage was hushed. Miscarriage is a common mystery, so regular and inexplicable it's hard to bring up as something unique to be decoded. Screaming and tears and agonizing won't change what this is, so I did none of those things.

The bleeding, quiet and steady, continued for a month. At first I twisted over the pace and wording of it all: miscarriage and pregnancy loss, phrases that imply I'd shaken loose the grip my body was supposed to have on the baby. Eventually I grew numb to it all, accepted it as fact that it had been a flawed pregnancy. Unsustainable. Noiseless.

Too much nothing.

I hear little giggles by the door and turn to see four sets of fingers wiggling underneath, looking for play. Four little sets of fingers that have never let me be completely alone or empty. I don't need to mark the time by hours or days or incomplete tasks. My time, be it agonizingly slow or impossibly frenzied, is best measured in stories and moments, drips and drops. Not in crossed-off tasks but in heartbeats. The heart is called a ticker, after all.

I tickle the little fingers under the door to the great delight of their owners. I swing open the door and am caught in a wave of arms and legs and hugs and joyful cries. I send them to get their shoes on so we can go out in the sun. I blink, surprised at the wetness in my eyes that has been absent for so long. I grab a blank journal, making sure the paper is heavy enough, and date the top of the page. I think for a moment and then quickly jot down:

Water is the most nourishing element. It is the stuff of life. We float in it before we are born. We are rejuvenated in it throughout our lives. We in ingest it to live. It cleanses and purifies. It renews. It is from water, not fire, that the Phoenix rises.

This is what it is.

The Day My Mom Stopped Talking To Me

Bethany Neumeyer

Knowing that my parents—two of the most wonderful people I know—did not love every moment of raising me or miss those moments once they had passed is one of the most reassuring things I've learned as a parent.

I distinctly remember the day my mother refused to talk to me.

I was an emotional teen: overdramatic, mouthy, and with enough attitude for at least three teenage girls. My mom was often at a loss for how to deal with me. Our arguments consisted mostly of me yelling while she tried in vain to reason with someone who was being completely unreasonable. So one day when I was about seventeen, in the middle of a "conversation" that was mostly just me being rude and irrational, she simply turned around and walked out of the room. She went into her bedroom, closed the door, and ignored me.

I was shocked. Moms aren't allowed to ignore their kids, are they? Wasn't it her job to want to be near me no matter how obnoxious and unbearable I was being? Why would someone even have children if they weren't going to be filled with ecstasy during every moment spent with them? I was overcome with righteous indignation at my mom's painfully obvious failure to understand how the whole motherhood thing was supposed to work.

Now that I'm a mom myself, the memory of that day still shocks me, but for an entirely different reason: how is it possible that in the twenty years I lived in her home, my mom only reached the point of refusing to talk to me *one* time? My oldest child is three years old, and I've already had plenty of moments where I don't particularly want to talk to him. When he gets out of bed at night for the eighteenth time. When he wakes his baby sister just minutes after I've finally gotten her to go to sleep. That time when he wrapped his arms around my waist for a hug and then, for no discernible reason, thought it might be fun to bite my stomach right above my still-tender C-section scar.

I love both of my kids madly, of course, but I've learned that it is not only possible but also fairly common to love your kids while simultaneously not wanting to look at them for a little while. I can waste time feeling guilty about it, or I can take a few minutes by myself to breathe and recover so that I can be a better mom when I'm ready to spend time with them again.

On a recent vacation, my mom and I chatted like the old friends we are—just two moms comparing war stories. I told her about some of the struggles I was having, and she told me that when we were younger, she sometimes felt guilty that she was never sad about my two siblings and me growing older and no longer being babies.

"I enjoyed all of the different ages with you kids for different reasons," she said, "but I never felt sad when they were over. I never wished that you could just stay little. I liked the good parts, but I was never sad to leave behind the challenges that came with each stage. I wondered sometimes if there was something wrong with me. Every other mom I knew seemed to mourn the passage of time, and I never did."

Later, my dad laughingly told me that sometimes after a particularly rough day, he would say to my mom, "Whose idea was it to have kids anyway?" To which she would respond, "Hey, don't blame this on me!"

Knowing that my parents—two of the most wonderful people I know—did not love every moment of raising me or miss those moments once they had passed is one of the most reassuring things I've learned as a parent. I will not miss the diaper blowouts. I will not miss cleaning up vomit. I will not miss potty training or being woken up at 3am or the way my teething daughter sometimes chomps down on my nipple while nursing. And whether I want it to or not, time will keep moving forward at the same deceptive speed: each day plodding along so slowly that it seems like bedtime will never arrive, while the years pass in a blur that leaves me wondering how the baby girl who I could swear was a newborn only yesterday is already starting to crawl and the little boy whose first words I just finished marveling over is somehow old enough to start preschool.

Someday my children will be adults, and maybe they will each have children of their own. Perhaps they will confide in me that sometimes they just want to close the bedroom door and not have to see their kids until they've had a moment to breathe. And I will tell them the same thing that I've learned from my own parents: I did not love every moment of being your mom. But, oh, my precious babies, I have loved *you* every second of your lives.

The Lonely Suburban Mom Club

Kristi Rieger Campbell

"Finally!" I thought. "Now, I can become a part of the mom club!" It wasn't as easy as I thought.

Before I became pregnant, I didn't have much use for my neighbors. Their children playing outside were cute and energetic, but rather than seeing their tenderness and vulnerability, I noticed only that having to slow my car down while they chased a ball—or a sibling—into or out of the street was going to make me late for work. Again.

Almost six years ago, I planned to birth and bunker down for three months of nursing and bonding. I was sure that I'd then re-embrace work with fewer hours and pumping while hidden beneath my desk. I wondered about how to obtain a lock for the door to my office, whether my team would be able to hear my breast pump pumping beneath my desk, and whether my cruel boss would say "fuck you" to me or, worse, to somebody on my team that week. He usually did both.

As most motherhood stories tend to do, my obsessions about pumping and the "fuck you's" at work shifted after weeks and weeks of pregnancy bed-rest. They shifted more once my son was born. Four days and fourteen phone calls later, I was completely untangled from my job, my team, and my boss's "fuck you's."

I became entangled in a new reality, one littered with scraps of sleeping in accidental snippets. A nap here, a stolen snore there. When I look back on those times, I remember the urgency with which I worried about the number of hours my son slept compared to the hours I'd read that he'd be expected to sleep. I don't remember how much I slept, because that didn't feel as important. I recall baby poop, and reeling over how suddenly, after living a longish life, I finally knew that the love I thought I knew in years before was nothing like the love I felt now, for my son.

I felt that love while acknowledging that I'd fallen asleep—again—in my green cushioned rocking chair with my exposed breast hanging heavily over my sleeping son's tiny face. Startled and relieved to hear my husband whisper my name, "He's sleeping. Come to bed." I can still feel the exhale that came from shifting my son from my arms to his crib. Relief. And also an unexplained reluctance to leave while I stood over him, marveling at the curve of his cheek, at the shape of his ear.

One hot July day, feeling lonely and needy, I strapped my two-week-old son into his Baby Bjorn carrier, his head and his bottom cradled by my hands for extra safety. I went outside and I walked. I walked the familiar sidewalks of my neighborhood.

"Hello, neighbors!" I thought. "I'm ready to be a part of your mom club now!" I passed women who did not say hello in return, and stopped to compare ages of children and favorite playgrounds with others.

I waited for my mom club pass while shifting from foot to foot, engaged in idle conversation about the weather and other things I didn't care about with mothers at the playground. They chilled on a blanket while their children—obviously older than my son—slid, and swung, and climbed. They didn't invite me to sit, and I was too shy to ask whether I might.

And so I walked.

Over time, my son grew, and he learned to walk but not to talk. By then, I was living with doctors, evaluations, hearing tests, early intervention, and an eventual short bus that pulled up to my front door. My son attended 27.5 hours a week of preschool autism classroom while my neighbors drove their children to the community co-op preschool that I thought I'd be taking my own son to three mornings each week. I said hello at the playground and didn't share our journey.

Today, almost six years later, I can see more broadly and realize that I could have been the mom who brought a blanket to the playground, sat down, and invited others to join me while their children slid, and swung and climbed. I could have told them, had they wanted to listen, about what it felt like to have the short bus come when I, too, imagined co-op preschool. It never got to that, though. Nobody ever asked, and I never shared.

This year, my son went to the regular bus stop for kindergarten.

"Finally!" I thought. "Now, I can become a part of the mom club!" It wasn't as easy as I thought.

I remain awkward while tentatively connecting. I answer imaginary phone calls while walking home from the bus stop, choosing to not trip into a conversation that's been going on for years before I wanted to pay attention. And yet, I want to be in that conversation. I want to be a part of the Mom Club that is made up of my neighborhood moms.

Toward the end of this year, the one that marked our first experience of going to the bus stop where the mom club gathered, one of the moms asked about our plans for this summer. I mentioned private swim lessons and camps. "You should join the Swim Team," she replied. "He'll be swimming by the end of the summer with this group!" I wanted to believe her. But she doesn't know my little boy, and she doesn't know that he has delays and that while he's larger than her daughter, who is older than he is, his motor skills are behind.

I think about it, and am ready to reply "But, my son can't swim?" wondering whether he might still fit in, or that I might. But she'd already moved on, speaking to one of the moms she's known for years, and I'm reminded that we're new to this bus-stop clique that I walk away from each day, wishing and hoping and wondering.

I imagine the bus stop, come September, and me, trying to connect. I imagine my son walking up to the champion swim fish named Julie, the daughter of the mom who mentioned Swim Team in the spring, and saying "Hi!" as confidently as he did before this summer.

I also imagine taking a blanket to the playground, and asking the tentative new mama who may be shifting from foot to foot whether she'd like to sit. I'll bring lemonade, and my son will be swinging, sliding, and climbing. Maybe, she'll be hoping to become a part of the mom club. I imagine inviting her into mine.

Like So Many Icebergs

Mandy Hitchcock

This line resonated with me deeply when I first read it, and I have repeated it to myself again and again since those dark first days. And I have repeated it again and again to other grieving mothers who have followed after me:

"I hope you take comfort in knowing that this path is not uncharted."

I stood, but just barely, my body wilted against the doorway of my daughter Hudson's private room in the pediatric ICU, listening to the incessant beeping of so many different machines monitoring her respirations, her oxygen saturation, her blood pressure. The odors of antiseptic, rubber, sweat, and anxiety saturated the air, mingling in that way that only occurs in a hospital. I stared at my little girl on the bed, all seventeen months and twenty-five pounds of her, a ventilator taped to her mouth, sensors taped to her forehead, an IV taped to her arm. She seemed so much bigger than I'd realized she'd become, and yet she seemed so small lying there motionless on the hospital bed. Her head drooped down and to her left, and her eyes were closed. They'd been closed for hours and hours, ever since the ICU staff put her into a coma, desperately trying to relieve the pressure on her brain caused by an aggressive bacteria that had bullied its way into her cerebrospinal fluid.

I didn't know then that she would be brain dead sometime within the next several hours, that right at that moment, those menacing bacteria were perpetrating a catastrophic, irreversible injury to her brain. All I knew was that her pupils had stopped responding to the hourly checks the ICU nurses conducted with their tiny flashlights, and I knew enough to know that was a very, very bad sign.

As I stood there watching her, a thought burrowed its way into my head, and once it took root, I could not excise it.

All I could think was this: I don't want to be "the one who lost her child."

My mother died when I was twenty-six, so I had no built-in resource for advice when I had children of my own. I couldn't ask her whether my pregnancy symptoms were normal, or what labor was like, or how to soothe my burning nipples when breastfeeding, or how to keep myself from going crazy with a crying baby, or how to get a baby to sleep through the night, or how to introduce solid foods, or when to call the pediatrician, or how to keep my cool when my toddler was pushing my very last button. My mom couldn't answer any of these ordinary questions for me, so I had to develop a cadre of other mothers who could—women who'd already finished having babies or those who, like me, were deep in the trenches of first-time motherhood. Those mothers helped me feel less lost, less alone, less completely out of my mind during that long, hard, first year.

But then my daughter died. And none of those other mothers could help me. In one swift motion, my experience of motherhood was cleaved from theirs like a calving iceberg. I was adrift. I was totally alone. I feared I would sink. None of them could tell me how I was supposed to get out of bed every day in a silent house. None of them could tell me how I was supposed to watch the world continue to spin on its axis when my daughter did not exist in it. None of them could tell me what it is like to be "the one who lost her child."

I was terrified of that identity, even before it became a reality. I didn't want to be that person. The notion continued to reverberate inside the walls of my mind, and I suddenly felt deeply ashamed. There my daughter lay, feet from me, very possibly dying, and there I was, thinking about how others might perceive me if she actually did die.

What I didn't know then, what I couldn't have known, was that though I'd never asked for that identity, though I'd never wish it on anyone, though I was dragged by my hair into it, my fingernails clutching desperately at the ground giving out beneath what used to be my life, I would come to accept that identity, even though I would never welcome it. I would come to understand its value, even though I would never embrace it. I would come to feel honored and humbled to walk in the steps of so many other "ones who lost their children" before me, and I would come to feel a deep sense of responsibility to mark the path well for those who came behind me.

It began with one line of a message I received from the only person I'd ever known to lose a child, ten years before Hudson died. This line resonated with me deeply when I first read it, and I have repeated it to myself again and again since those dark first days. And I have repeated it again and again to other grieving mothers who have followed after me:

"I hope you take comfort in knowing that this path is not uncharted."

Later, as letters and cards and notes began to pour in, as I began to explore the world of grieving online, I discovered that not only was I not alone, I was accompanied on this new, terrible, unmapped journey by more women than I could possibly have imagined.

In those bleakest early days after Hudson died, this was exactly what I needed to know. I am not "the one who lost her child." I am one of countless others. This path is not uncharted. Others have walked it before me and lived to tell me about it. I will live through this. I will not die.

The road a parent must walk after the death of a child is a harrowing one. It is dark. It is endless. It is utterly unfathomable in every sense of that word. There are moments, days, weeks, when you feel you may have turned to putty, that your feet don't touch the earth but instead plunge through it, that perhaps you will never find solid ground beneath them again.

And it is during those moments, days, and weeks when you most need to know that you are not walking the road alone. That others are walking it in front of you, leaving little cairns here and there to show you where they have been and that they have survived. That others are walking it right beside you, ready to pull you back out when your feet plunge through. That others are walking it behind you, giving your child's life and death new meaning, because now you are the one who builds the cairns, the one who retrieves the despairing. Even as you, too, still sometimes stumble unknowingly through the dark, even as you, too, still sometimes plunge straight through the earth beneath you.

What I didn't know when my daughter died is that when icebergs calve from the giant glaciers that tethered them for so long, they don't sink. They float. And there are thousands and thousands of them making their slow but persistent way through the seas.

The Day My Son Forgot He Was Shy

Katia Bishops

Help arrived in the form of a resounding message: we were struggling too, but we're slowly figuring this thing out.

I wish I could show you the photograph.

He is two-and-a-half years old with a head full of dark hair. He's sitting on a chair with his arms raised, stretching up as high as he can reach, and his entire body seems to long to join the tips of his fingers, an impression further enhanced by his facial expression—teeth exposed, nose scrunched, eyes sparkling. If I had to summarize this image in one word I'd choose "soar," and it wouldn't be just because of the position of his body.

If I wanted instead to give you the full background story of the image, this is what it would say:

Imagine your toddler is so shy he never responds to questions like "What is your name?" or "How old are you?" asked by people at the store or on the street. Imagine he is so shy he averts his eyes and only repeats "Mama?" whenever somebody speaks to him and he wishes they didn't. Imagine he didn't want to say "Ahh" when he opened his mouth at the doctor's office because that, to him, would constitute a conversation. Imagine he's been going to the same community center for the last six months and has yet to respond to an instructor's "hello," "goodbye," or high five. Now imagine he did *this* yesterday at circle time while singing his favorite song (instead of whispering it) and maybe you'll be able to appreciate the pure elation I still feel whenever I look at this photo.

The little boy in the photograph is my younger son, Daniel, and the background story I shared with you was posted alongside his image on my Facebook wall.

The momentum reaching its peak on camera must have been building itself up internally. Up until that moment, I would typically observe him in social interactions and cringe, because I can still remember. Not necessarily the details, but the place he is in. That dark, empty, hollow, borderless space deep within. I know how much he wishes they would look away, how much he wishes he were invisible.

Then a scene constructs itself around that dark pit and I remember the bus during my first year of high school. I remember how out of place I felt listening to their conversations, the sickening fear of being expected to participate in them and the adolescent- logic-driven decision to remove myself from the situation altogether, only to feel doubly exposed sitting a few rows down with their eyes, as I imagined them, on my back. I remember how it felt walking into that pit every afternoon. I wonder how deep a two-year-old's pit might be.

"*He probably can't get a word in edgewise,*" say those who've met his older brother, and I smile politely, but I know. I know how he hardly ever pauses for a breath at home. I see his defenseless gaze when his eyes meet mine as another child approaches him. I anticipate the appearance of his animal-like natural defense mechanism—a grimace of pout and furrowed brow when strangers smile at him. I constantly worry about his ability to take on a world unfiltered by me. I've had to be a lot of things for my older son, serve in many different capacities, but never as his voice.

When I posted that photograph on my Facebook page, I wasn't doing so to alleviate my concerns or to seek support. On the contrary, it was a moment of celebration and I wanted to share this private triumph—tiny and monumental at the same time—and the contagious happiness emanating from the photo. I forgot that my addressees were mainly other mothers and that the wonderful thing about moms is that they're trained to read between the lines. And so it happened that these women extended the support I didn't know I was looking for by way of opening up and sharing their private experiences.

"*I was that child,*" and "*my son/daughter is/was that child*" poured my way through Facebook comments from blog readers and private conversations with friends.

"*I've noticed how quick I was to answer for her and I had to make myself stop.*"

"*Some of us just need time to observe and warm up.*"

"We live in a society that holds up extroversion as the ideal, which just adds to the pressure. Small groups were easier for me."

Each comment illuminated a different, new facet of the child I was once the world's leading expert on and they had one thing in common. They all reminded me of a sentence I once heard quoted: Do not compare and equate somebody else's external to your own internal. I was looking at what my son was doing and projecting my own history onto it, but what if the fact that he is my child was obscuring my vision rather than sharpening it?

In the weeks to follow I did pause more to allow my son the opportunity to answer questions directed at him. We went to one-on-one play dates with children who behaved similarly. I continued to encourage him to practice independence and I observed his tremendous changes. I wish I could take some credit for those, but I can't. I view them as part of a bigger process already in motion, the beginning of which was documented on camera.

I've received some of the most thoughtful, kind, diplomatic, and insightful advice I could ever hope for, yet I don't attribute the change that occurred in my son to the advice I've received either. This is not the story about the mother who received great advice, implemented it, and they all lived happily ever after. It is, however, a story about how advice—not only of its own merit, but because of some of its attributes—can be helpful even if it does arrive slightly too late.

Sometimes the kindest thing you can do for someone who puts herself in a vulnerable position is to expose your own vulnerability. Posting something so personal and watching it generate care and support from mothers I've never once met or even chatted with online before was to me the equivalent of a modern day letter in a bottle. Help arrived in the form of a resounding message: we were struggling too, but we're slowly figuring this thing out. And the gift of care, support, and empathy from friends and strangers was the second greatest thing that happened on the day my son forgot he was shy.

How To Get Out of Bed Again and Again and Again

Allison Barrett Carter

But no one ever told me that motherhood would actually be exhausting for years.

There were days when I didn't want to get out of bed.

There are still days when I don't want to get out of bed.

I have been a mom for six years now and I am still waiting for the mental, physical, and emotional exhaustion to fade. Six years in to motherhood and there are mornings when I can't get my body to face one more second of parenting.

Even this morning, the wakeup call came (as it usually does, in the form of a child yelling, a fight forming, a little body tripping) and my bed was perfect. It was soft and fluffy. The indentations in the mattress conformed to support my body in ways I never imagined possible. The sheets caressed me like a warm, comforting touch.

My limbs were heavy and I was exhausted down to my core, my weariness at a cellular level. I felt as though I could not give one more breath to motherhood. I was out of reserves and resources to mother and I wanted so badly to stay in my bed.

I lay there, in a state of half-slumber, begging and pleading with whatever power would listen (God, Buddha, Allah, the sun, my husband, my child), for just a little longer, please. Please don't make me get up again. Ever.

That feeling has invaded my body so many mornings during my season as "mom."

Oh, I knew before we embarked on this journey that mornings of heady exhaustion were awaiting me. I understood that there would be mornings I would be so groggy I would put the milk in the pantry and the cereal in the fridge and not even notice. That was widely shared in all the *What to Expect* books and on the pregnancy blogs.

And I felt those feelings.

In those early exhausting mornings I couldn't imagine baring my breast one more time, letting my raw nipples be torn up by a toothless mouth . . . hooking up to a machine that made me look, and feel, like a bovine…rocking, bouncing, and shushing for one more far-too-long second . . . cooing softly to a human being who would wail through my lullaby . . . changing one more diaper praying that it would finally stop the crying . . .

Everyone told me to sleep while the baby slept, that it got better. They told me to hold on. But no one ever told me that motherhood would actually be exhausting for years.

Of course, I have stopped worrying about milk supply and whether or not I am well-stocked in diapers. Those weeks of newborn haze after my firstborn son made his way into this world ended.

But why, then, didn't the exhaustion?

Why didn't they tell me that the bone-weary fatigue and emotional rollercoasters weren't ready for their finale?

What I have now realized, on my own, is that as the years march on, there will always be days a mother will gladly sacrifice anything to stay in bed and not be a parent for just one day.

For shortly after that newborn haze lifted there were days when I couldn't imagine chasing a crawling toddler around a restaurant while cringing at what I removed from his mouth . . . trying desperately to teach him not to hit, scratch, pull hair, bite . . . wondering why I was failing so miserably at parenting and what other mothers must think.

There were mornings I would cast a wary eye at the sunlight slipping through the bedroom window and frantically try to figure out if there was a way I could avoid spending the day at yet another germ-infested indoor playgym and one more sun-sweltering playground full of arm-breaking obstacles.

Soon those mornings morphed into first hours spent getting the oldest to school on time while the new baby needed a bottle warmed, a diaper changed, to be rocked, bounced, shushed, and hugged . . . where my guilt for not mothering my second son the way I did my first overwhelmed me . . . where the newborn haze returned full force, this time with an older child who needed his lunch packed.

Today, with a first grader and a three-year-old, there are still some mornings my body just won't go. There are days when I am so weary of the fighting, tired of being a referee to two children that I equally love and lose my temper with.

They never told me about these exhausting days.

Not a single mother ever told me how to handle them. "Work out, eat healthy, do something for you, shower every day!" I learned the battle hymn. But where is the book simply titled, *"How to Get Out of Your Bed, Again and Again and Again"*?

I asked my dear friends, other mothers, if maybe I should see a doctor for postpartum concerns. Technically, I passed all the screening tests just fine. But six years in to parenting and here I am, with 6 AMs where getting out of bed is simply unimaginable.

"No," they have said. "No, you are normal. We feel the same way."

We come together over coffee while our children run around and we squeeze snippets of supportive words in. We assure each other that we are emotionally and physically exhausted from mothering and that it is okay.

So why didn't they tell us? Why didn't anyone have the bravery to admit that they were sickly exhausted most of their mothering days?

They still haven't told me that one day in my future, on the day that my sons are leaving and moving away forever, that I will have to face the future of not hugging them every morning or telling them to pick up their socks every night. How exhausted will my heart be then?

My hope is that, as mothers, we can admit to being more exhausted than words can describe. I pray (to God, Buddha, Allah, the sun, whomever) that we will absorb the fact that the pure exhaustion of the thankless, unrelenting task of being a mother is permissible. There is nothing to be ashamed of when we need a nap every day for six years.

It means are doing something right: we are all in. We are committing 110% each day.

The fact that there are days when the act of simply raising out of the bed is a feat of formidable strength does not mean that we are weak women. Indeed, mothers are strong because we continue to get out of bed, day after day after day, because our children need us.

No one ever told me that being a mom meant days of not wanting to get out of bed across the years.

So I am here to tell you that you will have those days, mothers, for the rest of your lives. But I promise you will get out of bed. Because we always get out of bed.

Learning To Tune Out the Noise

Dana Robertson Halter

*I wish I could go back to my pregnant self and tell her to nod
and smile when people told her how motherhood would change
her. Having kids changes your life, but you control how it
changes—and no one gets to tell you how you'll feel or what
you'll do.*

When the other girls were painting their nails and playing house, I
tucked my purple cords into my rubber boots and went frog-hunting
with my mom. Net in hand, I'd silently wade through the cattails
and scan for amphibian eyes. I caught mainly tree frogs and garter
snakes, but our family vacations usually resulted in some "critter
catching"—geckos and toads in Hawaii, crabs in the San Juan Islands,
crayfish and turtles in Michigan.

When I talked enthusiastically about my frog-hunting adventures,
people gave me a knowing smile and told me I'd grow out of my
childish hobby as soon as I started liking boys. Thinking about my
future "boy-crazy" self perplexed and frightened me. Would my
interests change so dramatically that I'd fill my time with makeup and
hair and swooning over the cute boy in math class? Would I no longer
enjoy exploring, climbing, running, and catching critters? I felt like the
world was telling me to say goodbye to all the things I loved and get
ready for the next chapter: boys, boys, and more boys. Puberty—and all
the unknowns that came with it—terrified me.

Fast forward more than two decades, and those same feelings
of fear and apprehension around growing up were back when I got
pregnant for the first time. As my belly grew, my friends, family,
and perfect strangers converged on me to help set expectations. "You
won't ever want to leave your baby." "You can kiss bike racing and
triathlons goodbye—after the baby comes, you won't have time to
exercise anymore." "Are you sure you want to go back to work? I
bet you'll decide to be a stay-at-home mom." "Coming back from
maternity leave is so awful—get ready to cry every day at your desk."

"Your values will change after you have a child. You'll probably become a Republican." Apparently, becoming a parent is so transformational that I'd be shedding my old belief system like a snake sheds its skin, and emerging shiny and . . . Republican.

Much like the twelve-year-old girl who couldn't fathom a future without frog-catching, I couldn't see myself being happy as a stay-at-home mom. I couldn't imagine no longer wanting to race my bike, hang out with my friends, or go out on dates with my husband. I was confused by friends who lost themselves in their children and became people I couldn't relate to or understand anymore. Was that in the cards for me, too? Would I become an automaton who could talk about nothing but her baby? Would I lose interest in my friends without children and throw myself into play dates and the PTA? If my baby looked like Homer Simpson, would I be so smitten that I'd tell everyone how beautiful he was? The more I thought about it, the more I worried that my personality wouldn't survive the gauntlet of motherhood.

So many women described motherhood as the missing piece that made them whole. After I had my first daughter, I fell madly in love—but she didn't fill up a space that was empty. I wondered if there was something wrong with me because I needed more than just my husband and children to be happy. I once asked my amazing mother-in-law what she wanted to do for a living when she was younger. Without hesitation, she answered, "Be a wife and a mother—it's the best job in the world." I wanted those things, too, but I also wanted to work, be a competitive athlete, and have an active social life. I was ashamed that motherhood wasn't enough for me.

When becoming a mother didn't turn me into the person that everyone told me I'd be, the guilt set in. And it was all-consuming. I felt guilty during maternity leave because I looked forward to my husband getting home so I could get a break from the baby. I felt guilty because the idea of being a stay-at-home mom sounded awful. I felt guilty that I liked working outside the home. And I felt guilty because having a baby didn't lessen my competitive drive.

I wasn't fully present as a mother during my daughters' early years because I was constantly feeling guilty that I wasn't someone else. I was ashamed that parenting a newborn didn't come naturally to me, that my husband did all the cooking, and that I missed being able to go out on a spontaneous girls night. I didn't want to be the mom my family, friends, and society described to me, but I felt guilty nonetheless.

All those years of guilt were exhausting and demoralizing. But as I look at my three-and-a-half and six-year-old daughters, I realize that I must be doing something right. My girls are kind, loving, outgoing, and strong. They make friends easily. They eat almost everything. They work hard in school. They're affectionate with our family and friends and tell me they love me five times a day. On the rare occasions that I say something negative about another kid they correct me and tell me to be nice. I'm working on letting go of the mama guilt and recognizing that part of the reason my girls are fabulous little people is me.

I wish I could go back to my pregnant self and tell her to nod and smile when people told her how motherhood would change her. Having kids changes your life, but you control how it changes—and no one gets to tell you how you'll feel or what you'll do. Besides adding "mama bear" to my resume, I'm still the same immature, crass, high-energy girl I was before kids. I work full time, I make time for my friends, and I'm training for my first Half Ironman Triathlon next month. At the end of both my maternity leaves, I was excited to go back to work and I didn't cry at my desk once. And I'm still a liberal Democrat, to the core.

In the summertime, I go frog-hunting at the pond by my work (in dresses and heels) at least once a week. And, obviously, that liking boys thing eventually worked out. I'm finally hitting my stride and realizing that being the best mom I can be means giving my all, being myself, and tuning out the noise.

The New Not Normal

Tamara Bowman

I'm so glad they told me not to stay silent—and to find that so many others can relate to these transitional pains—and to these small and wide pieces of my story, emphasis on small, but a bigger emphasis on wide.

It crept in quietly during one of our achingly long New England winters.

"It's so normal to freak out and get nervous about kindergarten! I'm freaking out too! I could just cry. Every day. I could just cry," my friends assured me.

No, this wasn't normal. Not for me, and not for what I believed was anyone. It was my not normal and it was fast becoming my new normal.

I didn't tell them the scope of it—that my "kindergarten nerves" about my daughter, Scarlet, were something completely different and with a different name.

My new/not normal was losing my breath at the kindergarten info session and not getting it back until I pushed through the double doors out into the icy night and I gulped in the air. I skipped the classroom tour, which didn't matter because my daughter was zoned for a different school than the one that held the meeting, and I drove home with my head hanging out the window.

In February.

My new/not normal was carrying my toddler son through the middle school parking lot as the first person there on the first day of kindergarten registration. My new/not normal was to be flustered, despite my punctuality and my diligent paperwork, and to be five seconds away from crumpling on the ground when the school committee members welcomed us with water, snacks, and more paperwork.

What I did was take deep breaths, smile, and push through.

My new/not normal was to be so nervous before kindergarten buddy day that I couldn't eat breakfast. Some parents had tears in their eyes as they let their preschool children go into kindergarten classes for forty-five minutes. I had nausea and shallow breathing.

I had delivered two children and gotten us through two newborn periods. I had seen my son, Des, wheeled away by ambulance to a NICU, only two days after birth for a suspected infection, and I had met my husband and toddler daughter in the ER after a dog bite had left her beautiful right cheek needing to be sewn up. I had rushed my three-year-old to the hospital after she had gotten her hand stuck in our minivan door, and I had brought first birthday cupcakes to the hospital staff that had sent my newborn son to another hospital after his birth. I wanted them to see just how happy and healthy he had grown to be. I wanted them to see how far he had come.

I wanted them to see how far I had come.

I had come so far, hadn't I? I had come so far until I stopped coming any further.

It was Scarlet's preschool graduation on the same day as Des' second birthday. It was feeling worn out and not knowing which scenario was taking away my breath and my energy, but just figuring it was both. It was everything. It was too much and it was memories of births and small babies and losses and gains, and what I'd never get back, and what I stood to lose. It was the passing of time. It was the humid heat of summer that tends to fog our minds with allergies and haze.

I could explain it away as anything, and everything. I worried that I was losing my mind and my slip on control and parenting and mental health. Before Scarlet blew out the candles on her fifth birthday, my heart raced and my breath grew shallow. I carried her small five-year-old body to her birthday surprise—an unlimited amount of fun at Build-A-Bear Workshop—and I was having that same trouble again. I couldn't catch my breath. The walls seemed to quiver and close in on me and the loud mall noises were a buzz in my ears.

As always, I deep-breathed it out and smiled through it—if not for me, for my daughter. What I didn't want was to have to smile through pain for her. What I didn't do was tell anyone how much pain

I seemed to be processing during this transition from four to five, and from preschool to kindergarten. What did this transition mean to me? And what did it mean about me? I could tell it was more about me than it was about my daughter.

She was ready for kindergarten. She was unflappable, charming, and excited.

For the first time since I had become a mother, I couldn't rise above pain and anxiety. I couldn't shake it. I couldn't feel magical or powerful or brave, which were all feelings I had felt many times—during the rough hospital parts of motherhood, and through the tiny miracles that make up my patchwork story of maternal love.

As September inched closer, I figured that getting through that first morning of kindergarten would begin and end the whole ordeal. We wore matching sundresses and I took photos and I watched her clasp hands with a new friend and I saw her readiness and I stood by and let silent tears fall, and I took more photos.

She walked into the building, the smallest kid in her class, and with a backpack that looked (and still looks) impossibly large on her frame, and she marched in.

Forward facing, and without a backwards glance.

My friends met me for coffee that afternoon; I had looked forward to the date but I was so nervous all day that I had a near panic attack while ordering my coffee at the cash register. The loss of air and the loud buzzing sounds. I didn't tell my friends who would have surely understood—one as a mother of three, and the other as a doctor who had surely seen her share of parents freaking out about transitions.

I wasn't ready yet to string together the words and to give it a name.

If I could have started my healing process earlier, I would have started right then.

I would have reached out and told my friends. Right then. Right there.

The pickup on the first day was the most painful point of the whole experience. I didn't find the words to tell my husband in time, that I was ailing and breathless, and I dragged behind him, panicked and pained, while he scooped up our daughter into his arms and asked her all about her first day of kindergarten. I wanted to be the kind of mother to scoop up my child. I wanted to be the kind of mother to assure her I would always be present and strong for her. I wanted to be the kind of mother to assure myself I would always be present and strong for her. Ultimately, that afternoon was the turning point in which I finally decided to seek extra support.

I had told my story before, in detail, but had I ever explored it enough to heal from it? Had I ever sought help for anxiety about such a specific and traumatic event?

My father had passed away suddenly of a heart attack when I was just about four years old. I had been sitting and eating dinner, and suddenly the house had been shaken by his fall to the floor. Our lives were forever shaken. While I know the experience was beyond painful, my young mind couldn't process the situation without confusion and then help. When I was five years old and registered for kindergarten, my mom remarried my now-dad and I suddenly had a new parent, three new siblings, a new home, and a new school in which to begin my kindergarten year—only two weeks after my parents' wedding. I don't remember being a five-year-old very well, but I was only now, at thirty-three, experiencing bodily memories of that striking transition, or sets of transitions, in my early life.

For the first month or two of her kindergarten year, I couldn't walk into my daughter's elementary school without a near panic attack. I needed support. I needed help.

I began to share my pains and fears—through writing, through friendship, and through therapy. I was able to peel back situations, layer by layer, about what had happened in my past to make the kindergarten transition far more painful for me than any other mothering scenarios had ever been. That was just one step of many, of potentially a lifelong set of steps to stay healthy and present for my family.

It isn't just about therapy and piecing together these hidden bodily memories. It's about learning coping strategies, and exploring the sights, sounds, and feelings of what life was like when I was five, and how it contributed to a PTSD diagnosis. Most importantly, it's about being able to talk to my husband about anxiety and triggers, since it can't be my children. Not yet, anyway. Someday I'd love to tell them about how my love for them is so great that I powered through even on the toughest days and that I fought battles often to be the best mother I could be to them.

Someday, I'll tell them. I still fight these battles, now smaller. Maybe I always will.

I'm so glad they told me that the shaky and breathless darkness has a name: PTSD. I'm so glad they told me that it's painfully treatable, emphasis on painfully, but a bigger emphasis on treatable.

I'm so glad they told me that transitions would hurt, some more than others, and I'm so glad they urged me to explore these feelings with my husband and family.

I'm so glad they told me not to stay silent—and to find that so many others can relate to these transitional pains—and to these small and wide pieces of my story, emphasis on small, but a bigger emphasis on wide.

I'm so glad they told me that she is not me, ten fingers and ten toes and deep hazel eyes. Shirley Temple curls turned into waves, and the second shortest kid in school too.

She is not me, though. She is not my pain and I am not my pain.

Let the Good Times Roll

Hannah Harlow

No one tells you that even some of the good times hurt.

With the birth of my kids, I was prepared for the sleepless nights, food woes, kicking wailing tantrums, the endless whys, and problems I wouldn't be able to think up until they happened. But no one mentions the heartache of seeing the people you love most in the world grow and succeed with or without—or in spite of—you.

On the first day of kindergarten the two-year-old and I waited with my older son at the bus stop, in the driveway across the street from our house. We came out too early because that's a problem I have. We kicked rocks and told stories while we waited, then I said, "Give me a hug and a kiss now."

"Why?" Huck asked. "The bus isn't even here yet."

"But when it does arrive you might feel rushed and forget."

"I won't forget."

"Give me a hug anyway."

He obliged and we played for a few more minutes until the bus rounded the corner and pulled to a stop in front of us. While I said hello to the driver, Huck bounded up the steps and into the first seat.

He forgot, but I reminded myself that it was okay because I had remembered and he was excited and he wasn't scared. I had heard plenty of stories about kids who cling and cry. Huck did that for a week when we changed daycares when he was two-and-a-half, but that was it. I cried more than he did the first time we ever left him with someone who was not family. I stepped out of the door, walked down the stairs, and made it around the corner before I wailed into my husband's chest. Huck was six months old; Huck was fine. He has been mostly fine ever since.

Once a week my husband drops Huck off at school instead of having him take the bus. On one of these days, I came home from work and my husband said, "He doesn't turn around at all."

"What do you mean?"

"He just gets out of the car and walks to the door and he never once looks back."

I dropped Huck off too sometimes. I knew what he meant, but I guess I had gotten used to it.

"I'm sorry, babe."

"I know it's a good thing, that he's confident and well-adjusted and all that crap," but the way he said it, it didn't sound like a good thing.

We stood there together in the kitchen wondering why he didn't need us more. And wondering why some of the times he did still need us felt like a burden. Now I can't drop off my son without watching him walk away and waiting to see if he'll turn around. He never does. He goes off to school bouncing on the balls of his feet, his giant black backpack bumping, his little blond head reminding me of a crocus.

* * *

One glorious fall day I arrived home in the late afternoon to find our nanny, Katie, outside with my two boys, building up leaf piles for them to jump in and scatter over and over again. I relieved her of her duties, took up her place with the rake, and was feeling pretty happy as she got in her car and drove away. We could play out here for maybe another hour before we needed to head inside and start the whole routine: dinner, bath, PJs, teeth, books, bed. But almost immediately the boys said they wanted to go inside. I was disappointed; I tried to cajole them into staying outside. There were whines, slumped shoulders, the throwing of things.

"Fine," I snapped. "Let's go."

The nanny got the best of them; they got the worst of me.

I made them dinner and as they sat at the counter eating, my two-year-old said, "Me miss Katie."

"She'll be back tomorrow," I said and forced a smile, like his words didn't hurt at all.

Do you miss me when I'm gone all day? I wanted to ask and felt pathetic.

"Me want her." I could hear the tears in his voice.

"Well, I'm here now," I said, feeling anxious, feeling defiant, feeling heartbroken.

"Me love her," Wells then announced.

"You do?" I asked, then recovered: "So do I."

But do you love me more? I shamelessly wondered.

"Yes," he agreed and rubbed a strawberry across his teeth. "I'm brushing my teeth!" He laughed. All was right with his world.

I need to work to live where we live and have the things that we have, but I also *want* to work. I like my job. I like who I am because of my job and I like the places it's going to take me that I wouldn't be able to get to if I gave it up now and then tried to come back.

"You want them to love the nanny," my husband reminded me later.

"I know."

"You want them to be happy."

"Of course."

"But it still sucks," he said.

* * *

Changes are imperceptible. So many go by unnoticed. When we reach the top of a staircase, the two-year-old reaches instinctively for my hand and his palm rests comfortably against my own. Then, as two approaches three, on occasion he wants to try the stairs himself. A short staircase becomes nothing to fear, even longer staircases he can do by himself with the help of a railing. But if I'm there, he holds out his hand and waits for me. I love that he is so sure of me and his skin is so soft and so smooth I want to hold it always. When will be the last time? Which staircase? Will I even know?

I have a dream in which one of the boys is calling my name: "Mama! Mama!" It wakes me up and I throw back the covers and run up the stairs. I know nothing is wrong halfway up because of the quiet, but still I go into each room and check. My older boy often sleeps sideways in a crescent, the covers bunched beneath him. I usually straighten him out and pull the blanket over him; he's a sound sleeper, a good sleeper: even if he wakes he'll go right back to sleep. The younger one sleeps on his stomach, like I do. As he falls asleep he puts over the top of his head a tiny brown blanket that has the head of a monkey on one corner. We call him ChiChi. Sometimes when I walk in ChiChi still covers his face and I panic for a moment because I can't find him in the dark. Then I move the lovey to the side so I can see his mouth, his nose, his eyes. At first I worried he wouldn't be able to breathe, now I just want to see him.

I sit beside each of their beds for a few minutes and stare at their faces, trying to remember the curves of their cheeks and the way their eyelashes splay against their pale skin in the blueness of the night. I try to memorize the purse of their lips, how sometimes their foreheads crease in dreams and sometimes all is smooth, the way the forward-motion of the day never is. I want to remember them just like this and just like this and just like this.

They come down in the morning already different and I have already forgotten because this is them now, this is them new, but it looks so much like yesterday.

My Special Education

Shannon Drury

He can't have autism because he's smart.
He can't have autism because he's extroverted.
He can't have autism because he's charismatic.
He can't have autism because he can't. He just can't.
Even though I knew he did.

The school psychologist requested a meeting with me in February as part of the lengthy process to assess my first-grader's "special needs." This phraseology, usually rendered with air quotes and a depressed shrug from one or both of his parents, was growing more tiresome with each use. Still, there was no kinder way to talk about a little boy who knocked over chairs, ate the class crayons, and kicked anyone who stood too close to him in the lunch line.

I met Linnea Hughes, PhD., in an empty classroom, shaking her hand after an uncomfortable few minutes in which I struggled with the removal of several layers of woolen clothing. "Brisk out there, isn't it?" Linnea said. The air temperature was twenty below zero.

"Something like that," I answered, taking two tissues from the nearby Kleenex box: one for my dripping nose and another to wipe the condensation off my fogged glasses. As soon as I could see where to sit, Linnea started her interview. Her questions were intended to probe my memories, to shake out the dust of my subconscious for clues that would explain the unexplainable.

Was Elliott premature? Had I smoked while I was pregnant? Did I ever catch him licking the flaking paint off our century-old radiators? Was he constipated? Did he meet my eyes when I sang to him? Linnea brightened when I mentioned several allergies (pollen, mold, cats) and DNA testing (though she seemed disappointed to learn Elliott was Fragile X negative), and nodded sympathetically as I admitted to my family's long history of mental health disorders. I failed to add, however, that I was slightly high myself, having downed a Percocet with my coffee that morning. My jaw, tender since a diagnosis of anxiety-triggered TMJ in the mid-nineties, was locking up again.

"I have observed him in class," Linnea said, "and he's a very bright boy. I don't know that I've ever seen a first grader reading the Hardy Boys on his own before. It's really incredible how advanced he is."

"He learned to read when he was three," I said. "I guess we didn't realize how unusual that is."

"But you don't have any other insights?" It occurred to me in that moment that I was also being evaluated, and probably found wanting. I had the advantage of knowing not to kick anyone I pleased, but I was nowhere near as gregarious as my six-year-old.

"No," I sighed, "I really don't." I rolled my fuzzy tongue around my mouth, already feeling the drying effect of the pill.

***

"Come on in, take a seat," said Jennifer Wilson, the school social worker, as she ushered my husband Matt and me into her closet-sized office. Linnea sat at the head of the table, beside Elliott's classroom teacher Mrs. Vanderwerf, whose crossed arms lay atop her ample belly to avoid jabbing either Linnea or her enormous stack of paperwork. I slid into the student-sized chair, grateful for my black shirt and sweater, as the dark layers might conceal the sweat beginning to trickle out from each armpit. Matt sat next to me, bumping my hip with his leg. I didn't mind.

Linnea dug into her paperwork with the relish of a seasoned school administrator and policy wonk, detailing her personal interview with me as well as her observations of Elliott in his classroom. "I also interviewed him myself," she added, "and I think Shannon was absolutely right: Elliott *is* smart enough to know exactly what he's supposed to tell an adult in a one-on-one situation. He has to be one of the most charming children I've ever met."

Matt nodded. "That's why no one believes us when we tell them he's a challenging kid." The corner of Mrs. Vanderwerf's pinched mouth dipped slightly—apparently *she* knew.

Jennifer sighed. Three small creases appeared between her thick black eyebrows, deepening as she spoke; I knew this was the part of the meeting she had been dreading. "It's our determination that Elliott fits all the characteristics of Asperger's Syndrome," she said.

***

"You know what I'm saying," drawled the skinny young woman to my left. "The character's a real Asperger type."

"What does that mean?" I didn't like to be the one in a class to ask questions, preferring to project my hard-earned air of unflappability—aside from the professor, I was the oldest person in the creative writing workshop offered as part of Hamline University's MFA program. The rest of the group were recent English B.A.s, some of them so youthful they bore cheeks full of pimples, hair with greasy parts, and instantly detectable angst. At thirty, with stretch marks carved in my belly and a screaming infant left at home with my husband, I no longer held my vanity as close to the surface. I too was on edge, but for different reasons: only the most selfish, unworthy mother in the world would go to a writing class instead of therapy.

The woman, a twenty-two-year-old with silver rings on each finger and another through her septum, sniffed audibly. "You know about Asperger's Syndrome, right?" she said. She had the wiry build of an avid cyclist and eschewer of television. I didn't care for her overly emotive prose, and she didn't care for my plain sentences. Now she knew something about the world that I, an actual *adult*, did not, and this pleased her.

"Nope," I said. The professor shifted in his chair, interested in how I would handle this. He'd already told us that we were all getting As, even with four weeks left in the semester. I was very glad that I'd tested the class before committing to getting a degree there. I would burn off the rest of the classes and go back home, to my real job: Mom.

"Asperger's is a kind of autism," she said. "Not Rain Man-style autism or anything, but autism. Higher functioning. But weird. Definitely weird."

I nodded, and the discussion went on. For reasons unknown, this tiny conversation stayed embedded in my memory even as everything else about the course faded. The minute-long encounter remained unburied, fresh, and readily available so that I could answer honestly whenever someone asked me when I heard the words "Asperger's Syndrome" for the first time.

***

"But he's not like these kids," I argued with Matt over a stack of books from the library with titles like *The Spirited Child*, *The Fussy Child*, *The Explosive Child*, all aiming for my Elliott bull's-eye but always falling short of the mark. Matt found all of this too stressful, but as Elliott's mom I couldn't leave all of the research to Jennifer and Linnea. They barely knew him! How could they expect to understand him? No one loved him more than his heroic, intrepid mother.

But unlike Elliott's true heroes, the calmly rational Hardy brothers, I wouldn't go near the books with clinical diagnoses. I preferred the titles that waded carefully on the shore but wouldn't dive too deep. I checked out books about toxins in wheat, vaccines, dairy products, fluoridated water, waxed apples. I chased down explanations and theories with the ferocity of Frank and Joe Hardy tracking Chet and Biff in *The Missing Chums*.

He can't have autism because he's smart.

He can't have autism because he's extroverted.

He can't have autism because he's charismatic.

He can't have autism because he can't. He just can't.

Even though I knew he did.

***

There was a rapping on the door, starting softly but growing more urgent. "MOMMMM," I heard Elliott call.

I jumped from my tiny chair to open the office door, and there I greeted my son, my beautiful, impulsive, brilliant, definitely weird son. "I ran out of Fruit Roll-Ups," he said, smacking his sticky, cherry red lips.

"Did you eat the whole box?" I slipped out the office door and closed it gently behind me. We left Elliott, with snacks and books aplenty, in the child-friendly meeting space outside the school's administrative offices. His food supply was supposed to last until 3:00, when the meeting would be over and the three of us would drive home to meet his one-year-old sister and the babysitter.

He smacked again, but a little louder this time. "Yep." Two red, gummy fingers held his place in *The Secret of Skull Mountain*, #27 in the Hardy Boys series. He was devouring the books gleefully but meticulously, careful to read them in the order Franklin W. Dixon intended. *The Sign of the Crooked Arrow*, #28, was in his backpack in case he finished *Skull Mountain* during our meeting. He could read as fast as he could eat.

"Help me understand," I said. "You ate eight Fruit Roll-Ups in twenty minutes?"

"I ate eight," he cackled. "That's a homophone, Mom." Instead of basking in the glory of teaching his mother figures of speech, he asked, "do you have any more food?"

I dug a chocolate chip granola bar out of my purse and handed it over. "You're still okay out there, right?"

"Yeah," he said, unwrapping the bar and taking a hefty chomp. "What are you guys talking about?"

"It's like we told you, honey," I said, bending down to wipe a smear of chocolate from his cheek. His impossibly soft, round, six-year-old cheek. I kissed the spot that my fingers cleaned. "We're talking about stuff that's going to help you have a better time in school."

"Okay," he said. "See ya," he added, turning to a navy corduroy beanbag and landing in its center with a satisfying *whump*.

My boy. My beautiful, sticky, impulsive, kicking, brilliant, definitely weird boy. I loved him so much that I would crack my own skull in half to make him happy.

He *was* happy. All of the evaluations in the piles in that room said so. Where were the evaluations for anxious, uncertain mothers? If I asked Elliott for a progress report, what would he say? I watched him inhale the bar, chomping steadily as he read his book.

I opened the door to Jennifer's office and slid back into my chair, apologizing for the interruption. "We were talking about some of the adaptations we can offer Elliott so he can be successful for the rest of the school year," Linnea said.

Jennifer looked at me in a way that showed she understood why I was crying. "And we were talking about Asperger's Syndrome," she said gently.

"Yes," I said. I took Matt's hand and squeezed it. "I want to hear more about it."

My Single Parent Secret

Tara Dorabji

Ever since I became single, I have more time for me. It's easier.

I'm a single parent and I have a secret.

It's not that being a parent is hard. We know that. Your kids won't stop whining. Every step is a battle. They are screaming. You feel like you've waged a war and all you've done is dropped your kids at school and made it to work. The dishes are still dirty; yogurt is smeared down your shirt; you got your cup of coffee, but it spilled in your bag and now your laptop won't turn on.

Lately, a lot of dads have been telling me how hard parenting is. Maybe it's a sign that they are more involved. These fathers talk about what having children has done to their lives, their marriages, their work. Most don't get into their sex lives, but I can tell by the omission that there is none. I get what they are talking about. You become a new being as a parent, even your brain changes.

But I can't resist telling these dads my secret. Sometimes I lead with, *I probably shouldn't say this, but* ...

The dad will pause and then nod for me to go ahead.

Ever since I became single, I have more time for me. It's easier. And I smile. There is a brightness so true in me, I know they feel it. It makes no sense. It goes against everything they know. They cannot imagine doing this without their wives—there would be no one to wash the crusted yams off of the booster seat, or schedule dental appointments, or pick up the kids when they are sick at school; nothing would be prepared for potlucks; new clothes would not appear in drawers; dinners with friends would be left unscheduled; who would remember that Tuesday is an in-service day and someone needs to find a babysitter?

I raise my beer to these married dads. The bottles clink and we take another swig.

Maybe it is because my kids aren't toddlers. Or maybe I realized that if my needs weren't part of the equation, we weren't going to be floating down the river. We'd sink.

It's easier being a single mom, I say. There is less to clean, less to cook, and in a way, less to argue about. In the morning, there is no hair sprinkled across the bathroom sink from a shave. If my kid is crying in the middle of the night, I get up, or the kid keeps crying. There is no elbow thrown, no whisper in the sheets, *Are you going to get up?*

I mess up a lot and then I deal with it, because I know that no one will clean up after me.

Still, sometimes, being single is hard. Once my six-year-old daughter said, *When Papa moved away, I didn't understand what was happening. It hurts my heart. I want him to come back.*

I hugged her and kissed her. She fit right into my arms. *Papa is always in your heart,* I said, placing a hand over it.

There are other times, too, like the summer when my twins were four and had days of high fevers. My daughter got a nose bleed—the type of nose bleed where clumps are coming out and I didn't know that her thirty-three-pound body could hold that much blood. *It's okay, baby. Just take a deep breath,* I said.

But really, *I* needed to take a deep breath because at that moment, my other daughter's nose started bleeding, and I was sitting there with my arms stretched apart, trying to keep the blood from pouring out of my twin daughters' noses. I didn't have a third hand to grab another wad of toilet paper. Both their fevers were going up and the Tylenol was empty. I had no idea how I was going to get us to the store to buy more.

Once I stopped the noses from bleeding, I went in my room and cried. After eight years of living in San Francisco, there was no one I could call and say, "Could you pick me up some Tylenol and bring it to my house?"

I was alone. Yet so responsible for caring for others. A few minutes later, I zipped up my girls' sweaters, put on their hats, and grabbed a roll of toilet paper in case their noses started bleeding on the drive. We were off to Walgreens.

I'm not saying it's easy. I'm not saying that I'm always sane or that

I don't yell, because I do. But damn if being a single mom doesn't give me more time for myself.

It took me years to fight off the guilt, to resolve my mommy martyr syndrome.

I still get caught in a web of everyone else's needs. I still lose myself, giving until I lose my balance. Still, I find hot springs and waterfalls, Thursday night reggae shows, dive bars, and rum. Sometimes I seek solace, sometimes attention, but I don't find guilt in my solitude. I build a life marked by both separation and nourishment.

When my kids are at their dad's house, sometimes I'll wake in the middle of the night. I listen through the silence for the sounds of them sleeping, but I am alone. Rain splatters against the skylight. My girls don't have their rain jackets. They will be wet tomorrow. They pack extra clothes in their backpack. My daughter returns her blue folder late every week, so that I can see it. Our lives are split.

In the beginning they were with their dad one day a week, then one-and-a-half days, now two days a week with his new baby on the way. There are even occasional weekends with him.

I'm not saying that I don't have a village. My mom helps me, too. She is in my corner willing to give and give and give. I wonder if this is a trait we breed into women?

I have time that I never imagined before. When I was with my kids' dad, I never got a night off. Work, kids, home. For four years, I lived my life in twenty-minute increments. It took a complete composting of my life until I could just sit and drink a cup of coffee in the morning.

My kids' dad retained that quiet coffee ritual even with two infants. He had Friday night radio. There were his evening and morning rituals in the garage that filled the house with smoke. I ceased to exist beyond what others needed from me. I couldn't see what I needed because I was wired to give. I wonder if we raise our young men to be wired to take?

It's taken a lot to reclaim these pieces of me. To relish quiet, me-time in all of its forms. Against all odds, it has everything to do with being single and my nights off when my kids are with their dad. I guard this part of myself. I am faithful to it. I hold it close.

I am grateful for my girls. The way that they punctuate my days. How my schedule forms around them. I am used to the drone of bickering. Arms that reach up around my neck—their thin, long limbs that fold into my lap. They are not too old to be cuddled. Most things can still be solved with a hug.

I think of their infancy. I would do it over (but not again) in a heartbeat. My daughters taught me how to give in a way that I could not have conceived of before. It is the greatest gift—to know love like this.

My girls are older, now. I don't feel guilty about spending a weekend away, sweating in the lodge, or just spending a day in bed with my lover.

My girls nourish me. We admire our independence and interdependence.

But I can't help but wonder if we are failing our boys?

How can it be that we silently train girls to notice all those small things? To stretch and accommodate and fill in all those spaces. No one asks. I just shape my life to meet unspoken needs. I see my daughters learning these ways. And I take this support from the women around me who offer, who give.

The biggest gift of all is to give. I want my daughters to learn the beauty of this—how to give without fear of depletion. But it's not so simple, in a world of taking. Sometimes an end is our beginning.

Franklin

Lisa Pawlak

Unfortunately, there are still occasions when I just need to wait it out. There is nothing like mothering a tween boy to make nursing, sleeping, and screaming seem like simple things of the past.

When my son Joshua was a baby, he had exactly four states of being—nursing, sleeping, screaming, and moving.

According to the baby books, Joshua nursed much more than he was supposed to—sometimes for hours. While nursing, he was quiet and sweet, cuddly and content. I suppose he was like that when he was sleeping too, but the sleeping-state always seemed so fleeting. Quite in contrast to the ample hours spent nursing, Joshua slept a mere fraction of the recommended amount. When awake, he'd scream until picked up and bounced, rocked, or nursed again.

I discovered that Joshua craved perpetual motion. He was unusually active in-utero, rolled over five minutes after birth, crawled by four months, and walked by nine. Since happiest when moving—in my arms, the stroller, the swing—we spent a lot of time in motion.

I spent many of Joshua's earliest days listening to his baby screams of duress and figuring out how to appease him. By "screams," I do mean the ear-splitting, back-arching, red-faced, eyes-squeezed-closed, break-a-mom's-heart-sort. I'd methodically go through my mental checklist: Uncomfortable? Hungry? Dirty diaper?

I'd make sure all of the obvious reasons for his misery were resolved. Often, something would work. More often than not, that something involved putting him in motion. But there were other times when I just couldn't figure out the problem. I simply had to wait it out.

It was during those times that I started calling him "Franklin." After all, *my* sweet baby Joshua wouldn't act like *that*. Franklin became the name of Joshua's alter-personality, his evil twin, a possessed demon who would rear his ever-demanding, screaming self quite regularly. It

219

wasn't much fun to mother Franklin and somehow, the identification of Franklin as a separate person than Joshua made the whole thing easier.

As the years went on, Franklin appeared less often. He was, of course, around a lot during the terrible-twos-and-threes, but after that? Many peaceful years passed without Franklin.

Now, Joshua is twelve—almost thirteen. He has turned out to be a pretty nice, well-rounded kid, about whom I am apt to brag incessantly. He makes straight A's, plays the clarinet in his school's band, loves to quietly read, has a good sense of humor and competes on a swim team. I couldn't be happier or prouder to be his mom.

Franklin, of course, is also twelve—almost thirteen. He, unlike Joshua, is not a very nice kid. Often seized by hormonal fits of rage, he is prone to yelling at the top of his lungs about how unfair life is, then mumbling, sulking, complaining and—finally—dramatically slamming doors. Franklin joins us uninvited, without any warning of an impending visit, often in the late afternoons when there is homework to be done and his blood sugar needs a pick-up. When Franklin arrives, I go through my updated mental checklist: Hungry? Stressed? Tired?

Again, I look to the magic of motion to soothe his angst and often, in the late afternoons, I drive Franklin to swim practice.

Pure motion typically does the trick and chases Franklin away. An hour-and-a-half and thousands of yards later, it is Joshua who emerges from the swimming pool. And since Joshua has, fortunately, expanded his states of being—he will then laugh and joke, play music, study, eat dinner, and put himself to sleep. He even stays asleep—for ten hours or more—like he's supposed to.

Unfortunately, there are still occasions when I just need to wait it out. There is nothing like mothering a tween boy to make nursing, sleeping, and screaming seem like simple things of the past. Massive mood swings, challenging power struggles, and a vibe of general defiance force me to admit that mothering Franklin is not, and never has been, easy.

On the other hand, mothering Joshua—my pride and joy—is a pleasure.

Adult Accompaniment

Ann Cinzar

*Women often talk of how they lose themselves in motherhood.
How their sense of self gets lost, blended into the homemade
baby food, or swallowed up by the diaper genie.*

Sometimes I'm more shocked by how I haven't changed.

I had all the stuff.

The loot bags overflowed with candy and toys. The cake was iced.
The balloons hung in colored bouquets around the room. My mother
had helped me with the setup and now all that remained was to wait
for the pint-sized guests to arrive for my son's birthday party. He was
turning five. It was a big year.

"Well, I'm going now," my mom said.

"What? What do you mean?" I asked.

"Everything's ready. You can take it from here," she replied.

"You mean you're not staying for the party?"

"No, I think I'll go."

"But . . . " I said, my voice trailing. "Who will be the adult, then?"

My mother titled her head and gave me a look that denoted either
slight amusement or pity. Perhaps both.

"You'll be fine. Call me and let me know how it goes," she said as
she walked out the door.

Was this happening? She left me in charge? Nine little boys, and
I am the adult? Not for the first time since I became a mother, I was
struck by a feeling: *This is crazy.*

Back when I had a professional life, I suffered from a pervasive case
of imposter syndrome. It was as though I was play acting and any day,
someone might walk into my office and say, "Okay, Ann. The jig is
up. We've figured it out—you are not equipped to do this job."

I assumed being a mother would be different. By the second
trimester, the nesting instinct had set in, and I had immersed myself

221

in the preparations: decorating the nursery, buying the crib bedding, ordering diapers. I had no doubt I would fall naturally into my role of rearing these children who were one with me. Wasn't motherhood the most natural thing in the world?

It turned out, for me, the physical day-to-day of being a mother was easy. But the mental part proved more difficult, the part where you try to reconcile the fact that it is no longer about where to go for dinner, but about ensuring another being doesn't starve for lack of one. Because now, you are the adult.

When my kids were quite young, I took them on a transatlantic flight. As we settled into our seats, the flight attendant came over. She smiled in that friendly yet assertive manner and asked, "Are you in charge of these children?" I looked over my shoulder, searching for an older, better dressed adult in the next row. Certainly she wasn't speaking to me? I turned back to find her eyes still trained on mine. "We're going to have to move you," she said. "These children are too young to be sitting in an exit row." I stared back at her, stunned, and thought, *So am I.*

I waited until my thirties to have children, so I was well into adulthood when they came along. Yet, there continue to be moments when my feelings and actions don't match my age. The times when I enter a parent-teacher meeting and start wise-cracking about a wayward art project on display in the class. Until I realize I am the parent—I'm here to have a serious discussion with a teacher about my child (who quite likely created that art project). Or when an impromptu dance party erupts in my kitchen, and I'm the one playing DJ. Or when a few families come over for dinner and the kids finally track us down in the living room to say, "Don't you parents know it's eleven o'clock? We need to go to bed!"

Intellectually we know, before the kids arrive, we are becoming parents. We've read all the books, watched the shows, gone to prenatal classes. But the reality that you're no longer the child doesn't hit you until your daughter falls from the swing set and you rush her to the Emergency Room, or when it (literally) hits the fan when food poisoning strikes on a trip down south. It's then you realize: this is on me. There is no one else to rely on.

The funny thing is, my mom was younger than I was when she started her family. I wonder whether she ever had feelings of being an imposter—of being responsible for children and yet still feeling like a child? If she did, she never expressed those feelings, at least not to me. She always seemed so competent, so self-assured. Did she ever let her mother façade yield to the girl who wants to cut a rug on the kitchen floor?

Nine little boys made it through that 5th birthday party, surviving with—or despite—only me for adult supervision. There have been many more birthdays since. At times, I look at these beautiful little creatures, growing before me, and think *Who is responsible for you?* Other times, I look at these squabbling creatures, yelling and fighting with each other and think, *And where is she? Because someone needs to get you guys in line.* And in both cases, even now, years into this journey, at times I am still shocked by the answer: Me. I am responsible. I am the parent. I am a mother.

Women often talk of how they lose themselves in motherhood. How their sense of self gets lost, blended into the homemade baby food, or swallowed up by the diaper genie.

Sometimes I'm more shocked by how I haven't changed. Even with the parent-teacher conferences, the trips to the ER, the stretch marks, I haven't fully embraced the persona of an adult. We sometimes say that having children allows us to see the world through a child's eye. More and more, I'm inclined to believe we never let go of the child we were in the first place.

Because despite all the external markings of an adult life, the undeniable evidence that I am the parent, underneath, in many ways, I am still the same girl. I'm that carefree kid skipping down the street, her head in the clouds. The girl who wants someone to brush back her hair and place a cool washcloth on her feverish forehead. The kid who does not want to share her piece of cake.

The daughter who wants to hear her mother say, "Of course I'm staying for the party, honey."

My Kid Does That Too

Laurie Foos

"Don't feel alone," she said. "Listen to me. You don't have to feel alone."

My son was standing at the window looking out at the cars when I knew. He was nearly four years old and repeating bits of dialogue from television and things he'd heard during the day. It was one of his favorite things to do, stand by the front window and talk to himself. Ever since the pediatrician had suggested I have him tested for a speech delay, I'd been puzzled by why he could recite lines of dialogue from television but not answer the question, "What is your name?"

That morning I'd sat next to him by the window as he leaned against the glass. Together we watched the cars whizzing by on the busy road in front of our house.

"See that blue one? Look at the red one," I said, and he kept looking out at the cars, not at me, and said, "See that blue one? Look at the red one."

I tried to get him to look at me, but he wouldn't, even when I said his name. *Zachariah.*

"The world is a confusing place for you, buddy, isn't it?" I said, and for a moment it was just the two of us looking out at the cars. I leaned my head against his while he quietly spouted lines from "Dora the Explorer." When I got up, he didn't turn away from the window.

That morning the speech teacher at his developmental preschool had called, a call I realized much later she must have rehearsed many times before picking up the phone. I no longer remember her name, but I know she was young and pretty, as most of my son's favorite therapists were, and as soon as I heard her voice on the other end, I knew why she was calling. Ever since the pediatrician had asked me, "Does he say *Mama* and mean it?" at his eighteen-month checkup, what had begun as a speech delay seemed steadily to be morphing into much more.

"I wanted to touch base with you about Zachariah," the speech teacher said. She paused, as if waiting for me to cut in, and when I didn't, she said, "I'm seeing some of the things we talked about, some of those things I mentioned back in January."

At our conference a few months before, she'd mentioned his lack of imaginative play, his self-direction, his inability to engage in reciprocal conversation, his poor eye contact. When I'd searched for these issues online late at night, I'd pieced together that all of these things classified as red flags for autism.

I won't make you say it, I thought, even though, since everything had begun, the Early Intervention, the hours each week with my son strapped in a booster seat while the therapist traipsed in and out of the house four times a week, trying to coax him to say new words, to feed bottles to baby dolls and send Diego spinning on a miniature carousel, that all along, I'd been trying to make someone say it. *Your son is on the Autism spectrum.*

When I ask him where his nose is, I asked one therapist, *why does he miss the mark?* "Could be something called 'poor motor planning,'" she said, but wouldn't elaborate when I pressed her. *Why was pointing at objects in books so important? What were they all getting at?* I'd wanted to know. *And why did they keep saying I shouldn't worry?*

"I understand," I said to the speech teacher that day on the phone, "because I'm seeing them, too."

In those few minutes at the window with my son looking at the cars, I suddenly saw all the signs at once. And as I later told people, once I did see them, I could not un-see them ever again.

The speech teacher recommended a developmental pediatrician who interviewed my husband and me and then scheduled an ADOS test. The actual test itself happened rather uneventfully in the basement of the doctor's office. The nurse practitioner tried to get him to do the things all the other therapists had been trying to do: to comb the dolly's hair, to point at the cat and the cow in the book, to answer the questions, "Can you show me the pig?" and "Zachariah, what's this?"

For his part my son spent much of the test looking up at the basement window where a lawn mower blared outside. As I sat watching from my plastic chair in the corner of the room, even I could see how distracted he was. As he drifted back toward the window over and over, the nurse practitioner would gently try to redirect him back to the blocks or the doll, but inevitably he'd get up to check on the mower outside.

"That lawn mower is very loud," I said. "He's worried about the lawn mower." I wanted to say, "Loud noises bother him," but knew that was another of the signs and didn't want to give the test any more reason to show what I already knew it would say.

I sat and counted the minutes until the test was over. Mostly I wanted the noise outside to stop, for my son to do just one of the things he'd been asked to do, or to scoop him up and run out of away from the office, from the school, the therapists, from all of it.

Finally the nurse practitioner wrote the letters, "PDD-NOS"—Pervasive Developmental Disorder Not Otherwise Specified, a disorder on the Autism spectrum—in block letters. She reached over and touched my arm.

"Mild, though," she said, as if it mattered. "Mild."

That night after the kids went to bed, I went and sat by myself in the bathroom on the edge of the tub. My father had died a year and a half earlier after a seven-year battle with colon cancer, and I wondered how many times over the past few years I'd sat there worrying about someone I loved: my father, my bereaved mother, my son. I thought that day of writing emails to friends about what had happened that day at the office, about the lawn mower, about seeing all he could not do, about what had finally been confirmed about my son—this was before the wildfire of texting—but I didn't write any of them. What would I say, anyway, and what would any of them say in return?

What was there, after all, to say?

Eventually I told people about the diagnosis. Many of my friends and family members told me stories about this or that friend who had a child who used to be in a resource room but now was earning a Master's degree, or about a child we both knew who had struggled in school but had triumphed later in life.

"What can they really tell about a kid at four?" one friend said. "He could grow out of this."

"Look at Einstein," another friend said. "He didn't talk at all until he was four or five."

"Maybe he's just tuning you out," one said. "My kid does that all the time."

It seemed every mother I met had a story of a child who had overcome some sort of early disability. Did I watch the kid on kid on YouTube who suddenly spoke full sentences at six-and-a-half after being completely mute? Had I seen the "48 Hours" story on those non-verbal children who couldn't utter a word but could type those lines filled with striking images and turns of phrase? And what about that diet that one friend had read about, the one where the child had eaten nothing but eggs and special minerals? That kid no longer had autism.

"He's only four," they'd say, and I'd try to feel reassured, as I knew they wanted me to, but what I really wanted to say, even to my own mother, still in grief and feeling protective of her only grandson was, "You just don't understand."

Not long after the diagnosis, the developmental preschool he attended held a fundraiser that my husband and I attended. After the diagnosis, he received ABA therapy in addition to the speech and occupational therapy, and other therapies that are offered to children like my son. During the break from bidding on the baskets of gift certificates wrapped in cellophane and festooned with all-too-cheerful ribbons, we followed the other parents to the cafeteria where they were serving coffee and donuts and taking membership for the Special Ed PTA. At my typical daughter's preschool—my kids are sixteen months apart—the moms often walked by each other in the hallways and gave each other a nod or a half smile but rarely exchanged more than a few words at pick-up. In fairness, I had kept to myself as well.

"Hi," I said to the woman with the membership information. "I'm Laurie, and my son is four, and I just found out that he is on the spectrum . . ."

Before I could even finish the sentence, this woman I'd seen at drop off with two boys, one on each arm, a haphazard ponytail and bags under her eyes, reached across the table and took my hand.

"Don't feel alone," she said. "Listen to me. You don't have to feel alone."

I almost stopped her and said, "Oh, no, really, I'm fine," mentally going through the list of friends who had listened to me talk about my son. But I didn't pull my hand away or try to protest. Instead I stood there and let her hold my hand. In all this time of doing Google searches and convincing myself that I was okay with this new reality, I had never realized how deeply alone I had felt.

I don't know what happened to that woman, as our sons ended up in different districts after aging out of the developmental preschool. I never had the chance to thank her. Today my son is nine years old and in a self-contained class, a small class made up of children like him, children with cognitive and social delays that render them unable to be fully integrated into typical classroom settings. He speaks constantly and has made great strides, reads and writes and is distinctly much more engaged with other children and in the world around him, though he struggles when things change and with social and cognitive issues that my friends with "typical" children don't experience. There are many things he simply does not understand.

With the advent of Facebook and other social media outlets, support groups, and the like, I have found a way to remind myself when I need to that there are other moms out there who "get it," other moms like me with kids who occasionally eat napkins or the collars of their shirts, who scream and cry when the bus has a substitute driver, or when it rains, or when there is some other change in routine.

Sometimes at night when I lay my head on my pillow, there are worries that course through my head, worries that are hard to stop. They move through my mind like the news ticker on the bottom of a television screen: worries about how the world will treat him when he's no longer little and cute, when it's time for girlfriends, jobs, and worst of all, what will happen when I am no longer here to protect him. When those moments happen, I turn back to that woman at the preschool and wonder what her worries are, and I think about all the other mothers like me in this club no one asks to belong to.

I've had many other moments since then, with mothers on park benches, in dressing rooms, and in line for the ladies' room. We spot each other; we know our own kind. My son may hold his hand over his ears at the sharp sound of the hand dryer, and another child may walk on tiptoe or say nonsensical things. We talk about a fear of ceiling fans or an obsessive need to open and close doors. On the days when there are meltdowns or when my son eats the wash cloth or lies down on the floor during homework time, I'll go into the bathroom before I get into bed, sit on the tub, and think of that woman who took my hand and reminded me that I'm not alone. I know that somewhere another mom is nodding and saying to herself, "My kids does that, too."

Motherhood, Divorce, and Seeking Grace

Tracy Jensen

I didn't recognize it at the time, but in the three years since my marriage ended, I have learned that ultimately, you have to stand up on your own.

"Aren't we supposed to be fighting?"

Those were the words from my soon-to-be ex-husband as we drove to the Arboretum with our kids. It was Mother's Day, but neither of us was feeling celebratory.

I had filed for divorce three days earlier, but Sunday arrived with both of us unsure of how to act. We stumbled around the house—full of family photos—our life together pushing inward with oppressive weight.

We decided that being anywhere but home was the best plan of action, and got in the car with our two kids, Austin, not quite two years old, and Abby, only three.

"I want a divorce."

Those are words I had never expected to say when I got married, nor as I had rocked in the nursery, rubbing my belly, excited to meet each of my two children. I knew that shards of our life would cut and embed in our skin. I knew that, despite the pain and anger that was ever-present between us, I was leaping into an unfathomable darkness.

Divorce is painful—of course I had known that abstractly when I filed. I had been told that people would judge me, how difficult it would be to heal, and that it would wreck us financially.

The assault of emotions still surprised me. I mourned the life we had planned. I mourned the loss of my spouse. I learned a new level of heartbreak as I watched my decision cause a ripple effect of pain through my children and the people we loved most.

It was the depth of the isolation that I didn't expect. Because of my kids, I limited the information I shared with friends and family. When questioned about the reasons for our split, I was vague, redirecting the conversation to how we were keeping focused on the kids. I thought I was doing my best so people didn't feel compelled to take sides.

They did anyway.

After a particularly harsh conversation with a friend who tore apart my character, I talked to my ex-husband, sitting in our basement as we had countless times over the previous eight years. He rallied support, taken aback at the acrimony of the conversation I was trying to shake off.

It was during those moments of kindness that I felt most vulnerable. I was letting go of the one person who was theoretically required to care at the same time that my support network disintegrated around me.

When you are a mother, divorce tethers you. I have no way to walk away from my children's father. There is no "clean" start. My life for years will have an element of living in a fish bowl, with him walking in and out of my home, examining my decisions, and texting my phone. I am exposed in everything I do, and each time I have to interact with my ex, regardless of how cordial, the failure of our marriage is in front of me.

I discovered I no longer fit in the life I had carved for myself. My shame kept me from church, or even private prayer.

Friends backed away. For some, it forced too much light on their own fears and fragile homes. Others could not understand my decision and turned their backs. Most common was the awkwardness of not knowing what to say, so they avoided contact and conversation.

Other friends stepped up in truly lifesaving ways. They opened up their homes, made sure I had plans for holidays, listened with open hearts, and gave my children extra love that they needed as much as I did.

The morning after I broke our world, I hid in my room, curled on the floor by my nightstand. My daughter walked in and out with purpose, each time placing another stuffed animal by my side. Once she was satisfied with the size of her plush army, she curled against me, her lovey clutched tight. She didn't say anything, just snuggled, soft and warm.

I didn't recognize it at the time, but in the three years since my marriage ended, I have learned that ultimately, you have to stand up on your own. Friends cannot carry you through 2:00 a.m. doubts, nor can they force you to shower, go to work, or take care of your children.

My life is now about the three of us. I push myself to be strong for them, and in the moments I am not, they provide the giggles and hugs that reset my focus. Abby is always ready with her stuffed animal fortress and Austin's bedtime songs are a calming elixir. I have shed drama for simplicity, and learned the value of genuine friendship. I forced myself to examine my role in my marriage's demise, and I work daily to live differently for myself, and for these two kids who are my foundation.

A woman recently told me she was inspired by how much grace I had shown throughout my divorce. I've turned that word over a lot in my mind, thinking about its meanings. While I always felt clumsy, I can hope that my children felt the grace and stability that my friend saw. And while the pain has receded, the grace of my own forgiveness is still in the distance.

Mostly Me

Pamela Valentine

*I wished I could be anywhere in the whole world but in this
room, at this moment, waiting for the answer to a question that
no parent should have to hear their child be asked.*

"Do you . . . want to be a boy?"

Parent-teacher conferences. Second grade. The yellow plastic
chair groaned in protest as I shifted, built for a person two feet smaller
and a hundred pounds lighter. The teacher, principal, and social
worker sat across the table. My six-year-old child sat beside me. I stared
hard at the fake wood tabletop, my eyes tracing the grain of the wood.
I wished my husband was there. I wished I hadn't brought my child.
I wished I could be anywhere in the whole world but in this room,
at this moment, waiting for the answer to a question that no parent
should have to hear their child be asked.

"Do you want to use male pronouns?"

I could just make out a face in the whorls of the wood on the
tabletop. It looked a little like a smiling turtle. With dread locks. I lifted
my eyes to the face that I've loved so completely since the moment
I saw it. There was a question in those bright blue eyes, a desperate
unspoken longing that I've known deep in my soul for years.

I had no words. What could I say? It wasn't my question to
answer. God, I'd avoided even asking it for fear of what the answer
might be. My breath caught in my throat and all I could do was stare,
like a deer caught in the middle of the highway at night, staring down
the headlights that would bring nothing but tragedy. I could feel the
weight of disappointment, fear, uncertainty, all of ours, not just my
own.

But mostly my own.

This wasn't my question to answer. It wasn't even my question to
ask.

"Do you?"

I looked back down at the turtle in the tabletop. What would you do, I asked him inside my head. Would you shout out, "No, you can't! Don't! We're not ready for this! What will people say, or think, or do? There's too much at risk, we can't just do that."

"Can I?"

The voice was so small and scared, like a tiny mouse cowering in the corner. I didn't recognize it. But it's how I felt inside too. Helpless and frightened. Frightened for all of us, not just myself.

But mostly myself.

"You can if you want to. Do you want to?"

My eyes flew from the turtle's winking smile to that cherub's face, as I watched the world fall apart in the dip of a chin, the slightest of nods. All of our worlds, not just mine.

But mostly mine.

They looked at me now, waiting. I needed to respond in some way, in some appropriate, supportive way. They were waiting. I looked down at the smiling turtle, he waited too. He would smile at them, say something warm and intelligent and sincerely supportive. They'd never know how his heart was breaking, crumbling away inside at everything he was losing. At the enormity of this decision, this seemingly simple decision, that right now opened like a chasm, wanting to swallow us all up, not just me.

But mostly me.

A good parent would be like the turtle. I'm a good parent. So what if all my dreams of mother-daughter lunches, girls' weekends, wedding dress fittings, and baby showers are all disappearing before me. A good parent wouldn't ever let them know. A good parent would smile and say, "If that's what you want, then let's do this. Whatever it takes, I support you."

I looked back down at the turtle in the grain of the wood and he smiled in approval. Only he would ever know. Know how much it hurt to say those words, know how much I meant them but just not yet. Know how much I love this child but how much I was mourning the loss of my daughter. No . . . the loss of the idea of my daughter, even I couldn't sell myself on that lie.

"I want to be a boy."

I smiled like the turtle, wooden and strained. I willed myself to not cry, not cry, not cry. I looked up into her . . . *his* eyes, his beautiful clear blue eyes and I could see that just as I was sinking into my own despair and deceit, he was rising out of his for the first time. A fierce feeling of pride at being witness to this transformation filled all of us at that table, not just me.

But mostly me.

The Hitting Stage

Wendy Kennar

The biggest sigh of relief came from hearing others tell me that hitting happened. It wasn't just us.

During a period of time that took us through the latter part of pre-school and into kindergarten, my son hit me. Usually with his hands. But sometimes with a book, a stuffed animal, a pencil. Once with a golf club. He punched me and pinched me.

He hit me with the desire to hurt. He hit me until I cried. Until I bruised. Until I sought refuge by locking myself in my bedroom, the only room in the house with a working lock.

We aren't a family that hits. Ryan had never been struck before. Ryan didn't watch violent movies. He didn't even own a toy gun or sword.

And yet he hit me. Over and over.

I was ashamed. After all, I was the mother of a precious, smart, gentle little boy. A little boy who didn't get into trouble at school. A little boy who was described as "easy" and "mild-mannered" since he was born. In fact, when I first held him, he was calm as could be, with wide-open Hershey brown eyes looking around the room, as if to tell me, "Let's do this," (something he says today).

I was an elementary school teacher in a Los Angeles public school. A school that was ethnically, linguistically, and socio-economically diverse. I was used to maintaining order and control with a group of thirty-plus fourth graders. I knew how to handle kids who threw items across the room, who drew violent sketches, who played "M-rated" video games on a daily basis. In fact, they were put into my room because I was gentle, because I was patient, because I was nurturing, because I loved them no matter what.

I did it at work. Why couldn't I do it at home?

My parents were my first line of contact. *What do I do now? What did I do wrong? How do I fix this?* My mom assured me it was a stage that

239

Ryan would outgrow. Meanwhile, I relied on my usual bag of teacher tricks—positive reinforcement for moments Ryan didn't get violent, withholding special privileges, taking away favorite toys and having him earn them back.

I finally turned to Ryan's pre-school teachers—three women who had worked together for more than a decade, who ran the class with confidence and structure. We communicated before and after school. Ryan received time-outs and verbal reprimands. He promised to "treat Mommy like a Princess"—a behavior one of his teachers spoke to him about often.

Ryan graduated pre-school and transitioned to kindergarten with the tears and apprehension that are quite common for most kids. I wasn't worried. (Before teaching the "big kids," I had been a kindergarten teacher for five years.) In school, Ryan was a model student. Polite. Obedient. Quiet. Hard-working. At home, he shifted between being a boy I could be proud of and a boy I couldn't stand the sight of. I felt guilty for not liking my child, for not knowing what brought my child to such extreme behaviors, and for not knowing how to help him.

I spoke to Ryan's kindergarten teacher. We had a student-teacher-parent conference explaining that the no-hitting rules at school were the same no-hitting rules at home (and everywhere). Ryan's kindergarten teacher was a mom of three. She told me that she herself would hear that her son behaved one way for his teacher and a completely different (and not as flattering) way for her at home.

My son hit me, rarely his dad, because I was his safe person. The person who would love him no matter what. The person who wasn't going anywhere.

We finally went to see a clinical psychologist. Our sessions involved a lot of play for Ryan, a lot of hand-wringing for me. I wanted a fix: a "do-this" and then "that stops."

And it was during those sessions that we got a sense of what was going on. There had been one recent big change in our family that had served as a catalyst for several small changes: I was no longer teaching.

Near the end of Ryan's pre-school experience, I left my twelve-year teaching career at the advice of my doctor. I suffer from an autoimmune disease and although I had tried to keep working, I just couldn't. I was now a stay-at-home mom. There was no more nanny. There was just Mommy. All the time. Mommy who didn't teach because of her "boo-boo leg." (My pain generally shows up worst in my left leg, and Ryan refers to it as my "boo-boo leg.") And Ryan didn't have the words to express his confusion or his acceptance, his anger, or his excitement about me being at home.

Our therapist helped me see that teaching is not the same as parenting. What works in a classroom—reprimands, phone calls home—don't automatically work at home. At home, I am not Mrs. Kennar. I am Mommy. The two are not the same. I hadn't fully understood that.

And our therapist told me that this didn't just happen to our family. All kids can hit. Kids who have never been hit can hit. I hadn't done anything wrong. I didn't need to "fix" anything. We needed to work through it. All of us, as a family.

Maybe our family would have made it out of this phase sooner if I had asked for help sooner. But I was embarrassed. I was overly optimistic thinking I could handle it on my own. And I was in denial that my son could behave in such a revolting manner. The biggest sigh of relief came from hearing others tell me that hitting happened. It wasn't just us.

Ryan doesn't hit any more. He gets angry and walks away. He gets really angry and he might hit a pillow or yell. But he doesn't hit me. Now, as he holds my hand when we walk, he'll reach over and kiss my hand. And I want to cry. But now it's for different reasons. Out of relief, pride, and joy.

V Is For Vegetables and Video Games

Kim Tracy Prince

I suddenly flash forward to the possible future—texting, friends, bullies, drugs, alcohol. Things that a pre-teen will face too early and over which he will clash with me and my desperate need for control. Vegetables and video games are easy.

"I want you out of my life!" he screams at me through tears, red-faced and gap-toothed. He is six years old, and I am nearing forty, and we are locked in a battle of wills. When he lets that last one loose, I decide the battle is over. I'm the mother, and I get to say so.

But he is, it is increasingly clear, turning out to be just like me. We stomp through the house, chasing and following, continuing the argument, which began over how nasty he is to his little brother when they are playing LEGO Star Wars on the Wii. It is the activity he loves the most, but when my four-year-old plays too, he slows the action down.

I tell the big brother it is time for bed. End of discussion, and there will be no video games tomorrow. His breath comes in hitches as he calms down from the full angry cry of just minutes ago. He reluctantly dresses in pajamas, brushes his teeth, asks me to get out of his room. But I am his mother, and he is not allowed to speak to me that way. I sit at the foot of his bed as he tells me that I am not the best mother in the world, and indeed, he reasserts, he wants me out of his life.

As his eyes are closing I say, "That hurts my feelings," and I get up and walk out of the room, closing the door behind me so I can hear the click on the closing of the argument, which I believe I have lost. Seconds later he follows me into the other room and sits in my lap and apologizes. I am not the best mother in the world, though, he says. I feed him too many vegetables, and he's already eaten enough vegetables to last his whole life.

In the same way that I can make an argument about housework mean that my husband doesn't love me anymore, my child has turned a spat about video games into judgment of my motherhood and my use of vegetables to torture him. I suddenly flash forward to the possible future—texting, friends, bullies, drugs, alcohol. Things that a pre-teen will face too early and over which he will clash with me and my desperate need for control. Vegetables and video games are easy.

I relax, allowing my body to become soft, to provide the safe haven for my child that I want myself to be. I let him tell me why he hates vegetables so much. I let him suggest alternative foods, tell me his favorites. His face, still hot from the recent tears, warms my arm. He is long and lanky, more like an eight-year-old than a new first grader. I ask him to remember why I feed him vegetables.

"Because you love me and you want me to grow," he whimpers. Yes. Yes, I do. Even though it hurts my heart to see the pictures of his fat baby arms, his carefree baby smile, his golden toddler hair flash on my computer screen as I walk by in the dark. It hurts to compare the strong boy limbs to the squishy preschooler thighs. Even though I miss who he is every day as he disappears into someone new, yes. I want him to grow.

Hourglass

Julie C. Gardner

*I wait for her to promise me that one day I'll wake up and know
I made the right choice. That someday soon I will be sure.
Instead, she shakes her head.*

We sit together at a table in my mother's sunny backyard. Or perhaps
we are in my sunny backyard. Or in her kitchen or in my kitchen. The
location of our conversation has blurred for me now but what sticks in
my memory are her words: *You may never get over it.*

It is a dozen years earlier. I rock my one-year-old son while he
naps, his scalp sweet and damp above the crook of my arm. Beside
us, a Noah's Ark lamp. In my head a lullaby plays, along with these
thoughts: *You will always have this moment. No one can take your
memories away.*

Another year passes and my postnatal room is dark and quiet, the
scent of soap sharp in the air. Shuffling across the room in a pair of
stiff, treaded socks, I have never felt more powerful, more alive. My
daughter sleeps in her hospital bassinet. Rosebud lips. Tiny knit cap.
Remember this, I tell myself. *Hold on to every detail.*

Although I'm still sporting the mesh underwear of the newly
delivered, I cannot wait to make another baby. I know it's crazy. I do
not speak the words out loud. But inside, I wonder. *What will he look
like? Who will she be?* I nurse my son for eleven months and his sister
well past her first birthday. When she weans, it does not occur to me
this is the last time. Forever.

We gather often in these early days, my female family members
and friends. Every one of them seems confident about the number of
children she desires. *One and done. Two is plenty. We're embracing zone
defense, then stopping at three.* A friend touches my elbow. Her eyes
are gentle. "You are not finished," she says. "You love being a mama.
You've got another one in you."

But I have two young children and a husband who works long, irregular hours. My teaching career affords me little flexibility. It would be insane to add to our chaos and smug to presume I could easily get pregnant again. *Trust me,* she says. *You'll have one more.*

My insides churn and I believe her. She has seen into my heart. So what if we're barely hanging on?

We can always have a third. If not now, then sometime. When we're ready.

Except we are never ready.

We're off-balance, exhausted and crazed. Planning another baby would be irresponsible—not to mention unfair—to the children we are struggling to manage already. Every day, these words on my lips: *Mommy is tired. I am losing my patience. Please don't push me. I'm begging you. Please.*

Still, at night I lie awake hoping to become pregnant by surprise. On the rare occasions when my period comes late, I harbor a private joy. *Of course we didn't expect it,* I will say, *but we are absolutely thrilled.* I wait a few days to purchase the EPT two-pack.

There are never any surprises.

My children meet me on the playground after school, talking over each other as they skip across the blacktop. There is mustard on Jack's shorts and Karly's shoes are full of sand. He says, "They wouldn't let us trap bees at lunch!" She tells me, "Today, we learned a new song!" Both of them begin to sing. "How can I marry such a pretty thing as you when I have no pants to put on?"

There comes a burst of giggles and I grin at them, laughing, too. I take in this moment, absorb their light. I have loved every one of my children's stages. Each has been hard in its own way but also beautiful. *Beautifully hard.* I try to sort between the two, sift out the bad and keep the good, but when I do, it all slips from my hand like so many grains of sand.

My friends and I grow older. We hear about "oops babies" and the jokes come fast: *Better her than me! She'll be sixty when this kid goes to college. Damn! Can you even imagine?* I blush and avert my eyes.

I imagine it. Yes, I do.

A "more mature" actress becomes pregnant. I Google her age,

searching for proof it's not too late. See! Halle Berry did it. And Gwen
Stefani. Kelly Preston was forty-seven. There is still more time.

More time.

I seem unable or unwilling to face the fact that the ship of my
childbearing years might have sailed. Maybe it's a stubborn refusal to
admit my own aging. Perhaps I still want to feel like the fertile young
woman I used to be. How ridiculous! How vain! I don't want to be
vain or ridiculous.

These are thoughts I rarely share, and when I do, I am
embarrassed. I have so much for which I should be thankful. How
dare I not be content? There are women everywhere unable to have
even one child. Women who have lost children. Women for whom
motherhood has meant unbearable pain. *You are selfish, Julie, and
ungrateful.* But I can't help how I feel.

I turn forty and take a leave of absence. It is a lifelong dream come
true, this chance to focus on our family and my writing. And yet, in a
corner of my brain lurks another possibility. I mention the idea to my
husband and he is, to my shock, on board. Between us, Bill has always
been the voice of reason. I don't want to disappoint him. So. *What do I
do now?*

I dig deep, explore the consequences, admit to him this sad
conclusion: If we have a baby, I will never write.

Of course other mothers balance work and small children but they
are strong and I fear I might be weak. A newborn would provide a
too-ready excuse, the valid reason why I never achieved my goals.
The thought is paralyzing. I am afraid to fail at both writing and at
parenting. We hem. We haw. We do not take the leap.

Instead, I write and write. I focus on my *book baby.* All the while,
I look at families with three children, at loved ones who were the
third child in line, and I think this: "Life wouldn't be the same without
Bryce. Linda. Aiden. Emma. Tommy. Who is missing that we don't
yet know we want?"

There is no answer. There never will be. Only restless doubt.

I blink twice and Jack and Karly are young adults, funny and
kind and smart. They are each other's best friends, their two-person
boat never rocked by another sibling. It is a fortuitous default. *Luck.*

Gratitude. Good fortune. These words dominate exchanges between four generations of my family. The message: *Do not change a thing.*

My parents hailed from the generation of Zero Population Growth. Their philosophy? Do not add more people to the planet than you'll take with you when you leave. It is a sound goal and conscientious. For my entire life, I assumed raising two daughters was an easy decision for my parents. My sister Nancy and I were enough. I envied my mother her certainty.

One afternoon, I tell her this in her backyard (or my kitchen or her kitchen or my backyard).

"When will these feelings end?" I ask. "When will I stop wondering? Questioning? Thinking . . . maybe?"

I wait for her to promise me that one day I'll wake up and know I made the right choice. That someday soon I will be sure. Instead, she shakes her head.

"You may never get over it."

In her tone, I hear. In her eyes, I see. About motherhood, she has had her own doubts. She didn't know if she was getting everything right. She simply kept her chin up, did her best. And like the rest of us, she hoped it was enough.

I am flabbergasted. Humbled. Freed.

I may never get over it. And that's okay.

It's okay to miss Jack's little boy voice rambling gruffly about his Legos. And Karly's toddler reach, her small grasping hands. *Mama, carry me?* The tug remains for me still, this longing for my babies. But these are precious images from the past, not visions of my future.

First steps. Second grade holiday performances. *Velveteen Rabbit* teas. T-ball games. Karate lessons. Some other mother is living this now. I will step aside to cheer her on.

I am forty-six (and a half) when the internet explodes with the breaking news: a fifty-six-year-old British woman has given birth to twins. I lean back in my chair, away from my writing desk.

Fifty-six. Really? That gives me ten more years.

Another voice echoes in my head: *You may never get over it.*

My mother was right. I get to work again.

A week later, I take a five-mile hike with a friend whose children are also teenagers. We discuss prom and SAT scores and driving lessons. High school graduation. If Mammoth gets decent snow next year, our families will ski together for the last time before our sons leave for college. The fall of 2016 looms. Neither one of us wants to miss a moment.

This is the good stuff. The best. I am soaking it up.

Home from the trail, I dump the sand out of my shoes.

It Doesn't Get Easier

Alice Jones Webb

It's not any easier. I've just traded kissing scraped knees for nursing broken hearts. I've traded sleepless nights nursing a hungry, restless baby for sleepless nights worrying about the decisions they might make when I'm not around—important, earth-shattering decisions, decisions that can't be undone, ones we could all have to live with for the rest of our lives.

"Don't worry. It gets easier."

That's what mothers with children older than my own have always told me. It's like a motherhood mantra. It's repeated by grandmothers and aunts and friends and little old ladies at the grocery store. When I was a new mother, a sleep-deprived, incoherent zombie who smelled like sweat and sour milk; when I hadn't showered in three days because the baby would scream whenever I put him down; when I felt like little more than an animated milk bottle for my demanding, squalling infant; when I defined a productive day as one in which I'd actually gotten dressed, they told me, "Don't worry. It gets easier."

Stupid, isn't it? Telling a mother not to worry? It's like telling water to run uphill or pigs to sprout wings or mothers-in-law to mind their own business. It's just not going to happen. Worrying is wired in our maternal DNA. And there are so many things to worry about: whether the baby is pooping a sufficient amount, whether his teeth will be jacked up from using a pacifier, how much his future therapy is going to cost from just how much I'm bungling this motherhood thing on a daily basis.

"Don't worry. It gets easier."

I still grabbed on to that like a lifeline . . . because I *was* worried. I was worried that I might not make it through this motherhood gig with my sanity intact. Those assurances made me feel as if there was a light at the end of the tunnel that maybe I just couldn't see yet. It was like they were coaxing me on from the other side, like the roaring crowd cheering on the runners at a marathon. They could see the finish line even if I couldn't. If I just kept going, even as smelly and unshowered as I was, I would get to that wonderful promised land of "easier."

It was a lie.

As the baby that had been glued to my breast became a toddler who was glued to my leg, the doubts started to creep in. It wasn't getting easier, which made me worry that I was doing something wrong. Maybe I hadn't read the right parenting books or joined the right "Mommy and Me" group. Because I was drowning in smelly toddler diapers and broken family heirlooms and the Legos (Oh, my God! There were so many Legos!). I was completely overwhelmed by the night terrors and the grocery store temper tantrums and the scribbled marker wall art.

Sure, I was getting better sleep and showering with greater regularity, but it wasn't getting any easier. I had traded all-night breastfeeding marathons for carefully removing the crust from grilled cheese sandwiches which had to be cut into perfect triangles. There were so many boo-boos to kiss and questions to answer and goldfish to rescue from the curious hands of an overly interested toddler, so many toppled house plants and broken toys and verses of "The Wheels on the Bus" to be sung . . . and then sung again. And I had to worry about him learning his alphabet and then writing his name and then whether or not he would curse in front of Grandma.

And in the middle of it all, they still told me, "Don't worry. It gets easier."

I want to scream at those well-meaning grocery store grannies and smiling moms on the playground to "Please, Just Shut Up!"

Because it's bullshit.

It doesn't get any easier.

Now I am the mother of three teenagers. I assure you things are not any easier than they used to be. My life is filled with slamming doors and sarcastic eye rolls and broken curfews. It's filled with the constant questioning of my authority and challenged boundaries and friend drama. I spend my time worrying about their reputations and their grades and safe sex and date rape and why some total stranger sent my daughter half-naked pictures of himself.

It's not any easier. I've just traded kissing scraped knees for nursing broken hearts. I've traded sleepless nights nursing a hungry, restless baby for sleepless nights worrying about the decisions they might make when I'm not around—important, earth-shattering decisions, decisions that can't be undone, ones we could all have to live with for the rest of our lives. I've traded repeated verses of children's songs for the constant repetition of "Be responsible." I've traded incessant questions like "What's that?" for "How could he be so mean?"

And sure some things have gotten easier. I no longer smell like someone else's piss. I can leave the house without small humans attached to me like Velcro. I sleep for stretches longer than a few short hours, and I haven't been vomited on in quite some time.

But in some ways, it's so very much harder. Parenting teens is stressful. When they were little, I controlled all of the decisions in their lives—what they would eat, what television shows they could watch, who their friends were, what time they went to bed. How badly could I screw that up? What kind of long-lasting consequences are there for watching one more episode of *Sesame Street*?

Now there's a persistent, unending worry about things like internet safety and drug abuse and texting while driving and whether or not they remembered to put on clean underwear (because if they didn't and they get in an accident, everyone at the hospital will think I'm a horrible mother). Plus, they aren't as cute and easy to forgive anymore.

I assure you that this thing hasn't gotten any easier.

What I heard when those well-meaning women said, "Don't worry. It gets easier," is that life would get back to normal—that I would be able to not only sleep and shower without interruption, but that I could have a thought independent of how something might affect my children. That I could make decisions based on what I wanted, not on what was best for the family. That I could pursue selfish whims and not care about the future. I wanted the normal pre-kid me that wasn't stressed out by the responsibility of raising human beings, because that's what I imagined "easier" looked like, at least when I let myself daydream during naptime.

Things didn't get easier, but they did change. Once we have

children, we have to find a new normal. And sometimes normal is learning to dodge Legos in your bare feet, wearing washed-out yoga pants because nothing is clean or fits quite right, and learning to pretend you didn't hear that expletive your cherub-faced angel blurted out at the Thanksgiving table. Sometimes it's learning to function without coffee or a good night's sleep, but loving your life anyway. Sometimes it's picking up that toppled Christmas tree and dusting yourself off and putting on a brave face. And through it all, the new normal is loving them more than your pre-kid self could have imagined.

And when you're the mother of three teenagers, it's reinforcing those tough boundaries and watching them stumble and reassuring them that they are doing just fine. It's having the hard conversations and ignoring the sarcastic eye rolls and stepping back when they make mistakes instead of rushing in to save the day (which is one of the hardest things in the world to do). The new normal is trusting your kids to make good decisions, and loving them even when they don't.

Which definitely isn't easy. But it is normal.

I know those new mothers staggering through their days smelling like urine want to hear it. They want to hear that it's going to get easier. I won't tell them that it does. They will hear it enough from those grannies at the grocery store. Those ladies lie. They mean well, but they lie.

I'm sorry. It doesn't get any easier. But it changes. Those little human beings aren't the same as they were a year ago, a month ago, or even a week ago. The good news is neither are we. We become better. We learn. We adapt. We figure things out We change. We find a new normal.

But this parenting thing never gets easier. It just doesn't. I wish I hadn't wasted so much time sitting around trying not to worry, waiting for things to get easier like they promised it would. I wish I hadn't sat there covered in someone else's bodily fluids waiting for life to get back to normal. I want to tell the young mother that I was, dressed in those ratty, milk-stained yoga pants, to just suck it up. Life is never going to be the way it was before. In fact, it might just be better. I want to tell her that there isn't really a light at the end of this tunnel, that it's just a train called "the teen years." It's going to hurt, but parenthood is all about pain . . . the pain of child birth, the pain of sleepless nights and sore nipples, the pain of watching them walk slowly away from you through the years, the pain of that powerful, all-encompassing love that we feel for our children. It's okay to embrace that pain. I wouldn't trade that beautiful pain for easy. Not on your life.

This parenting thing, it isn't going to be easy, but I promise it will be worth it.

Turns Out It's Not the End of the World If They Don't Graduate

Mary Novaria

"As hard as this is to hear," she told me, "the school counselor told us it's not the end of the world if they don't graduate."

The summer before my daughter's senior year in high school, along with the college catalogues and SAT prep brochures, glossy postcards from local photography studios showed up in the mailbox every few days promising "cutting edge, artistic senior portraits that rock!"

"We'll capture your child's unique personality," they vowed, as I questioned whether they actually knew any high school seniors and wondered exactly which personality they planned to capture. The teenage models grinning from those slick pieces of advertising did not resemble my anxious and depressed seventeen-year-old daughter. They looked carefree and confident—poster children for senior year and beyond.

Ellie had a mood disorder that was often so paralyzing she couldn't get out of bed. She rarely made it through a full week of school. Her grades were suffering and so was she. I was concerned she'd be unable to manage on her own when she went to college. I hadn't yet considered the possibility she might not finish high school. That was unthinkable for the mother of a girl who was an honor student, promising athlete, and talented musician.

When the school first informed us she was "gifted," my overactive imagination flashed forward with lightning pace. It skipped high school graduation altogether and went straight to home video of Ellie getting her degree from an Ivy League dean in full academic regalia. Then, she was off to save the world. It was quite a contrast to the certified letter from the high school principal threatening to report my prodigy, now a truant, to the District Attorney's office.

Since being diagnosed with depression and anxiety, Ellie had quit just about everything. If you flipped through her high school

257

yearbooks, you'd find scant evidence of her existence. I think the only photo she showed up for in four years was her JV Basketball picture freshman year. If there were others, maybe a shot of her with the softball team or marching band, those picture packets must have piled up in the bottom of Ellie's locker because I never saw them. There were no wallet-sized portraits to tuck into Christmas cards or a 5×7 to frame for Grandma. Ellie didn't even have a picture on her student I.D.

I had unrealistic expectations for her senior portrait. Maybe on some level I thought if we had the perfect picture, it would be an assurance that all the rest—SATs, college applications, graduation—would fall into place. It was too devastating to think otherwise.

When our eldest, Ben, left for college, I had big plans for my daughter. Although I missed Ben terribly, I looked forward to the one-on-one time with Ellie. My job was to get her ready to go off to college and become a self-sufficient and productive citizen. Although I didn't outline my plans to her, my secret expectations ran high: varsity basketball, school dances, a National Merit Scholarship, and a cool liberal arts college like Reed, Bard or maybe Princeton, her dad's alma mater. I was sure we could put a bout of high school tardiness behind us.

When our psychiatrist recommended homeschooling in the spring of junior year, I couldn't fathom a world in which my daughter did not go to school. And even though Ellie insisted she wanted to go, when the alarm clock rang, it was the bell that signaled the next round in a prizefight. Who would win the morning mêlée? Would I succeed in getting Ellie out of bed and off to school? Or would her stubborn malaise prevail, resulting in yet another unexcused absence? It was a contest of wills and, no matter who won the daily scuffle, neither of us was winning the war.

I could see the high school from the window above my kitchen sink, and when Ben and Ellie were younger, I'd watched from the front steps of our two-story colonial as they walked to the elementary school at the end of the cul-de-sac. Unlike our old neighborhood in the city, there were lots of children on the block and everyone took care of their property. No peeling paint, unraked leaves, or out-of-control dandelions allowed. Our community showed up on lists like "Best Cities for Kids" and "Best Places to Live." Same with the schools. *Newsweek, U.S. News & World Report*—if there were rankings, our schools made the list. Weekdays were packed with school activities, music lessons and team practices. Moms racked up minivan mileage and weekends were infused with the combined aromas of freshly-cut grass, soccer sweat, and barbecue smoke. School and club team tryouts were fraught with rivalry and, thanks to a plethora of AP classes, even a 4.0 grade point average wouldn't place a kid at the top of the class.

This was suburbia and everything was a competition—including the pursuit of a perfect senior portrait, a challenge that had all the hallmarks of Annie Leibovitz photographing the queen. Many shoots were on location, placing kids at railroad stations, on fire engines, in Kansas cornfields, or in front of graffiti-covered brick walls on the edge of downtown. My favorite scene was an utterly charming Victorian sofa of cerulean velvet planted in a golden field of wheat before a dilapidated farmhouse that hadn't seen a coat of paint in fifty or more years. Once the stage was set, a girl would don expensive designer clothes. She'd be flawlessly made up and impeccably coifed, but not obviously so. It takes a lot of hard work and money to cultivate that Ralph Lauren casual chic.

By October of Ellie's senior year, I was getting antsy about that portrait. I knew my chances of luring Ellie to one of these fancy studios were very slim, but I had an idea . . . and a new Nikon. I figured in this digital age I could shoot frame after frame until I captured the perfect senior picture. Of course, it would require patience on the part of both the photographer and the subject, but I was confident we could pull off a cutting edge, artistic photo that really rocked! I scouted locations, driving around rural areas of our community in search of falling-down barns and rusty train tracks. Ellie's electric PRS guitar was a gorgeous shade of teal that I knew would make a stunning prop and look über cool in any setting, although I had no delusions of dolling her up like Taylor Swift in red lipstick and a flowery dress. I wasn't going to hedge my bets with anything too fancy—no wardrobe changes, no pink pedicure, no grandmother's pearls.

I'd settle for something other than the hoodie, which, along with skinny jeans and black Converse, had become her uniform. In dark times, she almost always had the hood pulled over her head, a condition my husband John called "hooded." When Ellie was hooded, I'd know not to expect much in the way of conversation, information, or interaction. She'd camp out on the sofa in the family room, ears plugged with iPod buds, alternately responding to phone texts and Facebook messages, head buried in her laptop. The hoodie swaddled Ellie like baby bunting. It was armor, shielding her from whatever it was she was avoiding.

"She's *double* hooded," John said one day and, sure enough, there was Ellie, sitting on the sofa, not one but *two* hoodies pulled up over her unruly, ginger mane—a very small monk seeking comfort in a cold, damp monastery. My mysterious little druid had emotionally cloistered herself, quiet and alone, but not at peace. A symbol of retreat, the hoodie was the silent decree, the universal sign for *Leave. Me. Alone.*

That fall, all I wanted was an hour with my daughter in a damn field of wildflowers. My schedule was flexible, but Ellie was elusive despite my frequent prodding. She had no intention of conforming to my expectations for a page in the high school yearbook, so with my subject unwilling, my fantasy photo shoot was postponed indefinitely. Ellie's lack of cooperation may have been symbolic, and not just because a contrary nature was one of those many teen personalities to be captured on film. Maybe the big deal senior portrait seemed pointless to Ellie because she just couldn't picture the future. That whatever lay ahead—graduation . . . college . . . the rest of her life—were things she simply could not see.

I envisioned those things for her, but as the calendar crept past New Year's I began to panic.

The Tuesday after winter break, school resumed without Ellie, but she rallied and went three days in row. Then, we had a storm. Snow days Monday and Tuesday and our momentum was lost. Unlike in the past, when I considered a snow day a reprieve from our morning battles, this time it was an obstacle. I viewed the snowstorm as my enemy, the force that was going to grind everything to a halt.

"There are no mistakes in this friendly universe," a friend encouraged me. "A snow day is just perfect and right on time."

The reprieve did stop the guessing game, for a time at least. I laid a fire, admired the pristine snow weighing down the boughs of the backyard trees, and exhaled. Ellie and I made cookies, drank hot chocolate, and watched movies. It was cozy and I relished our two days of snowbound togetherness, but I couldn't sustain those warm fuzzies when everyone went back to school—except my daughter, who slept all day and again the next.

Despite therapy, meds, an outpatient program, and six weeks of inpatient treatment, Ellie continued to rack up the absences. She withdrew from a couple of classes when it became obvious she'd missed far too much work to have a prayer of making it up.

As I flashed back to our morning battles and all my pleading and threats, I didn't know if I had any fight left in me. And I didn't want to fight at all. I wanted to figure out the perfect motivating and encouraging thing to say. I prayed for some semblance of forward motion and searched for inspiration, anything that would guide Ellie over the threshold in the morning and in the months to come . . . anything that would get us to the end of the school year.

Graduation was four months away and I was terrified she wouldn't make it to the finish line. Both Ellie's therapist and my best friend Jeanie had floated the idea that Ellie drop out and take the GED. I was appalled. I could not imagine a scenario in which my daughter did not finish high school, and I resisted the idea as if it were hemlock. Obviously, I needed to let go of the National Merit fantasy, but . . . not graduate? That was not part of my plan.

I bemoaned my terror to Linda, whose daughter had been in treatment with Ellie.

"As hard as this is to hear," Linda told me, "the school counselor told us it's not the end of the world if they don't graduate."

I wanted to plug my ears. How could she be so calm? Not the end of the world?! Of course it would be the end of the world! This sort of thing didn't happen in our family.

Despite my initial resistance to what Linda had said, I thought about her words every day. I repeated them to myself, trying them on like a mantra to see if I could really believe them. *It's not the end of the world if they don't graduate . . . It's not the end of the world . . . It's not the end . . .*

On a Sunday morning in May, we ran into the Bernsteins at a local breakfast place. Dani, a super sweet mom, was bubbling over with pride in anticipation of that evening's graduation ceremony. Her daughter, Nicole, had been a classmate of Ellie's since kindergarten.

"Such a BIG DAY!" Dani beamed.

The girls, who'd once played soccer together and had attended the same birthday parties, stood by in awkward silence while I went along with the charade. I forced a strained, fake smile, trying valiantly to beam right back at Dani, as I telepathically willed the hostess to hurry up and tell us our table was ready. I felt like a fraud, a big, fat phony, as I halfheartedly played along with Dani's excitement. I couldn't bring myself to tell her Ellie and Nicole wouldn't be walking across the same stage later that day to get their diplomas.

"I guess we'll see you later!" Dani's husband enthused as the Bernsteins headed for their car.

"In just a few hours!" Dani chirped.

The crack in my heart grew a little deeper, we waved, and they were off—probably headed for a mother-daughter mani-pedi. They'd be so pretty and perky in their family pictures. Nicole's older brother would be there. Ellie's would not. We wouldn't be there at all.

Four weeks earlier, Ellie had officially withdrawn from school. It felt like doomsday. There was no way I wanted that "dropout" stigma on her or our family. The paperwork sat on the kitchen counter with the school district's cornstalk logo mocking me: "Education Beyond Expectations." A high school career ended in a one-page, yellow carbon copy of an original signed by Ellie, each of her teachers, the guidance counselor, and the assistant principal. Since she was eighteen, John and I didn't even have to sign the forms.

Ellie's senior year was over. She was not going to graduate and, for a while, the forfeiture of that milestone stung me with loss, shame, and regret. But what choice did I have but to deal with it?

Linda was right. It was not the end of the world. In many ways, it was a beginning. A beginning of understanding and acceptance that my daughter—that all of us—have our own paths to walk, and that some of those pathways are narrower, rockier, steeper, and have more switchbacks than others. Ellie has to travel her own path, to live the experience she is destined to have. To prevent it would disturb the natural order of things.

Shortly after her class graduated from high school, Ellie passed the GED with flying colors. She is healthy, building a full life in a community she loves, and is enrolled in college. My pride in her independence and determination is no less than the day she was identified as "gifted."

It may have taken me a while, but ultimately I realized that whether or not we were in the auditorium on a particular day with 350 of her peers, my daughter and I each had something in common with those graduates: We were all going to move forward. And we didn't need caps and gowns or senior portraits to get on with our lives.

Pushing Back on Time

Alexandra Rosas

"Who pushes back on time to stop it, is pushed back by time in its march, but who yields to it—finds it on his side."

I carry a folded, worn piece of paper in my purse. It's become smooth, like felt, from years of opening and closing only to unfold and read once again. I transfer it from purse to purse as the seasons change. Every time I reach for it, it saves my life. I hear her voice again, so firm, and I see her gaze locking with mine. She is talking to me, taking me through to the other side, and I hear her through the black ink that now floats over fading blue lines.

"Who pushes back on time to stop it, is pushed back by time in its march, but who yields to it—finds it on his side."

It is the voice of my therapist. I haven't seen her for over ten years, since she left to practice in another state, but she lives in the words on this paper that she gave me.

I started to see Katy when my children were two and three years old. As soon as they were born, I began mourning them. I mourned each morning, each week, each month, each year with them. I felt the cold march of time blow through our days. How could I enjoy my children when I knew that every day with them was one less day I would be with them? I knew one day our time together would be only memories.

I felt the loss of my children even as I cradled them in my arms. When other mothers would celebrate milestones of crawling, then pulling up, on to walking and first words, I could only think of how the future was rushing at us and that these very days of gold would much too soon be the ones I would long for.

I couldn't look at pictures of my children without imagining them with lives of their own one day.

I couldn't save their artwork because I would think of the torture it would one day bring to look back on the red trees they had drawn with orange leaves growing underneath a smiley-face sun.

I wanted to be a happy mother, more than anything I wanted this. But without a way to enjoy my life without lamenting the loss of motherhood, I didn't know how. The thought of being without my children knocked the wind out of me and I found myself unable to breathe.

The first time I met with Katy, I brought along a picture of my three glorious children. I held the picture of their faces in my hands, and being away from them just for this session made my eyes well up with tears. "I love them so much," I told her, feeling the embarrassment of confession. "I've never been good at anything but this. This mothering—I am mediocre at everything I've tried, but motherhood, this is where I excel."

I felt foolish telling a stranger how I cry over something that I cherished, and still had. I knew that I must have sounded like a fool.

"You pre-mourn your life without them," Katy said gently.

I nodded yes. She was right. I wanted to tell her so, but the words wouldn't come out.

I steadied my emotions and explained, "I have everything I want, and yet I'm so scared of what I'll do without it. I have heaven on earth right now, but I'm crying for the day I won't. I'm so stupid."

"It's pre-mourning, and you have every right to your feelings about your life, your children. Nothing you feel is stupid. What you are is in love with your children."

With her words, my tears became a river. It was just as she was saying: I was in love with my children and my life and I dreaded the heartache of being without them. I was scared of not knowing how to live if not as a mother. There was no shame in feeling this way, was there? The tears that came hot and fast now were from having someone there to hold my hand. I had a person in my life when I needed one as much as I needed anything, and she was telling me what would soon be like oxygen for me. "It's okay to feel what you feel as a mother."

"When you feel something so strongly, it's natural to fear a life without it. Who wouldn't? You will be fine, and I will help you.

Together, we will work on ways for you to enjoy what you have now and not live dreading the future."

What Katy tried so delicately to tell me was that my sadness existed because of not living in the moment—actually being there in the day captured in the pictures. Missing the present for lamenting the passing. At that age, at that stage, with them. She told me that I would be all right, that I wasn't going to dig through this alone. Her words of acceptance and understanding brought a trembling smile to my face.

I had something. Katy had given it a name. It was pre-mourning and she was going to help me. With her at my side, I would find my way through to a place where I could create happy memories and look forward to looking back on a life spent in joy.

"Who pushes back on time to stop it, is pushed back by time in its march; who yields to it—finds it on his side."

I would be okay, and I would find a way to love these golden days in the very moments that I was living them. Right here, right now, with Katy telling me I would find my way back again.

This Too Shall Pass

Julianne Palumbo

She explained to me that, in mothering, like in everything else, there would be times of joy and times of worry and sorrow. "Just always remember," she said, "this too shall pass."

This too shall pass. Four single-syllable words that hold so much. It's an old adage—*This too shall pass*—suggesting that everything in life is temporary, whether good or bad. Nothing will last forever.

It is said that Persian poets in medieval times first wrote these words. Woven into a fable of a king who took great comfort in knowing that nothing bad was permanent, these words have survived the ages.

Famous people of Biblical times—the ancient King Solomon—and famous people of more recent times—Abraham Lincoln—have taken comfort in repeating them.

As have I.

During the birth of my first child, my uterus hemorrhaged, leaving me with severe anemia. Nearly two-thirds of my blood had poured out of my body before anyone noticed. Except my husband, a young, overworked medical resident at the time, who decided to spend that first night in the hospital with me, because something just didn't seem right. While I lay there sleeping from the exhausting labor and my tango with a pair of forceps, he sat next to me studying during the intervals between his hourly compressions of my swollen belly.

When I woke the next morning, I was gray-skinned and too weak to lift my head. I knew by the glower of the young obstetrician who bolted into my hospital room, that, had things been allowed to go any further, I might not have gone home with my child. I spent the next five days in that hospital bed on medication that simulated contractions to stop my uterus from bleeding. It was like going through never-ending labor.

My baby son was brought to me a few times a day and laid on the bed next to me. I was unable to lift him, but I could snuggle up to him and hold his bottle. At the time, I didn't understand the significance of what my body had done and the shape I was in. Focused, instead, on his fragility, I failed to comprehend my own. Much relief came from knowing that experts were watching over my newborn for his first days of life.

After five days in the hospital, we came home with our new son, Teddy, and my husband went off to work. Being a medical fellow, he wasn't afforded much time off, and the stress of handling my medical issues had been all-consuming. He had been away from his medical duties for too long and needed to get back to the hospital. I needed to find a way to care for my newborn.

Once home, my condition was not at all prime for a new mother. I couldn't do what a new mother was supposed to do on my own. I couldn't even safely be left alone with my child. When I stood, what little blood was left in me must have rushed somewhere other than where it was needed, because I would get dizzy and eventually pass out. As the days plodded, I noticed a loss of some of my word-finding ability. Certain words became jumbled with others. *Rug, towel, blanket, mat.* They were all the same. My hair began to shed, choking the shower drain. At night when the baby woke to feed, my vision was centered like a subway train squeezing through the narrowest of tunnels. I was forgetting things, like the way home after a short walk to clear my head and the last time I fed the baby. The mirror revealed a reflection the pale colors of yellow and gray. The doctor promised I would recover; I just had to wait it out.

My mom came over every day for the first two weeks. She arrived sunny and vibrant, immediately falling into the rhythm of washing and folding onesies and bleaching formula stains from little blue bibs. Baby bottles lined the kitchen counters like soldiers reporting for duty. Nipples, sterilized and untouched, almost hung from midair so that nothing could contaminate them. I loved when she was there because she moved with a breeze of confidence and comfort. I was supposed to be mothering, but, in truth, *I* was being mothered and Teddy was being lovingly grand-mothered.

One day my mom couldn't make it over so my older sister drove up from Connecticut with her son to stay with me. She had planned to spend the entire day with me. I loved being with her since, like my mom, she was so capable and I always felt safe and protected in her presence. My sister made the whole motherhood thing look fun and easy, so I relished the time to lean on her. And, I adored my wide-eyed nephew.

We were sitting on the couch, and my sister decided to trim my bangs in some new way she had read about. In truth, she was probably desperate to improve upon my ghastly appearance. Our sons were enjoying baby dreams nearby.

In the heat of the haircut, my sister shifted her position, trying to get a better angle from which to rescue my thinning hair. With one hand she pushed off the edge of the glass coffee table. When she did, the table cracked, as glass will do, producing a shard that cut into her wrist. Blood poured, and as she struggled to wrap her wrist tightly to stop the flow, I called for an ambulance. In minutes, she was off to the hospital, and I was left home alone, on a blood-stained couch surrounded by broken glass and not one, but two babies, one of which could walk and had no idea that, when he awoke, his mother would be gone.

I stayed oh so quiet on the couch that day, hoping, praying not to wake either one of these sleeping babes. How would I take care of my two-year-old nephew when I couldn't even stand up without falling down? Suppose he woke my son and the two of them started screaming? Suppose they needed lunch? Suppose he tried to touch the broken glass?

Sitting on the couch staring at the two of them, I observed the consistency of their breathing. I read every twitch and murmur as if tea leaves to the wisdom of how much longer I had until all broke loose. Would motherhood always feel this vulnerable, this out of my control? I hoped that, at some point, I would be able to care for my child on my own. I was an attorney with a busy law practice at the time, supporting our home while my husband worked the punishing hours of a doctor-in-training. It was surprising how much pregnancy and the first few days of motherhood had bruised and weakened me. Perhaps there was a secret to this mothering thing, and I had not been let in.

After an hour or so, my nephew woke and did a blue-eyed search for his mom. I leaned my way to the television and pushed in a video that my sister, in her motherly wisdom and experience, had brought with her. As grace would have it, the video calmed him, and my own child slumbered on. Within the second hour, my sister returned from the emergency room full of apologies for leaving me alone with two children and relieved, I think, to find them content. I felt so responsible for her trouble, for the hospital bill, for the ambulance bill, and for our lost day.

I don't remember what we did with the rest of our day together, but I do remember the words, her words, that rescued me from the gloom of my struggle and allowed the short afternoon to rebound into precious sisterly time. "This too shall pass," she said.

She explained to me that, in mothering, like in everything else, there would be times of joy and times of worry and sorrow. "Just always remember," she said, "this too shall pass."

I have repeated those words in my head so many times since that stressful day as a new mother on the couch surrounded by broken glass, unable to care for my child. When my son developed night terrors, screaming from his bed or roaming around the house like a wide-eyed zombie . . . *This too shall pass.* When my young children clung to me, crying in gasps as I left for work each morning, refusing to be left behind with the babysitter . . . *This too shall pass.* When my sons battled each other, for years not finding any common ground . . . *This too shall pass.* When high school pressures, mean friends, unfair teachers, nasty coaches, illness and injury all threatened to sabotage our happy home life . . . *This too shall pass . . .* And it always did. Ages and stages morphed into other, better ages and stages. Fears and worries outlived their relevance, and even the harshest of stories faded into happier tales.

Through the many years of motherhood, those four words have carried me far, reminding me to have patience, to wait with hope and faith, knowing that nothing good or bad or indifferent lasts forever.

I am counting on the wisdom of these words now as I face the inevitable emptying of my nest, the end of something wonderful, something I have relished and rejoiced in and held on to with every last fiber of my will. With one child about to graduate from college and engaged to be married, a second child in the midst of college, and the third quickly outgrowing high school, I fear the "this too" part. Suddenly, I don't want this stage, this lovely stage of motherhood, of being needed and involved, and entertained, and clung to, to pass. I fear this stage most because of what it means for me once it passes.

In fact, I'm not exactly sure how these words that have sustained me through the last twenty years apply to my current stage in life.

Is it a cruel twist in the old adage? Transience is a wonderful quality when we are facing hardship. Not so welcome, though, when life is grand. Those deceitful words, they've betrayed my trust and turned on me. Why are they no longer there for me when I need them most?

Empty nesters say that they enjoy the freedom that sits at the finish line of childrearing. That it is now time to do those things we parents have delayed for so many years in order to put their children first. But what exactly is this gem that I would trade for more time with my children?

This too shall pass. This too shall pass. This too shall pass . . .

As I relish each moment of parenting, I search for ways to rebrand myself while squeezing every last morsel from this tube of mothering. I'm learning that life marches on one way or another. Perhaps, it will take the wisdom of Solomon *and* the sage of Lincoln to convince myself that, even this time, at this tentative stage, *This too shall pass* is a good thing.

Or, perhaps that old saying simply means my empty nest won't be empty for long.

Always On My Mind

E.V. Hoffman

*Like teachers at the end of a school term watching their charges
wave goodbye, we know that our young will go on to other
adventures and we will go on to other endeavors of bestowing
hard earned wisdom and developed cheer.*

"I cried all the way home from Atlanta," my friend said on the phone.
"Some Mothers' Day!"

"Yeah," I muttered.

"I wanted her to be independent," she explained. "I told her to
pursue her dreams. Now I wonder if she'll ever marry. I wonder what
she thought of her dad's and my marriage that she doesn't seem to want
to find someone."

"It's hard to squeeze in visits when you live far from your kids," I
said.

Earlier that day I'd received an e-mail from another friend whose
son lives far away. She lamented that her boy hadn't bothered to send
a Mother's Day card. Yet on the phone he bragged about the money
he spent being a Big Brother to a needy kid despite the organization
discouraging outlays of money. "How much expense is a card?" she
asked. I sympathized. I told her I'd only received one but have four
kids who could have sent Hallmark greetings. Nonetheless, my two
sons who hadn't bought me a card reached me by phone to express
their intention for me to have a "good day." My daughter left a short,
obligatory, flat-sounding voice mail.

Not wanting to whine, I was uncharacteristically quiet when my
husband offered to take me out to eat. I told him I had no desire to go
to a Mother's Day buffet to witness other women aglow, surrounded
by children and grandchildren. Since my elderly father passed last fall,
my husband and I had eaten Easter lunch out alone and before that, the
Thanksgiving feast, alone while other boisterous families filled up the
room. I think the waitress looked pitifully at the two of us seated by

275

our lonesome at the sole table for two tucked in a corner of the dining room. Our kids live in different states now, hours and hours away from us and from their birthplace and the home where they were raised. They pursue careers and graduate studies. One is married.

I try to remember if I thought much about my own mother when I was in my twenties. Although it cost a lot more back then than now, I called her more. I wrote more. So did she. I bought her gifts for her birthday and Mother's Day. My four didn't bother with a birthday remembrance either, and my birthday was seven days before Mother's Day. A double whammy week.

My friend on the phone said, "I think we all should do away with it. This holiday causes misery. At church they always honor the mom with the most kids, the mom who is the oldest, the newest mom, the one with the most kids in attendance that day, etc. How does this make childless women feel?"

"Or ones who have lost their kids?" I added. Then, she and I fell silent as we thought of a mutual friend who had suffered that loss and is sadly estranged from her son's young widow, too. I next said, "I never liked it when the preacher honored all females—as if they had raised kids. Mothers make sacrifices that motherless women don't have to make."

She concurred. I expounded further. "The day makes me sad because I think of past Mother's Days. I no longer have my grandmas, my mom, my friends' moms. I miss those times. The memories aren't enough to sustain me. And now my kids are grown and gone. I no longer feel like a mommy."

"Not much to look forward to . . ." her voice drifted off.

"Yet, there might be . . . later . . . when we have grandchildren . . . maybe?"

I thought about my mother-in-law and her one son who has not called her in years. I thanked my lucky stars to have brought more than one kid into this world. What if one has only one child and it's a child who hasn't inherited the gene carrying compassion and gratitude? Psychologists say that everyone is a product of nurture and nature. I'm not sure. My mom used to declare that the meanest parents sometimes had the most delightful children, and the nicest parents often raised narcissistic brats. She was a teacher, so she saw a lot of parenting and had her opinions!

As I age, I realize life is a combination of joy and pain, closely connected. Childbirth is pain, which is followed by the joy of the baby, which is followed by the labor of raising him after which joy ensues when one sees the job well done. Yet, at the completion of their rearing, they go on their merry ways and you are left—left alone to grow old.

I depress myself if I think too much about this process. Therefore, the sane thing for an old mom to do is to discover new ways to find purpose. Other folks exist in this world, who may not be blood kin, but who nevertheless need nurturing. Maybe conjugal partners can become each other's mom and dad, and perchance a group of pals can act like each other's fan club. Simultaneously, we empty nesters must not bemoan our fate—that our kids are grown and gone—but instead we should be grateful for the gift of children and also realize they never belonged solely to us. We got to proctor them for a while. Like teachers at the end of a school term watching their charges wave goodbye, we know that our young will go on to other adventures and we will go on to other endeavors of bestowing hard earned wisdom and developed cheer.

So, I tell myself: don't wallow. Like a good meal that was enjoyed and is finished, recall it at leisure fondly but rise up from your chair and carry on. Find new pursuits even though that song, like a needle stuck in a record's groove, keeps replaying in your head. I bet y'all know the tune. The lyrics too: "You were always on my mind." And on Mother's Day the words envelop both the ecstasy and the agony of being a mom. No matter where they live or what they do or where you go or what you become, your children will always be on your mind.

The Way Is Through

Andrea Jarrell

*Yet I've learned again and again that I can't go over, under, or
around, and I can't turn back. No matter how high or how rough
the surf, going through every stage is where the living is.*

My mother was a "miracle baby." I learned this while folding laundry.
I must have been eleven or twelve, old enough to have my period
but still my mother's girl. Because it was just the two of us—no father,
no siblings—we were confidants. On the weekends we did laundry,
carrying armloads upstairs from the communal washers and dryers in
our Southern California apartment complex, picking up stray socks
along the way, brushing Jacaranda petals from fallen shirts, heaving the
clean piles onto our couch.

As we paired the cabled knee socks I wore with short plaid skirts,
groovy maxi dresses, and my Girl Scout uniform, we talked. We
separated my mother's lacy bras and panties from my days-of-the-week
cotton bikinis, some newly stained at the crotch.

"I always envied Grandmommy her pristine underwear," my
mother said, speaking of her mother. Pristine because my grandmother
had had a hysterectomy a few years after my mother was born. From
twenty-eight on, she'd never had to worry about period stains.

The doctor said it was a miracle my grandmother bore any
children at all. He said this before surgically removing any chance of
her having more. But after the operation, she became sick. So sick that
the hospital broke its own rule by letting my mother—a child, and so
not allowed into such solemn places—visit her dying mother.

My grandmother, the daughter of missionaries, later said that Jesus
had appeared to her when she was in the hospital. She'd seen him
standing across a green riverbank in his long white robe, extending his
hand. But she denied him. Refusing to leave her miracle baby behind,
she'd experienced a second miracle and lived.

The births of my own children were personal marvels but, in the grand scheme, nothing extraordinary. Both were easy conceptions and healthy pregnancies. Still, birthing my son was physically the hardest thing I've ever done. He came fast, too fast for my midwife to get to the hospital. Too fast to consider an epidural, like I'd had with my daughter. Numbed that first time, I was unprepared for the heaviness between my legs like a two-ton speculum dragging me down to some murky ocean depth as my son's head pushed its way into the world. "Open your eyes, Andrea," the doctor said, calling me back to the ocean's surface, back to that bright room and the present moment.

Like a version of the children's song, "We're Going on a Bear Hunt," I knew then that I could not shut my eyes against that ocean of sensation threatening to drown me. I could not go over it. I could not go under it. I was going to have to swim through it. I've understood that ever since.

I understood it when my two-year-old daughter was attacked by our dog, my husband carrying her in his arms to the ER. So much blood; a half an inch closer and her eye would have been lost.

I understood it when my son clung to my leg on the first day of kindergarten, until I pulled his little hands away and waved goodbye to him.

I understood it when my daughter was in high school and I glimpsed the hickey at the top of her breast. She turned to me and said, "Don't tell Daddy."

I understood it when the police called in the middle of the night because my son had been caught sneaking out with friends.

And I understood it when, after moving our daughter into her college dorm room, it was time to go. I'd kept it together for three days—during the cross-country flight, the trips to Target for supplies, the making of her bed and stowing of duffle bags she'd use to come home at Christmas. Not wanting her to see me cry—oh how I'd resented my mother's tears at my own drop off—I turned from her after a final hug and didn't look back.

Driving to the airport, a sinkhole of grief opened within me—great, keening sobs—oddly familiar. I'd cried once like this before. When my grandmother, only fifty-nine, at last took her Jesus's hand

and crossed over, leaving my mother and me behind. Missing her would be forever and we would have to live through it.

No! I told myself. How could I equate my child leaving home with death? It's just the opposite: the life force driving on, leaving behind our time together.

And what of my life force? On the other side of fifty, every month I wonder if this will be my last period, and I'm secretly relieved when it arrives again like clockwork, keeping me tethered to the self I've known so long. After I heard the news that singer Sophie Hawkins gave birth at fifty, I spent the next several days fantasizing about starting all over again.

With my history, I'm prone to believing in miracles.

Would having another baby salve my grief over my children leaving home? Or are such impulses simply vanity, wanting the world to think I'm still young enough to be making babies? Wanting to believe it myself. Forty years of period stains passed, the children of that laundry-folding girl grown and nearly gone, who am I becoming? Part of me wants to hold that woman at bay.

Yet I've learned again and again that I can't go over, under, or around, and I can't turn back. No matter how high or how rough the surf, going through every stage is where the living is.

Each month when my period comes, I tread water in that vast ocean a little while longer, waiting for a different kind of birth.

Open your eyes, Andrea. Open your eyes.

Thirteen Years

Robin Finn

It isn't that no one told me how fast it would go by... They told me. And I'm glad they did. But I wish they'd made me understand: my baby wasn't the only one growing older in a flash.

I sat at the kitchen table and previewed my daughter's Bat Mitzvah slide show. Her life, and mine, captured in color snapshots drifting by every four seconds to the soundtrack of "A Hundred Years" by Five for Fighting and "In My Life" by the Beatles. The lyrics really got to me. "There are places I remember . . ."

It isn't that no one told me how fast it would go by. Plenty of mothers did—my mother, my mother-in-law, women shopping with teenaged daughters at the mall or the grocery store. They'd stop and smile at my toddler, waving her chubby arms beneath a stained pink t-shirt. They'd say, "Enjoy it. It goes by so fast," and then point to the sixteen-year-old standing next to them in ripped jeans and earbuds. "That's my baby," they'd say.

They told me. And I'm glad they did. But I wish they'd made me understand: my baby wasn't the only one growing older in a flash.

I watched the slide show and saw myself on-screen. There I was, pregnant, for a moment, and then reclining on a blue couch, clutching an infant daughter to my chest. But before I could wonder where I was or remember the tiny yellow and green flowers printed on the edges of my new daughter's onesie, I was thirty-three and she sat cross-legged on a hospital chair, a blue and white bundle of brother nestled in her lap.

I glanced over at her hunched over her laptop—her long, dirty-blonde hair falling over her teen-aged shoulders, gold hoops in her ears, an iPhone perched to the right of her elbow. On the screen, the ball of baby brother dissolved into matching car seats in the third row of a silver minivan, a new baby sister strapped into an infant carrier in the seat ahead. Sippy cups and coloring books were strewn along the floor. I caught a glimpse of a box of orange goldfish crackers.

I wanted to compliment my thirteen-year-old on the perfection of the slide show she created—her photo selection, slide transitions, technical acumen—but there they were, my three children, skiing down a mountainside in white helmets and striped parkas and a well of emotion engulfed me.

Slide after slide spun by every four seconds and each song faded into the next. I lived at warp speed, I wanted to watch the slideshow in slow motion. I wanted to crawl back into every image and have each moment stretch out before me. I wanted to stick my nose into a baby blanket and inhale the scent of fresh diaper and baby thighs. I wanted to hold an infant to my chest, feel her nurse, feel the wonder of being a newly minted mother.

Many mothers warned me. But I thought the warning was for my kids, not for me. I watched my son and daughters move from preschool to elementary school to middle school, but I never saw myself grow older. Only them.

My girlfriends and I got teary at culminations, drank wine at book clubs, swapped stories while folding laundry. Her son was always at the nurse, my daughter never remembered her homework, none of them ever cleaned their rooms, all of them drove us crazy. We took pictures on iPhones, met for dinners and drinks, drove back and forth from endless activities. But then came thirteen and we were *those moms*—the moms of older kids, Bar Mitzvah moms.

I laid a hand on my daughter's arm. A temporarily tattooed gold bracelet wound its way around her wrist. "This is so well done," I told her. "I had no idea you—"

"Shh," she said, pointing to the screen.

They'd tried to tell me: my mother when she saw her daughter with a daughter, my mother-in-law as her son rocked a baby to sleep, my neighbor as she packed up her only child for college. "Enjoy it," they'd said. "It goes by in a flash." At supermarkets, birthday parties, holiday celebrations, they all repeated the same line. But it was thirteen years before I understood—it wasn't simply the baby years that flew by, it was all the years. Standing at the sidelines cheering, I'd forgotten that I, too, was subject to the rules of time.

I sat at the kitchen table, my daughter next to me, her laptop between us and wished I could wrap the moment around me, hold it close, inhale it like a favorite blanket, that singular moment when she was thirteen, and I was forty-three.

Author Bios

Elaine Alguire

Elaine Alguire is a mother of three, writer and photography lover. She pours her heart and soul out on her blog, The Miss Elaine-ous Life, and has since late 2006. She is a Co-Director for the Listen To Your Mother show in Southeast, TX. Her writing has been featured on several other sites such as *Mamalode*, *The Huffington Post* and *Bon Bon Break* and she is a Voices of the Year Honoree for 2016. In her spare time she loves to shop and eat delicious food.

Jennifer Berney

Jennifer Berney lives in Olympia, Washington with her wife, two sons, and a crew of dogs, chickens, and honeybees. She is a contributing blogger for *Brain, Child* and her essays have also appeared in *The New York Times Motherlode*, *The Washington Post*, *Brevity*, and *Mutha*. She is currently working on a memoir that chronicles her years-long quest to conceive a child.

Katia Bishops

Katia is the creator of IAMTHEMILK, a WordPress recommended blog in the family category between 2014-2015. Her writing was featured on *Yahoo News, RedBook Magazine, Huffington Post, Yummy Mummy Club* and other online publications. She is a past contributor to HerStories Project's first anthology. Katia is the mother of two boys and the wife of one.

Elizabeth Bobst

Elizabeth Bobst is a mother, a writer, and an educator living in Chapel Hill, NC.

Jeanne Bonner

Jeanne Bonner is a writer and journalist based in Atlanta, Ga.

She's contributed reporting to The New York Times and CNN. Her creative writing, including nonfiction essays and book reviews, have appeared online at *Literary Hub, Catapult, Consequence* and *Asymptote Journal*. She received a Bachelor's degree in Italian Literature from Wesleyan University and has an MFA in Creative Writing from Bennington College.

Tamara Bowman

Tamara is a writer/blogger, a professional photographer, a mama of two, and a nearly professional cookie taster. She has been known to be all four of those things at all hours of the day and night. She is a very proud contributor to the books, *The Mother Of All Meltdowns, Only Trollops Shave Above The Knee* and *Stigma Fighters Anthology*. After two cross country moves, due to her intense Bi-Coastal Disorder, she lives with her husband, daughter, son, and strange pets in glorious western Massachusetts.

Kristi Rieger Campbell

Kristi Rieger Campbell's passion is writing and drawing stupid-looking pictures for her blog, Finding Ninee. It began with a memoir about her special-needs son Tucker, abandoned when she read that a publisher would rather shave a cat than read another memoir. Kristi writes for a variety of parenting websites including Huffington Post Parents, has been published in several popular anthologies, received 2014 BlogHer's Voice of the Year People's Choice Award, and was a proud cast member of the DC Listen to Your Mother show.

Allison Barrett Carter

Allison Barrett Carter is a freelance writer in North Carolina. She is on a journey to keep learning and finding the best life, documenting it all on her website (http://allisonbarrettcarter.com). Her pieces have appeared in many places such as *New York Times' Motherlode, Washington Post's On Parenting, Role Reboot, Verily Magazine, The Good Men Project* and in several print anthologies such as *Chicken Soup for the Soul*.

Ann Cinzar

Ann writes about lifestyle, culture, and negotiating the complexities of modern life. Her work has appeared in various publications, including *The Washington Post, McSweeney's Internet Tendency,* and *The Globe* and *Mail.* Find her at anncinzar.com or connect with her on Twitter @anncinzar.

Christi Clancy

Christi Clancy's work has appeared in *The New York Times,* the *Chicago Tribune,* the *Milwaukee Journal, Glimmer Train Stories, Hobart, Pleiades,* and on *Brain, Child, The Mid, Literary Mama,* on Wisconsin Public Radio and elsewhere. She lives in Madison Wisconsin and teaches English at Beloit College.

Katie Coppens

Katie Coppens is a middle school English and science teacher. Much of her writing revolves around her three biggest passions: family, teaching, and nature. She lives in Maine with her husband and two daughters.

Amy Dillon

Amy Dillon is a writer and mom of two young boys. Her work has appeared in Brain, Child magazine, the *Mom for the Holidays* anthology and in short-form quips in *The Bigger Book of Parenting Tweets.* Her tweets, from @amydillon, are regularly included on lists by *HuffPost Parents, SheKnows* and *Babble.* A native of the Midwest, Amy and her family live in Durham, North Carolina.

Tara Dorabji

Tara Dorabji is a writer, strategist at Youth Speaks, mother, and radio journalist at KPFA. Her work is published or forthcoming in *Al Jazeera, Tayo Literary Magazine, Huizache, Good Girls Marry Doctors* (Aunt Lute 2016), *Center for Asian American Media, Mutha, Censored 2016, So Glad They Told Me* (Summer 2016), and *Midwifery Today.* Tara is working on novels, set in Kashmir and Livermore. Her projects can be viewed at dorabji.com.

Shannon Drury

Shannon Drury is the author of "The Radical Housewife: Redefining Family Values for the 21st Century," a memoir based on her experiences as a stay-at-home mom serving as president of Minnesota NOW. She is a columnist for the Minnesota Women's Press, and her writing has appeared in several anthologies. She lives in Minneapolis with her family.

Robin Finn

Robin Finn is an author, essayist, and advocate. Her work has appeared in *The Washington Post*, *The Huffington Post*, Disney's *Babble.com*, and *ADDitude Magazine*, among others. Robin's *BuzzFeed* article, "*28 Things Nobody Tells You About Having A Kid With ADHD*," had more than 96,000 shares and was a top- 100 story of the week. As an advocate, Robin consulted with the Centers for Disease Control and Prevention (CDC) on ADHD messaging for parents. She has master's degrees in public health from Columbia University and in spiritual psychology from the University of Santa Monica. Robin lives in Los Angeles with her husband and family. Visit her online at www.robinfinn.com and @RobinFinnAuthor.

Laurie Foos

Laurie Foos is the author of *Ex Utero, Portrait Of The Walrus By a Young Artist, Twinship, Bingo Under the Crucifix, Before Elvis There Was Nothing,* and most recently, *The Blue Girl.* Her non-fiction has appeared in *Brain, Child* and in the anthology, *At The End Of Life: True Stories About How We Die.* She lives on Long Island with her husband and their two children.

Emily Gallo

Emily was a career woman "Mommy!" with her ear on the pulse of culture and art, "Mamamamama!" engaged in the pedagogical "Mom!" conversation "Mahmeeeee!" Now, she knows what's really important. "Wipe me!"

Nina Garcia

Nina Garcia is a mom to three boys, including twins. She blogs about parenting at Sleeping Should Be Easy, where she writes everything she's learning about being mom and all its joys and challenges. Her book, *Parenting with Purpose*, has received five stars on Amazon and continues to inspire its readers to engage in mindful parenting.

Julie C. Gardner

Julie C. Gardner is a wife, mother, dog-owner and author. In her spare time she runs (which means she doesn't run often). She is a co-author of *You Have Lipstick On Your Teeth* and her essays have appeared in BlogHer: Voices of the Year 2012 and *Precipice Literary Magazine*. Her first novel, *Letters for Scarlet*, was released by Velvet Morning Press in April 2016.

Dana Robertson Halter

Dana Robertson Halter is a working mom of two little girls, triathlete, and a big "E" extrovert who loves living in Seattle, beer, oversharing, and making people laugh. She holds a master's degree in public administration from the University of Washington and majored in English at Colorado College. "Learning to tune out the noise" is the first personal piece that Dana's had published – and she's over the moon.

Hannah Harlow

Hannah Harlow has an MFA in fiction from Bennington College. Her writing has appeared in *Day One, Synaesthesia Magazine, failbetter*, and elsewhere. She promotes books for a living and lives outside of Boston with her husband and two sons. Find her online at hannahharlow.com.

Kelly Hirt

Kelly is a writer, elementary teacher, and a homeschooling mama. Kelly's work has been seen in *ParentMap, Mamalode, BrainChild*'s blog, *Huffington Post*, and many other sites as well as her own (http://mytwicebakedpotato.com). Kelly is currently working on a nonfiction book about supporting twice-exceptional children and working on two women's fiction manuscripts. Kelly loves coffee, chocolate, and spending time with her family.

Mandy Hitchcock

Mandy Hitchcock is a writer, bereaved mother, cancer survivor, and recovering lawyer. She is currently re-writing (for the third time) her first memoir, and her essays have been featured in *The Washington Post, The Huffington Post, The Sun Magazine's Readers Write, Modern Loss,* and others. She also tells stories live on stage at The Monti in North Carolina and was a cast member of the 2014 Raleigh-Durham production of Listen To Your Mother. A mom of three—two living children and one sweet spirit—she lives with her family in Carrboro, North Carolina, where she writes away in her basement and practices just a bit of law on the side. Read more at mandyhitchcock.com.

E.V. Hoffman

E.V. Hoffman writes personal essays that have appeared in multiple anthologies of the *Chicken Soup for the Soul* series. Her non-fiction stories have been published in other collections similar to the *Chicken Soup* brand. In addition, she pens articles on travel, caregiving, parenting and the craft of writing. Her features have appeared in *The Writer, Today's Caregiver, Australian Catholics, Sasee Magazine, Northwest Travel, You and Me Medical,* and many others. Her fiction has been published in the *Deadly Ink Anthologies, Page and Spine,* and *Tough Lit. Magazines.* She's working on a YA novel.

Sharon Holbrook

Sharon writes for *The New York Times, Washington Post, Brain, Child Magazine,* and for many other national print and online publications. She lives with her family in Cleveland, Ohio.

Marie Holmes

Marie Holmes' essays have appeared in *xoJane, Refinery 29* and the *Washington Post.* Her fiction and poetry have been published in several literary journals, and she is the recipient of awards from Gival Press and the Bronx Writer's Center. She lives with her partner and their children in New York City.

Sarah Hosseini

Sarah Hosseini is an introverted urbanite, temporarily hiding out in the suburbs, wondering, with a glass of wine in hand, where is everybody? (But secretly hoping no one comes out of their houses to talk to her.) She's been published in *Huffington Post, Scary Mommy, Your Tango* and many more. She writes profanity laced musings about motherhood on her blog, Missguided Mama. She lives with her 2 girls and husband in Atlanta-ish.

Ann K. Howley

Ann K. Howley is the author of the award-winning memoir, *Confessions of a Do-Gooder Gone Bad.* A regular contributor to *Pittsburgh Parent Magazine,* her articles and essays about the inevitable surprise and hilarity in life appear in publications nationwide, including *skirt!Magazine, Bicycle Times, Pittsburgh-Post Gazette* and others. In both 2015 and 2016, she won the First Place Prize for Nonfiction in the Pennwriters Writing Contest for her humorous essays about momhood. A popular speaker, Ann loves to convince moms and dads that their lives are worth writing about.

Vanessa Hua

Vanessa Hua is author of *Deceit and Other Possibilities* (Willow Books, September 2016). She is a columnist for the *San Francisco Chronicle* and her two novels are forthcoming from Ballantine. For nearly two decades, she has been writing about Asia and the diaspora. She received a Rona Jaffe Foundation Writers' Award, the San Francisco Foundation's James D. Phelan Award for Fiction, and was a Steinbeck Fellow in Creative Writing at San Jose State University. Her fiction and non-fiction has appeared in *The Atlantic, The New York Times, PRI's The World, ZYZZYVA, Guernica,* and elsewhere.

Andrea Jarrell

Andrea Jarrell's personal essays have appeared in *The New York Times* "Modern Love" column; *Narrative Magazine*; *Brain, Child Magazine*; *Full Grown People*; *Memoir Journal*; *Literary Mama*; *The Washington Post*; *The Huffington Post*, and the anthology *My Other Ex: Women's True Stories of Leaving and Losing Friendships*, among other publications. Her memoir *I'm the One Who Got Away* will be published in 2017.

Tracy Jensen

Tracy Jensen is a writer, fundraiser, marketing nerd, outdoor girl and runner. A single mom to two young kids, she is notorious for doing things the hard way. She spends her days juggling parenthood and her consulting business, putting more miles on her laptop than the running path. She has contributed to a number of publications and blogs, including *EverydayFamily*, *Scary Mommy*, *BonBon Break*, *Mamalode* and several regional publications. She was also a member of the 2013 Chicago cast of Listen to Your Mother. Jensen believes fresh air, a good cup of coffee and a compelling story can cure just about anything.

Wendy Kennar

Wendy Kennar is a freelance writer who finds inspiration in her seven-year-old son and from her experiences from her twelve-year teaching career. Her work has appeared in several publications, both print and online. She writes at www.wendykennar.com.

Alison Lee

Alison Lee is the co-editor of *Multiples Illuminated: A Collection of Stories and Advice From Parents of Twins, Triplets and More* (Spring 2016), a writer, and publisher. She is working on the second book in the anthology series to be published in 2017. Her writing has been featured in *On Parenting at The Washington Post*, *The Huffington Post*, *Mamalode*, *Mothers Always Write*, *Everyday Family*, *Scary Mommy*, *Feminine Collective*, *Sammiches & Psych Meds*, *Parent.Co*, *Club Mid*, and is one of 35 essayists in the anthology, *My Other Ex: Women's True Stories of Leaving and Losing Friends* (Fall, 2014). Alison lives in Malaysia with her husband and four children (two boys and boy/girl twins).

M.K. Martin

M.K. Martin is an Army vet who juggles her writing, school, and new baby with the heroic support of her husband. She loves long rides on her motorcycle and writing in cafes.

Janet McNally

Janet McNally is author of the young adult novel *Girls In The Moon*, coming in Fall 2016 from HarperCollins/HarperTeen, and a collection of poems, *Some Girls*, winner of the White Pine Press Poetry Prize. She has an MFA from the University of Notre Dame, and has twice been a fiction fellow with the New York Foundation for the Arts. Janet lives with her husband and three little girls in Buffalo, where she teaches creative writing at Canisius College.

Gargi Mehra

Gargi Mehra is a software professional by day, a writer by night and a mother at all times. Her short stories and essays have appeared in numerous literary magazines online and in print. She blogs at http://gargimehra.wordpress.com/ and tweets as @gargimehra.

Nora Neill

For Halloween when she was ten, Nora Neill dressed up as a writer. It's still her favorite costume. She wears it to teach composition at a community college in Michigan, minus the beret, and at home where she pleases her spouse and cats with made up lyrics to well-known songs.

Bethany Neumeyer

Before becoming a stay-at-home mom, Bethany worked in member services for a non-profit foundation, taught writing classes to adult ESL students, and was a substitute teacher (though not all at the same time). These days, she mostly uses her writing degree to make up impromptu songs for her two young kids and to answer the question "why?" 15,000 times a day. In her (limited) spare time, Bethany likes to nap, hang out with her ER doctor husband, read good books, and write; her work can be found on *The Huffington Post, Scary Mommy,* and her own blog, I Was Promised More Naps.

Ellen Nordberg

Ellen Nordberg's articles and essays have appeared in *The Chicago Tribune, The Denver Post, The Huffington Post*, and *NPR*, as well as on *Scary Mommy, Mom Babble*, and *Errant Parent.* A new Co-Producer for Listen to Your Mother, she performed in the Denver and Boulder shows, as well as in The Narrators and the Truth Be Told Boulder Grand Slam. Her essays have recently won the Stories on Stage Memoir prize and a Colorado Author's League award. She spends most of her day sweeping stinky athletic cups off her coffee table, and being grateful that no one really warned her ahead of time about the true realities of being a twin mom.

Mary Novaria

Mary Novaria is a mother, wife and journalist whose work has been featured in numerous print and online publications including the *Washington Post, Redbook, Country Living, Delish, Dr. Oz The Good Life, Good Housekeeping, Chicago Tribune, Feminine Collective, Kansas City Star, Huffington Post, The Good Men Project, Period!*, and *ParentCo.* She writes about family, friendship, and everyday life on her blog, A Work in Progress (www.marynovaria.com), and recently completed a memoir.

Navarre Overton

Navarre Overton is a stay-at-home mom to her toddler, two teens, and a very active terrier mix. When she isn't dealing with emotional meltdowns, enjoying her kids being awesome, or walking her dog, she is writing for her blog Raising Revolution which she launched in early 2015. Her hobbies include: geeking out on languages, playing video games, and winning the internet.

Julianne Palumbo

Julianne Palumbo's poems, short stories, and essays have been published in *Literary Mama*, *Coffee+Crumbs*, *MomBabble*, *Kindred Magazine*, *Poetry East*, *Mamalode*, *Manifest Station*, and others. She is the author of *Into Your Light* (Flutter Press, 2013) and *Announcing the Thaw* (Finishing Line Press, 2014), poetry chapbooks about raising teenagers. Julianne was nominated for a Pushcart Prize in 2013. She is the Founder/Editor-in-Chief of Mothers Always Write, an online literary magazine for mothers by mother writers.

Chantal Panozzo

Chantal Panozzo's essays have appeared in the *New York Times*, *Wall Street Journal*, *Washington Post*, *Vox*, *Brain Child*, and many other publications. The author of *Swiss Life: 30 Things I Wish I'd Known*, she is currently working on five books, including a memoir about surviving her daughter's first year while living 5,000 miles from home.

Lisa Pawlak

Lisa Pawlak is a San Diego based freelance writer and regular contributor to the *Chicken Soup for the Soul* series. Additionally, you can find her work in *San Diego Family*, *Hawaii Parent*, *Scary Mommy-Club Mid*, *Coping with Cancer*, the *Christian Science Monitor*, *Mothers Always Write*, *Mamalode*, *Sweatpants & Coffee*, *The Imperfect Parent* and *Working Mother*.

Jackie Pick

Jackie Pick is a former teacher who is now writing her way through what she nervously identifies as her "second adolescence." Her writing has been featured on various parenting sites including *Mamalode*, *The HerStories Project*, and *Scary Mommy*, as well as the literary art magazine *Selfish*. She is a contributor to *Multiples Illuminated* (2016) and to *Here in the Middle* (Fall, 2016). Jackie is the co-creator and co-writer of the upcoming short film Bacon Wrapped Dates, and occasionally performs sketch and musical comedy in Chicago. When she's not in one of her three children's school pick-up lanes, she can be found on Twitter (@jackiepick) apologizing for not updating her blog (jackiepickauthor.com)

Kim Tracy Prince

Kim Tracy Prince is a freelance writer whose work appears in *Notre Dame Magazine*, and on *Mamalode, Intuit's Mint.com, Business.com, Babycenter*, and elsewhere. She has been blogging through her adventures in motherhood and life since 2004. Kim lives in the Los Angeles area with her husband and two young sons.

Jennie Robertson

Jennie Robertson is an essayist and poet who lives and writes in rural New England. Her work has appeared in *Mary Jane's Farm Magazine* and *Literary Mama*. She is a regular contributor to Thinking Outside the Sandbox Business and Family and book review editor at Mothers Always Write.

Alexandra Rosas

Alexandra is a published author and storyteller with the nationally acclaimed live storyteller series The Moth. She is also the producer for Listen To Your Mother Milwaukee. She has been featured on *Huffington Post, Purple Clover, Brain,Child, Mamalode*, and several online websites. You can follow her on her personal blog, Good Day Regular People.

Ashley Roth

Ashley N. Roth is a writer, mother, and animal activist in Nashville, Tennessee. Her fiction has appeared in *The Molotov Cocktail* and *100 Word Story*, and her first children's book was released in November 2015.

Meredith Samuelson

Meredith is a writer and visual artist from Long Island where she lives with her husband and two delicious little boys. Her family inspires nearly everything she does, from portraits and collages to essays and

Facebook rants. She teaches middle school art in Brooklyn, NY, and she's been told (once) that she is Mindy Kaling's voice twin.

Dana Schwartz

Dana Schwartz lives in New Hope, Pennsylvania with her husband and two children. A lifelong reader and writer, she earned her MFA in Creative Writing from Fairleigh Dickinson University in 2008. Since then she has published short stories in several literary journals and this is her third anthology with the HerStories Project. You can find her at The Gift of Writing, in her online journaling course, Crossing the River: Writing Through Grief, and on her blog, Writing at the Table. She is currently working on a memoir.

Kristin Vanderhey Shaw

Kristin Shaw is a freelance writer, wife, and mother based in Austin, Texas. She is a co-producer of the Listen To Your Mother show in Austin, the Director of Social Media and staff writer for Airport Improvement magazine, and has been published at national sites like *The Huffington Post; The Washington Post; Brain, Child;* and *Scary Mommy.* Kristin owns Firewheel Communications.

Yvonne Spence

Yvonne Spence is author of *Drawings in Sand,* a novel about a mother in recovery, and of a short story collection: *Looking For America.* Her short stories and personal essays have been published in anthologies and magazines and one story was a prize-winner in a She Magazine contest. Yvonne has an MA in Creative Writing, which she was working towards when her second daughter was born prematurely. In 2015 Yvonne instigated the blogging initiative 1000 Voices Speak for Compassion, which unites bloggers worldwide to write about compassion, and for which she has won a BlogHer 2016 Voices of the Year Award. She lives in the UK with her husband and teenage daughters.

Brooke Takhar

Brooke Takhar blogs as missteenussr.com and runs so she can eat artisanal ice cream directly from the recyclable glass jar. Online you can read more of her stories at *Club Mid, Blunt Moms, Scary Mommy, In the Powder Room, Project Underblog* and *Coffee + Crumbs*. Currently she's drinking black coffee, sleeping or farting around on Facebook or Twitter.

Lisa Trank

Lisa began writing after many years of being a performing artist – an actress and singer. She's a former recipient of a Rocky Mountain Women's Institute Fellowship in poetry, and focuses on reimagining the stories she grew up as the first generation to be born in this country. Currently, she's completing her first young adult novel, entitled "*Tangled Chimes,*" a multi-generational, slightly fantastical, coming-of-age story. She's the proud mother of three wonderful teen-age daughters, is married to her best friend, and lives in Longmont, Colorado, with a constant view of the Rocky Mountains.

Pamela Valentine

Pamela Valentine shares the joys and challenges of raising a gender diverse child as Affirmed Mom through ChicagoNow. She was recently awarded a BlogHer 2016 Voices of the Year Award and an Excellence in Blogging from the National Gay and Lesbian Journalists Association. Her essays have been featured on *Scary Mommy, Cosmo, Good Housekeeping, Brain, Child Magazine* and in the upcoming anthology, *Here in the Middle.*

Meghan Moravcik Walbert

Meghan Moravcik Walbert's work has been featured in a variety of publications and websites, including *The New York Times, Mamalode, BlogHer* and *Brain, Child*. She was named a BlogHer 2015 and 2016 Voice of the Year and was a cast member of the 2015 Listen To Your Mother: Lehigh Valley show. She lives in Eastern Pennsylvania with her husband and son.

Alice Jones Webb

Alice Jones Webb is a homeschooling mom to four kids, a

wife, writer, bookworm, laundry sorter, black belt, nerd, procrastinator, history lover, free-thinker, obsessive recycler, nature lover, star gazer, a bit of a rebel, but definitely not your typical soccer mom. Her essays can be found on her blog, *Different Than Average*, where she writes about parenting outside of mainstream culture, as well as featured on sites such as *Brain, Child Magazine*; *Scary Mommy*; *The Mind Unleashed*; and *Elephant Journal* among others.

Vicky Willenberg

Vicky is a wife, mother, and obsessive volunteer at her sons' school. She chronicles the good, the bad, and the hysterical on her blog The Pursuit of Normal. You will most often find her on Facebook, sharing the daily shenanigans that go hand in hand with raising two boys while still growing up herself. Her work can be found in *Scary Mommy's Guide to Surviving the Holidays*, *The HerStories Project: Women Explore the Joy, Pain, and Power of Female Friendships* and *My Other Ex*; as well as on *TheMid, BlogHer, Mamapedia,* and *Mamalode*.

Liza Wyles

Liza Wyles is a TV writer and producer. She is also a reproducer, raising two children in her native Queens, New York. Her parenting and humor writing has been published on such sites as *Romper, Scary Mommy, Reductress* and in the flash fiction anthology, *Six-Word Memoirs on Jewish Life*.

Mimi Sager Yoskowitz

Mimi Sager Yoskowitz lives in suburban Chicago with her husband and four children. Her writing has been featured on *Brain, Child, Kveller, Mamanomnom,* and other sites. She also blogs at "Mimi Time" http://mimisager.com. In her previous life she was an editorial producer at CNN in New York, and a writer for local news broadcasts in both New York and Chicago. She holds a Master's from Northwestern's Medill School of Journalism and is a graduate of Brandeis University.

Kimberly Zapata

Kimberly Zapata is the creator and voice behind Sunshine Spoils Milk, a blog dedicated to mental health, motherhood, and everything in between. She is a staff writer for *Romper*, a regular contributor for *Babble* and *Sammiches & Psych Meds*, and her work has appeared on *The Washington Post, HuffPost, Scary Mommy, BLUNTMoms, Mamalode, Bonbon Break,* and *The Mighty*. In addition to this anthology, her work is also appears in the 2015 publication *Lose The Cape: Never Will I Ever (And Then I Had Kids)*.

About the Editors

Jessica Smock is a writer, editor, former educator and educational researcher, and mother to a son and daughter. She has a doctorate in development and educational policy from Boston University. She lives outside of Buffalo, New York with her family.

Stephanie Sprenger is a freelance writer, editor, music therapist, and mother of two daughters. Her work has been featured in *The Washington Post's On Parenting, Brain, Child Magazine, Redbook.com, Cosmopolitan.com, Motherwell Magazine,* and *The Huffington Post,* among others. She also contributed to the anthology *A Letter to My Mom* (Crown Archetype, 2015). Stephanie is co-producer of the Listen To Your Mother Boulder show and was named one of BlogHer's 2014 Voices of the Year. She lives in Colorado with her family and can be found online at stephaniesprenger.com

The HerStories Project is a writing and publishing community for women. We offer a variety of online writing courses, feature a bi-monthly personal essay column, HerStories Voices, to which writers can submit guest posts, and our HerTake advice column explores modern friendship through reader questions. We have previously published three books—*The HerStories Project: Women Explore The Joy, Pain, and Power of Female Friendship; My Other Ex: Women's True Stories of Leaving and Losing Friends,* and *Mothering Through the Darkness: Women Open Up About the Postpartum Experience* (She Writes Press, 2015). My Other Ex and Mothering Through the Darkness were both selected as Finalists in Foreword Reviews' IndieFab Book of the Year contest. Find out more about out books, our courses, and other opportunities for writers and readers at **herstoriesproject.com**.

Acknowledgements

We would like to thank our incredible contributors for sharing their stories with us, and with the many families who will read their words. You are all such gifted, courageous storytellers. We'd also like to thank the hundreds of women who submitted their essays for consideration in this book—we were blown away by how many powerful, important, relatable stories you shared with us, and we were honored to have read your submissions.

We want to thank everyone—friends, family members, and the media—who supported the #sogladtheytoldme social media movement to provide supportive advice to mothers. It was humbling and empowering to hear your messages of solidarity for parents—it is because of you that this project took flight.

Thanks also to our HerStories Project Community, which has grown considerably since our first few blog posts about friendship nearly four years ago! We are grateful for your continued support and inspiration.

Finally, and most importantly, thank you to our patient and supportive families, without whom this book would not have been possible. We appreciate you!

Made in the USA
Lexington, KY
03 September 2016